2019

Scouts BSA Requirements

THIS BOOK BELONGS TO

Harder   715 859 2901
    715 529 7787

BOY SCOUTS OF AMERICA®

*This booklet is designed
to bring together the
requirements for merit
badges, rank advancements,
and Eagle Palms, and to
highlight recognitions for
special opportunities. Your
comments and reactions will
be appreciated. Send them to
advancement.team@
scouting.org OR
Advancement, S272,
Boy Scouts of America,
1325 West Walnut Hill Lane,
P.O. Box 152079,
Irving, TX 75015-2079.*

33216
ISBN 978-0-8395-3215-6
©2019 Boy Scouts of America
2019 Printing

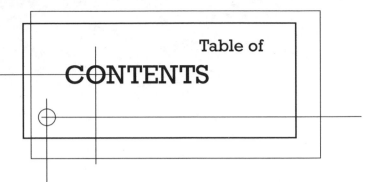

Table of

CONTENTS

Merit badges, badges of rank, and Eagle Palms may be earned by registered Scouts, including Lone Scouts, and by qualified Venturers or Sea Scouts who are not yet 18 years old. Venturers and Sea Scouts qualify by achieving First Class rank as a Scout or Lone Scout (or as a Varsity Scout prior to Jan. 1, 2018). The only exceptions for those older than age 18 are related to Scouts registered beyond the age of eligibility and those who have been granted time extensions to complete the Eagle Scout rank.

Rank Advancement
for Venturers and Sea Scouts

Any Venturer or Sea Scout who has achieved the First Class rank as a Scout or Lone Scout (or as a Varsity Scout prior to Jan. 1, 2018) may continue advancement up to their 18th birthday toward the Star, Life, and Eagle Scout ranks, and Eagle Palms. Qualified Venturers and Sea Scouts must meet the requirements as prescribed in the official Scouts BSA handbooks and the *Scouts BSA Requirements* book.

The Venturer may fulfill leadership requirements by serving as president, vice president, secretary, treasurer, den chief, historian, guide, quartermaster, chaplain aide, or outdoor ethics guide.

The Sea Scout may fulfill leadership requirements by serving as boatswain, boatswain's mate, purser, yeoman, storekeeper, crew leader, media specialist, specialist, den chief, or chaplain aide.

The unit leader conference will be conducted by the Advisor or Skipper. As the Venturer or Sea Scout fulfills requirements for the Star and Life ranks, a board of review must be conducted by the crew or ship committee according to the procedures established by the National Council as published in the *Guide to Advancement*. Eagle Scout boards of review are conducted in accordance with the *Guide to Advancement* and procedures established by the local council.

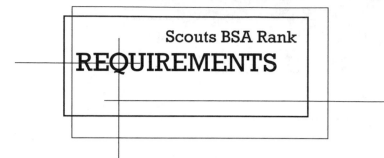

Scouts BSA Rank

REQUIREMENTS

The rank requirements in this book are official as of Jan. 1, 2019. If a Scout has started work toward a rank before that date using requirements that were current before Jan. 1, 2019, except as noted below, the Scout may complete that rank using the old requirements. Any progress toward a rank that is begun after Jan. 1, 2019, must use the requirements as they are presented in this Scouts BSA Requirements *book.*

SCOUT
Rank Requirements

All requirements for the Scout rank must be completed as a member of a troop or as a Lone Scout. If you have already completed these requirements as part of the Webelos Scouting Adventure, simply demonstrate your knowledge or skills to your Scoutmaster or other designated leader after joining the troop.

1a. Repeat from memory the Scout Oath, Scout Law, Scout motto, and Scout slogan. In your own words, explain their meaning.

1b. Explain what Scout spirit is. Describe some ways you have shown Scout spirit by practicing the Scout Oath, Scout Law, Scout motto, and Scout slogan.

1c. Demonstrate the Scout sign, salute, and handshake. Explain when they should be used.

1d. Describe the First Class Scout badge and tell what each part stands for. Explain the significance of the First Class Scout badge.

1e. Repeat from memory the Outdoor Code. In your own words, explain what the Outdoor Code means to you.

1f. Repeat from memory the Pledge of Allegiance. In your own words, explain its meaning.

2. After attending at least one Scout troop meeting, do the following:

2a. Describe how the Scouts in the troop provide its leadership.

2b. Describe the four steps of Scout advancement.

2c. Describe what the Scouts BSA ranks are and how they are earned.

2d. Describe what merit badges are and how they are earned.

3a. Explain the patrol method. Describe the types of patrols that are used in your troop.

3b. Become familiar with your patrol name, emblem, flag, and yell. Explain how these items create patrol spirit.

4a. Show how to tie a square knot, two half-hitches, and a taut-line hitch. Explain how each knot is used.

4b. Show the proper care of a rope by learning how to whip and fuse the ends of different kinds of rope.

5. Tell what you need to know about pocketknife safety.

6. With your parent or guardian, complete the exercises in the pamphlet *How to Protect Your Children From Child Abuse: A Parent's Guide* and earn the Cyber Chip Award for your grade.[1]

7. Since joining the troop and while working on the Scout rank, participate in a Scoutmaster conference.

Notes: The requirements for Scout, Tenderfoot, Second Class, and First Class ranks may be worked on simultaneously; however, these ranks must be earned in sequence.

Alternative requirements for the Scout rank are available for Scouts with physical or mental disabilities if they meet the criteria listed in the *Scouts BSA Requirements* book.

---

[1] If your family does not have internet access at home AND you do not have ready internet access at school or another public place or via a mobile device, the Cyber Chip portion of this requirement may be waived by your Scoutmaster in consultation with your parent or guardian.

TENDERFOOT
Rank Requirements

1a. Present yourself to your leader, prepared for an overnight camping trip. Show the personal and camping gear you will use. Show the right way to pack and carry it.

1b. Spend at least one night on a patrol or troop campout. Sleep in a tent you have helped pitch.

1c. Tell how you practiced the Outdoor Code on a campout or outing.

2a. On the campout, assist in preparing one of the meals. Tell why it is important for each patrol member to share in meal preparation and cleanup.

2b. While on a campout, demonstrate the appropriate method of safely cleaning items used to prepare, serve, and eat a meal.

2c. Explain the importance of eating together as a patrol.

3a. Demonstrate a practical use of the square knot.

3b. Demonstrate a practical use of two half-hitches.

3c. Demonstrate a practical use of the taut-line hitch.

3d. Demonstrate proper care, sharpening, and use of the knife, saw, and ax. Describe when each should be used.

4a. Show first aid for the following:
- Simple cuts and scrapes
- Blisters on the hand and foot
- Minor (thermal/heat) burns or scalds (superficial, or first-degree)
- Bites or stings of insects and ticks
- Venomous snakebite
- Nosebleed
- Frostbite and sunburn
- Choking

4b. Describe common poisonous or hazardous plants; identify any that grow in your local area or campsite location. Tell how to treat for exposure to them.

4c. Tell what you can do while on a campout or other outdoor activity to prevent or reduce the occurrence of injuries or exposure listed in Tenderfoot requirements 4a and 4b.

4d. Assemble a personal first-aid kit to carry with you on future campouts and hikes. Tell how each item in the kit would be used.

5a. Explain the importance of the buddy system as it relates to your personal safety on outings and in your neighborhood. Use the buddy system while on a troop or patrol outing.

5b. Describe what to do if you become lost on a hike or campout.

5c. Explain the rules of safe hiking, both on the highway and cross-country, during the day and at night.

6a. Record your best in the following tests:

- Pushups _____ (Record the number done correctly in 60 seconds.)

- Situps or curl-ups _____ (Record the number done correctly in 60 seconds.)

- Back-saver sit-and-reach _____ (Record the distance stretched.)

- 1-mile walk/run _____ (Record the time.)

6b. Develop and describe a plan for improvement in each of the activities listed in Tenderfoot requirement 6a. Keep track of your activity for at least 30 days.

6c. Show improvement (of any degree) in each activity listed in Tenderfoot requirement 6a after practicing for 30 days.

- Pushups _____ (Record the number done correctly in 60 seconds.)

- Situps or curl-ups _____ (Record the number done correctly in 60 seconds.)

- Back-saver sit-and-reach _____ (Record the distance stretched.)

- 1-mile walk/run _____ (Record the time.)

7a. Demonstrate how to display, raise, lower, and fold the U.S. flag.

7b. Participate in a total of one hour of service in one or more service projects approved by your Scoutmaster. Explain how your service to others relates to the Scout slogan and Scout motto.

8. Describe the steps in Scouting's Teaching EDGE method. Use the Teaching EDGE method to teach another person how to tie the square knot.

9. Demonstrate Scout spirit by living the Scout Oath and Scout Law. Tell how you have done your duty to God and how you have lived four different points of the Scout Law in your everyday life.

_____ _____ _____ _____

10. While working toward the Tenderfoot rank, and after completing Scout rank requirement 7, participate in a Scoutmaster conference.

11. Successfully complete your board of review for the Tenderfoot rank.

Notes: The requirements for Scout, Tenderfoot, Second Class, and First Class ranks may be worked on simultaneously; however, these ranks must be earned in sequence.

Alternative requirements for the Tenderfoot rank are available for Scouts with physical or mental disabilities if they meet the criteria listed in the *Scouts BSA Requirements* book.

SECOND CLASS
Rank Requirements

1a. Since joining Scouts BSA, participate in five separate troop/patrol activities, at least three of which must be held outdoors. Of the outdoor activities, at least two must include overnight camping. These activities do not include troop or patrol meetings. On campouts, spend the night in a tent that you pitch or other structure that you help erect, such as a lean-to, snow cave, or tepee.

1b. Explain the principles of Leave No Trace and tell how you practiced them on a campout or outing. This outing must be different from the one used for Tenderfoot requirement 1c.

1c. On one of these campouts, select a location for your patrol site and recommend it to your patrol leader, senior patrol leader, or troop guide. Explain what factors you should consider when choosing a patrol site and where to pitch a tent.

2a. Explain when it is appropriate to use a fire for cooking or other purposes and when it would not be appropriate to do so.

2b. Use the tools listed in Tenderfoot requirement 3d to prepare tinder, kindling, and fuel wood for a cooking fire.

2c. At an approved outdoor location and time, use the tinder, kindling, and fuel wood from Second Class requirement 2b to demonstrate how to build a fire. Unless prohibited by local fire restrictions, light the fire. After allowing the flames to burn safely for at least two minutes, safely extinguish the flames with minimal impact to the fire site.

2d. Explain when it is appropriate to use a lightweight stove and when it is appropriate to use a propane stove. Set up a lightweight stove or propane stove. Light the stove, unless prohibited by local fire restrictions. Describe the safety procedures for using these types of stoves.

2e. On one campout, plan and cook one hot breakfast or lunch, selecting foods from MyPlate or the current USDA nutritional model. Explain the importance of good nutrition. Demonstrate how to transport, store, and prepare the foods you selected.

2f. Demonstrate tying the sheet bend knot. Describe a situation in which you would use this knot.

2g. Demonstrate tying the bowline knot. Describe a situation in which you would use this knot.

3a. Demonstrate how a compass works and how to orient a map. Use a map to point out and tell the meaning of five map symbols.

3b. Using a compass and map together, take a 5-mile hike (or 10 miles by bike) approved by your adult leader and your parent or guardian.[2]

3c. Describe some hazards or injuries that you might encounter on your hike and what you can do to help prevent them.[2]

---

[2]If you use a wheelchair or crutches, or if it is difficult for you to get around, you may substitute "trip" for "hike" in requirement 3b and 3c.

3d. Demonstrate how to find directions during the day and at night without using a compass or an electronic device.

4. Identify or show evidence of at least 10 kinds of wild animals (such as birds, mammals, reptiles, fish, or mollusks) found in your local area or camping location. You may show evidence by tracks, signs, or photographs you have taken.

5a. Tell what precautions must be taken for a safe swim.

5b. Demonstrate your ability to pass the BSA beginner test: Jump feetfirst into water over your head in depth, level off and swim 25 feet on the surface, stop, turn sharply, resume swimming, then return to your starting place.[3]

5c. Demonstrate water rescue methods by reaching with your arm or leg, by reaching with a suitable object, and by throwing lines and objects.[3]

5d. Explain why swimming rescues should not be attempted when a reaching or throwing rescue is possible. Explain why and how a rescue swimmer should avoid contact with the victim.

6a. Demonstrate first aid for the following:
- Object in the eye
- Bite of a warm-blooded animal
- Puncture wounds from a splinter, nail, and fishhook
- Serious burns (partial thickness, or second-degree)
- Heat exhaustion
- Shock
- Heatstroke, dehydration, hypothermia, and hyperventilation

6b. Show what to do for "hurry" cases of stopped breathing, stroke, severe bleeding, and ingested poisoning.

6c. Tell what you can do while on a campout or hike to prevent or reduce the occurrence of the injuries listed in Second Class requirements 6a and 6b.

6d. Explain what to do in case of accidents that require emergency response in the home and backcountry. Explain what constitutes an emergency and what information you will need to provide to a responder.

6e. Tell how you should respond if you come upon the scene of a vehicular accident.

7a. After completing Tenderfoot requirement 6c, be physically active at least 30 minutes each day for five days a week for four weeks. Keep track of your activities.

---

[3]Under certain exceptional conditions, where the climate keeps the outdoor water temperature below safe levels year-round, or where there are no suitably safe and accessible places (outdoors or indoors) within a reasonable traveling distance to swim at any time during the year, the council Scout executive and advancement committee may, on an individual Scout basis, authorize an alternative for requirements 5b and 5c. The local council may establish appropriate procedures for submitting and processing these types of requests. All the other requirements, none of which necessitate entry in the water or entry in a watercraft on the water, must be completed as written.

7b. Share your challenges and successes in completing Second Class requirement 7a. Set a goal for continuing to include physical activity as part of your daily life and develop a plan for doing so.

7c. Participate in a school, community, or troop program on the dangers of using drugs, alcohol, and tobacco and other practices that could be harmful to your health. Discuss your participation in the program with your family, and explain the dangers of substance addictions. Report to your Scoutmaster or other adult leader in your troop about which parts of the Scout Oath and Scout Law relate to what you learned.

8a. Participate in a flag ceremony for your school, religious institution, chartered organization, community, or Scouting activity.

8b. Explain what respect is due the flag of the United States.

8c. With your parents or guardian, decide on an amount of money that you would like to earn, based on the cost of a specific item you would like to purchase. Develop a written plan to earn the amount agreed upon and follow that plan; it is acceptable to make changes to your plan along the way. Discuss any changes made to your original plan and whether you met your goal.

8d. At a minimum of three locations, compare the cost of the item for which you are saving to determine the best place to purchase it. After completing Second Class requirement 8c, decide if you will use the amount that you earned as originally intended, save all or part of it, or use it for another purpose.

8e. Participate in two hours of service through one or more service projects approved by your Scoutmaster. Tell how your service to others relates to the Scout Oath.

9a. Explain the three R's of personal safety and protection.

9b. Describe bullying; tell what the appropriate response is to someone who is bullying you or another person.

10. Demonstrate Scout spirit by living the Scout Oath and Scout Law. Tell how you have done your duty to God and how you have lived four different points of the Scout Law (not to include those used for Tenderfoot requirement 9) in your everyday life.

_____ _____ _____ _____

11. While working toward the Second Class rank, and after completing Tenderfoot requirement 10, participate in a Scoutmaster conference.

12. Successfully complete your board of review for the Second Class rank.

Notes: The requirements for Scout, Tenderfoot, Second Class, and First Class ranks may be worked on simultaneously; however, these ranks must be earned in sequence.

Alternative requirements for the Second Class rank are available for Scouts with physical or mental disabilities if they meet the criteria listed in the _Scouts BSA Requirements_ book.

FIRST CLASS
Rank Requirements

1a. Since joining Scouts BSA, participate in 10 separate troop/patrol activities, at least six of which must be held outdoors. Of the outdoor activities, at least three must include overnight camping. These activities do not include troop or patrol meetings. On campouts, spend the night in a tent that you pitch or other structure that you help erect, such as a lean-to, snow cave, or tepee.

1b. Explain each of the principles of Tread Lightly! and tell how you practiced them on a campout or outing. This outing must be different from the ones used for Tenderfoot requirement 1c and Second Class requirement 1b.

2a. Help plan a menu for one of the above campouts that includes at least one breakfast, one lunch, and one dinner, and that requires cooking at least two of the meals. Tell how the menu includes the foods from MyPlate or the current USDA nutritional model and how it meets nutritional needs for the planned activity or campout.

2b. Using the menu planned in First Class requirement 2a, make a list showing a budget and the food amounts needed to feed three or more youth. Secure the ingredients.

2c. Show which pans, utensils, and other gear will be needed to cook and serve these meals.

2d. Demonstrate the procedures to follow in the safe handling and storage of fresh meats, dairy products, eggs, vegetables, and other perishable food products. Show how to properly dispose of camp garbage, cans, plastic containers, and other rubbish.

2e. On one campout, serve as cook. Supervise your assistant(s) in using a stove or building a cooking fire. Prepare the breakfast, lunch, and dinner planned in First Class requirement 2a. Supervise the cleanup.

3a. Discuss when you should and should not use lashings.

3b. Demonstrate tying the timber hitch and clove hitch.

3c. Demonstrate tying the square, shear, and diagonal lashings by joining two or more poles or staves together.

3d. Use lashings to make a useful camp gadget or structure.

4a. Using a map and compass, complete an orienteering course that covers at least one mile and requires measuring the height and/or width of designated items (tree, tower, canyon, ditch, etc.).

4b. Demonstrate how to use a handheld GPS unit, GPS app on a smartphone, or other electronic navigation system. Use GPS to find your current location, a destination of your choice, and the route you will take to get there. Follow that route to arrive at your destination.

5a. Identify or show evidence of at least 10 kinds of native plants found in your local area or campsite location. You may show evidence by identifying fallen leaves or fallen fruit that you find in the field, or as part of a collection you have made, or by photographs you have taken.

5b. Identify two ways to obtain a weather forecast for an upcoming activity. Explain why weather forecasts are important when planning for an event.

5c. Describe at least three natural indicators of impending hazardous weather, the potential dangerous events that might result from such weather conditions, and the appropriate actions to take.

5d. Describe extreme weather conditions you might encounter in the outdoors in your local geographic area. Discuss how you would determine ahead of time the potential risk of these types of weather dangers, alternative planning considerations to avoid such risks, and how you would prepare for and respond to those weather conditions.

6a. Successfully complete the BSA swimmer test.[4,5]

6b. Tell what precautions must be taken for a safe trip afloat.

6c. Identify the basic parts of a canoe, kayak, or other boat. Identify the parts of a paddle or an oar.

6d. Describe proper body positioning in a watercraft, depending on the type and size of the vessel. Explain the importance of proper body position in the boat.

6e. With a helper and a practice victim, show a line rescue both as tender and as rescuer. (The practice victim should be approximately 30 feet from shore in deep water.)[5]

7a. Demonstrate bandages for a sprained ankle and for injuries on the head, the upper arm, and the collarbone.

7b. By yourself and with a partner, show how to:

• Transport a person from a smoke-filled room.

• Transport for at least 25 yards a person with a sprained ankle.

7c. Tell the five most common signals of a heart attack. Explain the steps (procedures) in cardiopulmonary resuscitation (CPR).

7d. Tell what utility services exist in your home or meeting place. Describe potential hazards associated with these utilities and tell how to respond in emergency situations.

---

[4]See the Swimming merit badge requirements for details about the BSA swimmer test.

[5]Under certain exceptional conditions, where the climate keeps the outdoor water temperature below safe levels year-round, or where there are no suitably safe and accessible places (outdoors or indoors) within a reasonable traveling distance to swim at any time during the year, the council Scout executive and advancement committee may, on an individual Scout basis, authorize an alternative for requirements 6a and 6e. The local council may establish appropriate procedures for submitting and processing these types of requests. All the other requirements, none of which necessitate entry in the water or entry in a watercraft on the water, must be completed as written.

7e. Develop an emergency action plan for your home that includes what to do in case of fire, storm, power outage, and water outage.

7f. Explain how to obtain potable water in an emergency.

8a. After completing Second Class requirement 7a, be physically active at least 30 minutes each day for five days a week for four weeks. Keep track of your activities.

8b. Share your challenges and successes in completing First Class requirement 8a. Set a goal for continuing to include physical activity as part of your daily life.

9a. Visit and discuss with a selected individual approved by your leader (for example, an elected official, judge, attorney, civil servant, principal, or teacher) the constitutional rights and obligations of a U.S. citizen.

9b. Investigate an environmental issue affecting your community. Share what you learned about that issue with your patrol or troop. Tell what, if anything, could be done by you or your community to address the concern.

9c. On a Scouting or family outing, take note of the trash and garbage you produce. Before your next similar outing, decide how you can reduce, recycle, or repurpose what you take on that outing, and then put those plans into action. Compare your results.

9d. Participate in three hours of service through one or more service projects approved by your Scoutmaster. The project(s) must not be the same service project(s) used for Tenderfoot requirement 7b and Second Class requirement 8e. Explain how your service to others relates to the Scout Law.

10. Tell someone who is eligible to join Scouts BSA, or an inactive Scout, about your Scouting activities. Invite this person to an outing, activity, service project, or meeting. Provide information on how to join, or encourage the inactive Scout to become active. Share your efforts with your Scoutmaster or other adult leader.

11. Demonstrate Scout spirit by living the Scout Oath and Scout Law. Tell how you have done your duty to God and how you have lived four different points of the Scout Law (different from those points used for previous ranks) in your everyday life.

_____ _____ _____ _____

12. While working toward the First Class rank, and after completing Second Class requirement 11, participate in a Scoutmaster conference.

13. Successfully complete your board of review for the First Class rank.

Notes: The requirements for Scout, Tenderfoot, Second Class, and First Class ranks may be worked on simultaneously; however, these ranks must be earned in sequence.

Alternative requirements for the First Class rank are available for Scouts with physical or mental disabilities if they meet the criteria listed in the _Scouts BSA Requirements_ book.

SCOUT, TENDERFOOT, SECOND CLASS, and FIRST CLASS RANKS
Alternative Requirements

A Scout with a permanent physical or mental disability or a disability expected to last more than two years or beyond the 18th birthday and who is unable to complete all of the requirements for Scout, Tenderfoot, Second Class, or First Class rank may, with his or her parent or guardian, submit a request to the council advancement committee to complete alternative requirements. Below are the procedures for applying for alternative requirements. To help facilitate this process, use the Individual Scout Advancement Plan, No. 512-936, which can be found at www. scouting.org/advancement. For more detailed information about alternative requirements, see the *Guide to Advancement.*

1. **Do as Many Standard Requirements as Possible.** Before applying for alternative requirements, a Scout must complete as many of the existing requirements as possible.

2. **Prepare a Request for Alternative Requirements.** Once the Scout has done his or her best to the limit of the Scout's abilities and resources, the unit leader or a troop committee member submits to the council advancement committee a written request for alternative requirements for Scout, Tenderfoot, Second Class, or First Class ranks. It must show what has been completed and suggest the alternatives for those requirements the Scout cannot do.

3. **Secure a Medical Statement and Provide Supporting Documents.** The request must be accompanied by supporting letters from the unit leader, a parent or guardian, and the Scout (if possible), as well as a written statement from a qualified health professional related to the nature of the disability. This may be a physician, neurologist, psychiatrist, psychologist, etc., or, when appropriate, an educational administrator in special education. Statements must describe the disability; cover the Scout's capabilities, limitations, and prognosis; and outline what requirements cannot be completed. Additional information such as Individualized Education Plans (IEP) provided to parents by schools, and various treatment summaries and reports, may help an advancement committee make an informed decision.

4. **The Advancement Committee Reviews the Request.** The council advancement committee reviews the request, utilizing the expertise of professionals involved with youth who have special needs. To make a fair determination, the committee may want to interview the Scout, his or her parent or guardian, and the unit leader. The committee's decision is then recorded and delivered to the Scout and the unit leader.

STAR
Rank Requirements

1. Be active in your troop for at least four months as a First Class Scout.

2. As a First Class Scout, demonstrate Scout spirit by living the Scout Oath and Scout Law. Tell how you have done your duty to God and how you have lived the Scout Oath and Scout Law in your everyday life.

3. Earn six merit badges, including any four from the required list for Eagle. You may choose any of the 17 merit badges on the required list for Eagle to fulfill this requirement. See Eagle rank requirement 3 for this list.

Name of Merit Badge	Date Earned
(Eagle-required) _____	_____
(Eagle-required) _____	_____
(Eagle-required) _____	_____
(Eagle-required) _____	_____
_____	
_____	

4. While a First Class Scout, participate in six hours of service through one or more service projects approved by your Scoutmaster.

Notes: For Venturers working on Scouts BSA requirements, replace "troop" with "crew" and "Scoutmaster" with "Crew Advisor." For Sea Scouts working on Scouts BSA requirements, replace "troop" with "ship" and "Scoutmaster" with "Skipper."

5. While a First Class Scout, serve actively in your troop for four months in one or more of the following positions of responsibility (or carry out a Scoutmaster-approved leadership project to help the troop):

Scout troop. Patrol leader, assistant senior patrol leader, senior patrol leader, troop guide, Order of the Arrow troop representative, den chief, scribe, librarian, historian, quartermaster, bugler, junior assistant Scoutmaster, chaplain aide, instructor, webmaster, or outdoor ethics guide.[6]

Venturing crew. President, vice president, secretary, treasurer, den chief, historian, guide, quartermaster, chaplain aide, or outdoor ethics guide.

Sea Scout ship. Boatswain, boatswain's mate, purser, yeoman, storekeeper, crew leader, media specialist, specialist, den chief, or chaplain aide.

Lone Scout. Leadership responsibility in your school, religious organization, club, or elsewhere in your community.

6. With your parent or guardian, complete the exercises in the pamphlet *How to Protect Your Children From Child Abuse: A Parent's Guide* and earn the Cyber Chip award for your grade.[7]

7. While a First Class Scout, participate in a Scoutmaster conference.

8. Successfully complete your board of review for the Star rank.[8]

---

[6]Assistant patrol leader is not an approved position of responsibility for the Star rank.

[7]If your family does not have internet access at home AND you do not have ready internet access at school or another public place or via a mobile device, the Cyber Chip portion of this requirement may be waived by your Scoutmaster in consultation with your parent or guardian.

[8]If the board of review does not approve the Scout's advancement, the decision may be appealed in accordance with *Guide to Advancement* topic 8.0.4.0.

LIFE
Rank Requirements

1. Be active in your troop for at least six months as a Star Scout.

2. As a Star Scout, demonstrate Scout spirit by living the Scout Oath and Scout Law. Tell how you have done your duty to God and how you have lived the Scout Oath and Scout Law in your everyday life.

3. Earn five more merit badges (so that you have 11 in all), including any three additional badges from the required list for Eagle. You may choose any of the 17 merit badges on the required list for Eagle to fulfill this requirement. See Eagle rank requirement 3 for this list.

Name of Merit Badge   **Date Earned**

(Eagle-required) _____

(Eagle-required) _____

(Eagle-required) _____

_____

_____

4. While a Star Scout, participate in six hours of service through one or more service projects approved by your Scoutmaster. At least three hours of this service must be conservation-related.

5. While a Star Scout, serve actively in your troop for six months in one or more of the following troop positions of responsibility (or carry out a Scoutmaster-approved leadership project to help the troop).

Scout troop. Patrol leader, assistant senior patrol leader, senior patrol leader, troop guide, Order of the Arrow troop representative, den chief, scribe, librarian, historian, quartermaster, bugler, junior assistant Scoutmaster, chaplain aide, instructor, webmaster, or outdoor ethics guide.[9]

Venturing crew. President, vice president, secretary, treasurer, den chief, historian, guide, quartermaster, chaplain aide, or outdoor ethics guide.

Sea Scout ship. Boatswain, boatswain's mate, purser, yeoman, storekeeper, crew leader, media specialist, specialist, den chief, or chaplain aide.

Lone Scout. Leadership responsibility in your school, religious organization, club, or elsewhere in your community.

[9]Assistant patrol leader is not an approved position of responsibility for the Star, Life, or Eagle rank.

6. While a Star Scout, use the Teaching EDGE method to teach another Scout (preferably younger than you) the skills from ONE of the following choices, so that the Scout is prepared to pass those requirements to their Scoutmaster's satisfaction.

   a. Tenderfoot 4a and 4b (first aid)

   b. Second Class 2b, 2c, and 2d (cooking/tools)

   c. Second Class 3a and 3d (navigation)

   d. First Class 3a, 3b, 3c, and 3d (tools)

   e. First Class 4a and 4b (navigation)

   f. Second Class 6a and 6b (first aid)

   g. First Class 7a and 7b (first aid)

   h. Three requirements from one of the required Eagle merit badges, as approved by your Scoutmaster

7. While a Star Scout, participate in a Scoutmaster conference.

8. Successfully complete your board of review for the Life rank.[10]

Notes: For Venturers working on Scouts BSA requirements, replace "troop" with "crew" and "Scoutmaster" with "crew Advisor." For Sea Scouts working on Scouts BSA requirements, replace "troop" with "ship" and "Scoutmaster" with "Skipper."

[10]If the board of review does not approve the Scout's advancement, the decision may be appealed in accordance with *Guide to Advancement* topic 8.0.4.0.

EAGLE
Rank Requirements

1. Be active in your troop for at least six months as a Life Scout.

2. As a Life Scout, demonstrate Scout Spirit by living the Scout Oath and Scout Law. Tell how you have done your duty to God, how you have lived the Scout Oath and Scout Law in your everyday life, and how your understanding of the Scout Oath and Scout Law will guide your life in the future. List on your Eagle Scout Rank Application the names of individuals who know you personally and would be willing to provide a recommendation on your behalf, including parents/guardians, religious (if not affiliated with an organized religion, then the parent or guardian provides this reference), educational, employer (if employed), and two other references.

3. Earn a total of 21 merit badges (10 more than required for the Life rank), including these 13 merit badges: (a) First Aid, (b) Citizenship in the Community, (c) Citizenship in the Nation, (d) Citizenship in the World, (e) Communication, (f) Cooking, (g) Personal Fitness, (h) Emergency Preparedness OR Lifesaving, (i) Environmental Science OR Sustainability, (j) Personal Management, (k) Swimming OR Hiking OR Cycling, (l) Camping, and (m) Family Life.

   You must choose only one of the merit badges listed in categories h, i, and k. Any additional merit badge(s) earned in those categories may be counted as one of your eight optional merit badges used to make your total of 21.

Name of Merit Badge   **Date Earned**

1. _____

2. _____

3. _____

4. _____

5. _____

6. _____

7. _____

8. _____

9. _____

10. _____

4. While a Life Scout, serve actively in your troop for six months in one or more of the following positions of responsibility[11]:

Scout troop. Patrol leader, assistant senior patrol leader, senior patrol leader, troop guide, Order of the Arrow troop representative, den chief, scribe, librarian, historian, quartermaster, junior assistant Scoutmaster, chaplain aide, instructor, webmaster, or outdoor ethics guide.

Venturing crew President, vice president, secretary, treasurer, den chief, historian, guide, quartermaster, chaplain aide, or outdoor ethics guide.

Sea Scout ship. Boatswain, boatswain's mate, purser, yeoman, storekeeper, crew leader, media specialist, specialist, den chief, or chaplain aide.

Lone Scout. Leadership responsibility in your school, religious organization, club, or elsewhere in your community.

5. While a Life Scout, plan, develop, and give leadership to others in a service project helpful to any religious institution, any school, or your community. (The project must benefit an organization other than the Boy Scouts of America.) A project proposal must be approved by the organization benefiting from the effort, your Scoutmaster and unit committee, and the council or district before you start. You must use the *Eagle Scout Service Project Workbook*, BSA publication No. 512-927, in meeting this requirement. (To learn more about the Eagle Scout service project, see the *Guide to Advancement*, topics 9.0.2.0 through 9.0.2.16.)

6. While a Life Scout, participate in a Scoutmaster conference.

---

[11]Assistant patrol leader and bugler are not approved positions of responsibility for the Eagle Scout rank. Likewise, a Scoutmaster-approved leadership project shall not be used in lieu of serving in a position of responsibility.

> In preparation for your board of review, prepare and attach to your Eagle Scout Rank Application a statement of your ambitions and life purpose and a listing of positions held in your religious institution, school, camp, community, or other organizations, during which you demonstrated leadership skills. Include honors and awards received during this service.

7. Successfully complete your board of review for the Eagle Scout rank.[12] (This requirement may be met after age 18, in accordance with *Guide to Advancement* topic 8.0.3.1.[13]).

Notes: For Venturers working on Scouts BSA requirements, replace "troop" with "crew" and "Scoutmaster" with "crew Advisor." For Sea Scouts working on Scouts BSA requirements, replace "troop" with "ship" and "Scoutmaster" with "Skipper."

---

[12] APPEALS AND EXTENSIONS

If a Scout believes all requirements for the Eagle Scout rank have been completed but a board of review is denied, the Scout may request a board of review under disputed circumstances in accordance with *Guide to Advancement* topic 8.0.3.2.

If the board of review does not approve the Scout's advancement, the decision may be appealed in accordance with *Guide to Advancement* topic 8.0.4.0.

A Scout who foresees that, due to no fault or choice of their own, it will not be possible to complete the Eagle Scout rank requirements before age 18 may apply for a limited time extension in accordance with *Guide to Advancement* topic 9.0.4.0. These are rarely granted and reserved only for work on Eagle.

[13] AGE REQUIREMENT ELIGIBILITY

Merit badges, badges of rank, and Eagle Palms may be earned by a registered Scout or a qualified Venturer or Sea Scout. Scouts may earn these awards until their 18th birthday. Any Venturer or Sea Scout who has achieved the First Class rank as a Scout in a troop or as a Lone Scout may continue working up to their 18th birthday toward the Star, Life, and Eagle Scout ranks and Eagle Palms.

An Eagle Scout board of review may occur, without special approval, within three months after the 18th birthday. Local councils must preapprove those held three to six months afterward. To initiate approval, the candidate, the candidate's parent or guardian, the unit leader, or a unit committee member attaches to the application a statement explaining the delay. **Consult the *Guide to Advancement*, topic 8.0.3.1, in the case where a board of review is to be conducted more than six months after a candidate's 18th birthday.**

If you have a permanent physical or mental disability, or a disability expected to last more than two years or beyond age 18, you may become an Eagle Scout by qualifying for as many required merit badges as you can and qualifying for alternative merit badges for the rest. If you seek to become an Eagle Scout under this procedure, you must submit a special application to your local council service center. Your application must be approved by your council advancement committee **before you can work on alternative merit badges.**

A Scout, Venturer, or Sea Scout with a disability may also qualify to work toward rank advancement after reaching 18 years of age if the guidelines outlined in section 10 of the *Guide to Advancement* are met.

EAGLE SCOUT RANK
Alternative Requirements

The Eagle Scout rank may be achieved by a Scout or a qualified[14] Venturer or Sea Scout who has a physical or mental disability by completing the Application for Alternative Eagle Scout Rank Merit Badges, No. 512-730, and by qualifying for alternative merit badges. This does not apply to individual requirements for merit badges. Merit badges are awarded only when all requirements are met as stated. See the *Guide to Advancement*, topic 10.2.2.3, for details.

The physical or mental disability must be of a permanent rather than of a temporary nature or a disability expected to last more than two years or beyond age 18. The application must include a written statement from a qualified health professional related to the nature of the disability. This person may be a physician, neurologist, psychiatrist, psychologist, etc., or, when appropriate, an educational administrator in special education.

Before applying, the Scout must earn as many of the Eagle-required merit badges as possible. However, where a permanent disability clearly precludes completing specific merit badges, a Scout who has earned at least First Class may apply for an alternative merit badge without waiting until all other Eagle-required merit badges are complete. Any alternatives must present the same challenge and learning level as those they replace, and must be completed prior to the 18th birthday unless the member is registered beyond the age of eligibility (reference *Guide to Advancement*, topic 10.1.0.1–10.1.0.2).

1. Obtain a clear and concise statement related to the nature of the disability from a qualified health professional.
2. The unit leader meets with the candidate and the Scout's parent or guardian to determine the alternative merit badges to replace those impeding the Scout's advancement.
3. The unit leader, parent or guardian, and the Scout (if possible) prepare supporting letters to accompany the application.
4. The district and council advancement committees, in turn, review the proposed alternative merit badges. They may choose to speak with the Scout, the Scout's parent or guardian, or unit leader. If the council advancement committee approves, then the candidate may start work on the approved alternative merit badges.

---

[14]In order to be an Eagle Scout candidate, a Venturer or Sea Scout must have achieved First Class rank as a Scout or as a Lone Scout.

Note: In approving the application, the district and council advancement committees must utilize the expertise of a health-care professional involved with youth who have disabilities.

5. Upon completion of the Eagle Scout rank requirements, using the alternative merit badges, the candidate appears before a board of review. The approved Application for Alternative Eagle Scout Rank Merit Badges must be attached to the Eagle Scout Rank Application.

6. Following a successful board of review, the council processes both applications and forwards them to the National Advancement Program Team. Local council action on alternative merit badges does not require national approval.

EAGLE PALMS

After successfully completing your Eagle Scout board of review on or after Aug. 1, 2017, and being validated as an Eagle Scout by the National Service Center, you will be entitled to receive an Eagle Palm for each additional five merit badges you completed before your Eagle board of review beyond those required for Eagle. In addition, all current Scouts who have completed their Eagle board of review and who had not passed their 18th birthday before Aug. 1, 2017, are entitled as well to receive Eagle Palms. For these Palms only, it will not be necessary for you to complete the requirements stated below.

After becoming an Eagle Scout and receiving the Eagle Palms you are entitled to, you may earn additional Palms by completing the following requirements:

1. Be active in the Boy Scouts of America for at least three months after becoming an Eagle Scout or after the last Palm was earned.[15]

2. Since earning the Eagle Scout rank or your last Eagle Palm, demonstrate Scout spirit by living the Scout Oath and Scout Law. Tell how you have done your duty to God and how you have lived the Scout Oath and Scout Law in your everyday life.

3. Continue to set a satisfactory example of accepting responsibility or demonstrating leadership ability.

4. Earn five additional merit badges beyond those required for Eagle or last Palm.[16]

5. While an Eagle Scout, participate in a Scoutmaster conference.

You may wear only the proper combination of Palms for the number of merit badges you earned beyond the rank of Eagle. The Bronze Palm represents five merit badges, the Gold Palm 10, and the Silver Palm 15.

Notes: For Venturers working on Scouts BSA requirements, replace "Scoutmaster" with "crew Advisor." For Sea Scouts working on Scouts BSA requirements, replace "Scoutmaster" with "Skipper."

[15]Eagle Palms must be earned in sequence, and the three-month tenure requirement must be observed for each Palm.

[16]Merit badges earned any time since joining Scouts BSA may be used to meet this requirement.

Introduction to
MERIT BADGES

On the following pages, in alphabetical order, are the requirements for all of the current merit badges.

You can learn about sports, crafts, science, trades, business, and future careers as you earn merit badges. There are more than 100 merit badges, and any Scout or any qualified Venturer or Sea Scout may earn any of these at any time (see page 5).

Pick a Subject. Talk to your unit leader about your interests. Read the requirements of the merit badges you think might interest you, and pick one to earn. Your leader will give you the name of a person from a list of counselors. These individuals have special knowledge in their merit badge subjects and are interested in helping you.

Scout Buddy System. *You must have another person with you at each meeting with the merit badge counselor.* This person must be either another registered adult or the parent/guardian of the Scout.

Call the Merit Badge Counselor. Get a *signed* Application for Merit Badge, No. 34124, from your unit leader. Get in touch with the merit badge counselor and explain that you want to earn the badge. The counselor may ask to meet you to explain what is expected and to start helping you meet the requirements. You should also discuss work you have already started or possibly completed.

> At the first meeting, you and your merit badge counselor will review and may start working on the requirements. In some cases, you may share the work you have already started or completed.

Unless otherwise specified, work on a requirement can be started at any time. Ask your counselor to help you learn the things you need to know or do. You should read the merit badge pamphlet on the subject. Many troops, schools, and public libraries have them. (See the list on the inside back cover.)

Show Your Stuff. When you are ready, call the counselor again to make an appointment. When you go, take along the things you have made to meet the requirements. If they are too big to move, take pictures or have an adult tell in writing what you have done. The counselor will test you on each requirement to make sure you know your stuff and have done or can do the things required.

Get the Badge. When the counselor is satisfied you have met each requirement, he or she will sign your application. Give the signed application to your unit leader so your merit badge emblem can be secured for you.

Requirements. You are expected to meet the requirements as they are stated—no more and no less. You must do exactly what is stated in the requirements. If it says "show or demonstrate," that is what you must do. Just telling about it isn't enough. The same thing holds true for such words as "make," "list," "in the field," and "collect," "identify," and "label."

The requirements listed in this book are the official requirements of the Boy Scouts of America. However, the requirements on the following pages might not match those in the Scouts BSA handbooks and the merit badge pamphlets, because this publication is updated only on an annual basis.

Once a Scout begins work, the Scout may continue using the requirements they started with until completion of the badge. Alternatively, they may choose to switch to the revised requirements. Sometimes, however—especially for more significant changes—the Scouts BSA handbooks, the *Scouts BSA Requirements* book, www.scouting.org/meritbadges, or official communications from the National Council may set forth a different procedure that must be used. The National Council may establish a new date for when use of the existing requirements must cease.

There is no time limit for starting and completing a merit badge, but all work must be completed when a Scout turns 18.

"Enhancing our youths' competitive edge through merit badges"

American Business

1. Do the following:

   (a) Explain four features of the free enterprise system in the United States. Describe the difference between freedom and license. Tell how the Scout Oath and Scout Law apply to business and free enterprise.

   (b) Describe the Industrial Revolution and tell about the major developments that marked the start of the modern industrial era in the United States. Discuss three people who had a great influence on business or industry in the United States and describe what each did.

   (c) Identify and describe to your counselor the five primary areas of business.

   (d) Explain the history of labor unions in the United States and the importance of labor unions and employers working together. Identify two major labor unions currently in existence.

   (e) Discuss with your counselor how business impacts the local, national, and global economy.

2. Do the following:

   (a) Explain the three basic types of financial statements (income statement, balance sheet, and statement of cash flows). Discuss with your counselor how each statement can help business leaders make better decisions.

   (b) Explain how changes in interest rates, taxes, and government spending affect the flow of money into or out of business and industry.

   (c) Explain how a sole proprietorship or partnership gets its capital. Discuss and explain four ways a corporation obtains capital.

   (d) Name five kinds of insurance useful to business. Describe their purposes.

3. Do the following:

   (a) Explain the place of profit in business.

   (b) Describe to your counselor green marketing and sustainable business practices.

   (c) Explain how ethics plays a role in business decision making.

   (d) Discuss the differences between operating a brick-and-mortar business versus an online business.

4. Describe the role of the U.S. Department of Labor. Discuss two of the following topics with your counselor:

(a) Fair Labor Standards Act (FLSA)

(b) Occupational Safety and Health Act (OSHA)

(c) Family and Medical Leave Act (FMLA)

(d) Employee Retirement Income Security Act (ERISA)

5. Choose a business and research how it applies each of the primary areas of business (accounting, finance, economics, marketing, and management). Share what you have learned with your counselor.

6. Do ONE of the following:

(a) Choose one of the primary areas of business and identify three career opportunities. Select one and research the education, training, and experience required for this career. Discuss this with your counselor and explain why this interests you.

(b) Select a business leader and interview this individual to learn more about his or her company and career path. Discuss the role ethics plays in making business decisions. Share what you have learned with your counselor.

 American Cultures

Choose THREE groups that have different racial, cultural, national, or ethnic backgrounds, one of which comes from your own background. Use these groups to meet requirements 1, 2, and 3.

1. Do TWO of the following, choosing a different group for each:

(a) Go to a festival, celebration, or other event identified with one of the groups. Report on what you see and learn.

(b) Go to a place of worship, school, or other institution identified with one of the groups. Report on what you see and learn.

(c) Talk with a person from one of the groups about the heritage and traditions of the group. Report on what you learn.

(d) Learn a song, dance, poem, or story that is traditional to one group, and teach it to a group of your friends.

(e) Go to a library or museum to see a program or exhibit featuring one group's traditions. Report on what you see and learn.

2. Imagine that one of the groups had always lived alone in a city or country to which no other groups ever came. Tell what you think the city or country might be like today. Now tell what you think it might be like if the three groups you chose lived there at the same time.

3. Tell about some differences between the religious and social customs of the three groups. Tell about some ideas or ways of doing things that are similar in the three groups.

4. Tell about a contribution made to our country by three different people, each from a different racial, ethnic, or religious background.

5. Give a talk to your Scout unit or class at school on how people from different groups have gotten along together. Lead a discussion on what can be done to help various groups understand one another better.

 # American Heritage

1. Read the Declaration of Independence. Pay close attention to the section that begins with "We hold these truths to be self-evident" and ends with "to provide new Guards for their future security." Rewrite that section in your own words, making it as easy to understand as possible. Then, share your writing with your merit badge counselor and discuss the importance of the Declaration to all Americans.

2. Do TWO of the following:

(a) Select two individuals from American history, one a political leader (a president, senator, etc.) and the other a private citizen (a writer, religious leader, etc.). Find out about each person's accomplishments and compare the contributions each has made to America's heritage.

(b) With your counselor's approval, choose an organization that has promoted some type of positive change in American society. Find out why the organization believed this change was necessary and how it helped to accomplish the change. Discuss how this organization is related to events or situations from America's past.

(c) With your counselor's approval, interview two veterans of the U.S. military. Find out what their experiences were like. Ask the veterans what they believe they accomplished.

(d) With your counselor's approval, interview three people in your community of different ages and occupations. Ask these people what America means to them, what they think is special about this country, and what American traditions they feel are important to preserve.

3. Do the following:

(a) Select a topic that is currently in the news. Describe to your counselor what is happening. Explain how today's events are related to or affected by the events and values of America's past.

(b) For each of the following, describe its adoption, tell about any changes since its adoption, and explain how each one continues to influence Americans today: the flag, the Pledge of Allegiance, the seal, the motto, and the national anthem.

(c) Research your family's history. Find out how various events and situations in American history affected your family. If your family immigrated to America, tell the reasons why. Share what you find with your counselor.

4. Do TWO of the following:

(a) Explain what is meant by the National Register of Historic Places. Describe how a property becomes eligible for listing. Make a map of your local area, marking the points of historical interest. Tell about any National Register properties in your area. Share the map with your counselor, and describe the historical points you have indicated.

(b) Research an event of historical importance that took place in or near your area. If possible, visit the place. Tell your counselor about the event and how it affected local history. Describe how the area looked then and what it now looks like.

(c) Find out when, why, and how your town or neighborhood started, and what ethnic, national, or racial groups played a part. Find out how the area has changed over the past 50 years and try to explain why.

(d) Take an active part in a program about an event or person in American history. Report to your counselor about the program, the part you took, and the subject.

(e) Visit a historic trail or walk in your area. After your visit, share with your counselor what you have learned. Discuss the importance of this location and explain why you think it might qualify for National Register listing.

5. Do ONE of the following:

(a) Watch two motion pictures (with the approval and permission of your counselor and parent) that are set in some period of American history. Describe to your counselor how accurate each film is with regard to the historical events depicted and also with regard to the way the characters are portrayed.

(b) Read a biography (with your counselor's approval) of someone who has made a contribution to America's heritage. Tell some things you admire about this individual and some things you do not admire. Explain why you think this person has made a positive or a negative contribution to America's heritage.

(c) Listen to recordings of popular songs from various periods of American history. Share five of these songs with your counselor, and describe how each song reflects the way people felt about the period in which it was popular. If a recording is not available, have a copy of the lyrics available.

6. Discuss with your counselor the career opportunities in American heritage. Pick one that interests you and explain how to prepare for this career. Discuss what education and training are required for this career.

American Labor

1. Using resources available to you, learn about working people and work-related concerns. List and briefly describe or give examples of at least EIGHT concerns of American workers. These may include, but are not limited to, working conditions, workplace safety, hours, wages, seniority, job security, equal-opportunity employment and discrimination, guest workers, automation and technologies that replace workers, unemployment, layoffs, outsourcing, and employee benefits such as health care, child care, profit sharing, continuing education, and retirement benefits.

2. With your counselor's and parent's approval and permission, visit the office or attend a meeting of a local union, a central labor council, or an employee organization, or contact one of these organizations via the internet. Then do EACH of the following:

   (a) Find out what the organization does.

   (b) Share the list of issues and concerns you made for requirement 1. Ask the people you communicate with which issues are of greatest interest or concern to them and why.

   (c) Draw a diagram showing how the organization is structured, from the local to the national level, if applicable.

3. Explain to your counselor what labor unions are, what they do, and what services they provide to members. In your discussion, show that you understand the concepts of labor, management, collective bargaining, negotiation, union shops, open shops, grievance procedures, mediation, arbitration, work stoppages, strikes, and lockouts.

4. Explain what is meant by the adversarial model of labor-management relations, compared with a cooperative-bargaining style.

5. Do ONE of the following:

   (a) Develop a time line of significant events in the history of the American labor movement from the 1770s to the present.

   (b) Prepare an exhibit, a scrapbook, or a computer presentation, such as a slide show, illustrating three major achievements of the American labor movement and how those achievements affect American workers.

   (c) With your counselor's and parent's approval and permission, watch a movie that addresses organized labor in the United States. Afterward, discuss the movie with your counselor and explain what you learned.

   (d) Read a biography (with your counselor's approval) of someone who has made a contribution to the American labor movement. Explain what contribution this person has made to the American labor movement.

6. Explain the term *globalization*. Discuss with your counselor some effects of globalization on the workforce in the United States. Explain how this global workforce fits into the economic system of this country.

7. Choose a labor issue of widespread interest to American workers—an issue in the news currently or known to you from your work on this merit badge. Before your counselor, or in writing, argue both sides of the issue, first taking management's side, then presenting labor's or the employee's point of view. In your presentation, summarize the basic rights and responsibilities of employers and employees, including union members and nonunion members.

8. Discuss with your counselor the different goals that may motivate the owners of a business, its stockholders, its customers, its employees, the employees' representatives, the community, and public officials. Explain why agreements and compromises are made and how they affect each group in achieving its goals.

9. Learn about opportunities in the field of labor relations. Choose one career in which you are interested and discuss with your counselor the major responsibilities of that position and the qualifications, education, and training such a position requires.

 # Animal Science

1. Name four breeds of livestock in each of the following classifications: horses, dairy cattle, beef cattle, sheep, hogs. Tell their principal uses and merits. Tell where the breeds originated.

2. List five diseases that afflict the animals in each of the classifications in requirement 1. Also list five diseases of poultry. Describe the symptoms of each disease and explain how each is contracted and how it could be prevented.

3. Explain the major differences in the digestive systems of ruminants, horses, pigs, and poultry. Explain how the differences in structure and function among these four types of digestive tracts affect the nutritional management of these species.

4. Select one type of animal—beef cow, dairy cow, horse, sheep, goat, or hog, or a poultry flock—and tell how you would properly manage it. Include in your discussion nutritional (feeding) concerns, housing, disease prevention, waste control/removal, breeding programs, and biosecurity as appropriate.

5. Explain the importance of setting clear goals for any animal breeding program. Tell how purebred lines of animals are produced. Explain the practice of crossbreeding and the value of this practice.

6. Complete ONE of the following options:

Beef Cattle Option

(a) Visit a farm or ranch where beef cattle are produced under any of these systems:

(1) Feeding market cattle for harvest

(2) Cow/calf operation, producing cattle for sale to commercial feeders

(3) Producing purebred cattle for sale as breeding stock to others

Talk with the operator to learn how the cattle were handled, fed, weighed, and shipped. Describe what you saw and explain what you learned. If you cannot visit a cattle ranch or farm, view a video from a breed association, or research the internet (with your parent's permission) for information on beef cattle production. Tell about your findings.

(b) Sketch a plan of a feedlot to include its forage and grain storage facilities, and loading chute for 30 or more fattening steers; or sketch a corral plan with cutting and loading chutes for handling 50 or more beef cows and their calves at one time.

(c) Make a sketch showing the principal wholesale and retail cuts of beef. Tell about the U.S. Department of Agriculture (USDA) dual grading system of beef. Tell the basis of each grade in each system.

(d) Define the following terms: bull, steer, bullock, cow, heifer, freemartin, heiferette, calf.

Dairying Option

(a) Tell how a cow or a goat converts forage and grain into milk. Explain the differences in feeds typically used for dairy cows versus those fed to beef cows.

(b) Make a chart showing the components in cow's milk or goat's milk. Chart the amount of each component.

(c) Explain the requirements for producing grade A milk. Tell how and why milk is pasteurized.

(d) Tell about the kinds of equipment used for milking and the sanitation standards that must be met on dairy farms.

(e) Define the following terms: bull, cow, steer, heifer, springer; buck, doe, kid.

(f) Visit a dairy farm or a milk processing plant. Describe what you saw and explain what you learned. If you cannot visit a dairy farm or processing plant, view a video from a breed or dairy association, or research the internet (with your parent's permission) for information on dairying. Tell about your findings.

Horse Option

(a) Make a sketch of a useful saddle horse barn and exercise yard.

(b) Tell about the history of the horse and the benefits it has brought to people. Using the four breeds of horses you chose in requirement 1, discuss the different special uses of each breed.

(c) Define the following terms: mare, stallion, gelding, foal, colt, filly; mustang, quarter horse, draft horse, pacer, trotter; pinto, calico, palomino, roan, overo, tobiano.

(d) Visit a horse farm. Describe what you saw and explain what you learned. If you cannot visit a horse farm, view a video from a breed association, or research the internet (with your parent's permission) for information on horses. Tell about your findings.

(e) Outline the proper feeding of a horse doing light work. Explain why the amount and kind of feed will change according to the kind of horse and the work it does. Describe what colic is, what can cause it, and its symptoms.

Sheep Option

(a) Make a sketch of a live lamb. Show the location of the various wholesale and retail cuts.

(b) Discuss how wools are sorted and graded.

(c) Do ONE of the following:

(1) Raise a lamb from weaning to market weight. Keep records of feed intake, weight gains, medication, vaccination, and mortality. Present your records for review by your counselor.

(2) Visit a farm or ranch where sheep are raised. Describe what you saw and explain what you learned. If you cannot visit a sheep farm or ranch, view a video from a breed association, or research the internet (with your parent's permission) for information on sheep. Tell about your findings.

(d) Describe some differences between the production of purebred and commercial lambs. Then select two breeds that would be appropriate for the production of crossbred market lambs in your region. Identify which breed the ram should be.

(e) Define the following terms: wether, ewe, ram, lamb.

Hog Option

(a) Make a sketch showing the principal wholesale and retail cuts of pork. Tell about the recommended USDA grades of pork. Tell the basis for each grade.

(b) Outline in writing the proper feeding programs used from the breeding of a gilt or sow through the weaning of the litter. Discuss the feeding programs for the growth and finishing periods.

(c) Do ONE of the following:

(1) Raise a feeder pig from weaning to market weight. Keep records of feed intake, weight gains, medication, vaccination, and mortality. Present your records for review by your counselor.

(2) Visit a farm where hogs are produced, or visit a packing plant handling hogs. Describe what you saw and explain what you learned. If you cannot visit a hog production unit or packing plant, view a video from a packer or processor, or research the internet (with your parent's permission) for information on hogs. Tell about your findings.

(d) Define the following terms: gilt, sow, barrow, boar.

Avian Option

(a) Make a sketch of a layer house or broiler house showing nests, roosts, feeders, waterers, and means of ventilation. Explain how insulation, ventilation, temperature controls, automatic lights, and other environmental controls are used to protect birds from heat, cold, and bad weather.

(b) Explain why overcrowding is dangerous for poultry flocks.

(c) Tell about the grading of eggs. Tell how broilers (fryers) are graded. Describe the classes of chicken meat.

(d) Do ONE of the following:

(1) Manage an egg-producing flock for five months. Keep records of feed purchased, eggs sold, medication, vaccination, and mortality. Present your records for review by your counselor.

(2) Raise 20 chicks from hatching. Keep records of feed intake, weight gains, medication, vaccination, and mortality. Present your records for review by your counselor.

(3) Visit a commercial avian production facility. Describe what you saw and explain what you learned. If you cannot visit a commercial facility, view a video from a poultry association, or research the internet (with your parent's permission) for information on poultry production. Tell about your findings.

(e) Define the following terms: chick, pullet, hen, rooster, cockerel, cock, capon; tom, poult.

7. Find out about three career opportunities in animal science. Pick one and find out the education, training, and experience required for this profession. Discuss this with your counselor, and explain why this profession might interest you.

 # Animation

1. **General knowledge.** Do the following:

(a) In your own words, describe to your counselor what animation is.

(b) Discuss with your counselor a brief history of animation.

2. **Principles of animation.** Choose five of the following 12 principles of animation, and discuss how each one makes an animation appear more believable: squash and stretch, anticipation, staging, straight-ahead action and pose to pose, follow through and overlapping action, slow in and slow out, arcs, secondary action, timing, exaggeration, solid drawing, appeal.

3. **Projects.** With your counselor's approval, choose two animation techniques and do the following for each:

(a) Plan your animation using thumbnail sketches and/or layout drawings.

(b) Create the animations.

(c) Share your animations with your counselor. Explain how you created each one, and discuss any improvements that could be made.

4. **Animation in our world.** Do the following:

(a) Tour an animation studio or a business where animation is used, either in person, via video, or via the internet. Share what you have learned with your counselor.

(b) Discuss with your counselor how animation might be used in the future to make your life more enjoyable and productive.

5. **Careers.** Learn about three career opportunities in animation. Pick one and find out about the education, training, and experience required for this profession. Discuss your findings with your counselor. Explain why this profession might interest you.

 # Archaeology

1. Tell what archaeology is and explain to your counselor how it differs or relates to other fields of study such as anthropology, geology, paleontology, and history. Explain how archaeology is different than artifact collecting or treasure hunting.

2. Describe each of the following steps of the archaeological process: site location, development of background research and a research design, site survey and fieldwork, artifact identification and examination, interpretation, preservation, and information sharing.

3. Describe at least two ways in which archaeologists determine the age of sites, structures, or artifacts. Explain what absolute dating and relative dating are.

4. Learn about a combined total of five archaeological sites located both within and outside the United States.

(a) For EACH site you research, point it out on a map and explain how it was discovered. Describe some of the information about the past that has been found at each site. Explain how the information gained from the study of these sites answers questions that archaeologists are asking and how the information may be important to modern people. Compare the relative ages of the sites you research.

(b) Choose ONE of the sites you picked and give a short presentation about your findings to a Cub Scout pack, your Scout troop, your school class, or another group.

5. Do the following:

(a) Learn about the federal laws and international conventions that protect archaeological sites. Find out if your state, county, or local government has regulations that apply to archaeological or historic sites.

(b) Identify a national, international, or local organization that helps to protect archaeological sites.

6. Do the following:

    (a) Explain why it is important to protect archaeological sites.

    (b) Explain what people should do if they think they have found an artifact.

    (c) Describe the ways in which you can be a protector of the past.

7. Do ONE of the following and discuss your findings with your counselor:

    (a) Visit a museum to observe how artifacts aid in conveying history.

    (b) Present to your counselor a significant family artifact/heirloom and discuss its history.

    (c) Make a list of the trash your family throws out during one week. Discuss with your counselor what archaeologists might learn about you and your family if they found your trash a thousand years from now.

8. Do either A or B of the following:

    (a) With your parent's and counselor's permission, assist a qualified archaeologist for at least eight hours with a project being worked on. Projects may include surveying, site monitoring, site stabilization, excavation, laboratory analysis, use of digital archaeological technology, or public outreach. Describe your involvement in the project, what you learned about archaeology, and the steps of archaeological inquiry.

    Note: Visiting an archaeological site will require advance planning. An archaeological site during study can be a dangerous place. While there, you will need to closely follow the archaeologist's directions and comply with all the safety procedures. Be aware of the changing conditions at the site.

    (b) With your counselor's approval, take part in a simulated archaeological project designed by a qualified archaeologist. The project must include the use of a simulated archaeological site including artifacts and features for the site. Using the steps of archaeological inquiry, analyze the "artifacts and features" and document the spatial relationships of the "artifacts and features" at the simulated site.

    Explain how the environment and time can affect the interpretation of an artifact and the overall archaeological site. Tell how you would share the results of your analysis with other researchers and the public.

    Note: To find out how to make a simulated archaeological site, talk with a professional archaeologist, trained avocational archaeologist, museum school instructor, junior high or high school science teacher, advisor from a local archaeology society, or other qualified instructor.

9. Under the supervision of a qualified archaeologist or instructor, do ONE of the following:

    (a) Help prepare an archaeological exhibit for display in a museum, visitor center, school, or other public area.

    (b) Use the methods of experimental archaeology to re-create an item or to practice a skill from the past. Write a brief report explaining the experiment and its results.

10. Research a group of people who lived in your area more than 100 years ago. Find out about their ways of life, including housing, clothing, arts and crafts, tools, trade and markets, rituals and religions, and diets, and their relationships with other groups of people in the area. Describe what you would expect to find at an archaeological site where these people lived. Explain how these people influenced your current community.

11. Identify three career opportunities in archaeology. Pick one and explain how to prepare for such a career. Discuss with your counselor what education and training are required, and explain why this profession might interest you.

 **Archery**

1. Do the following:

   (a) State and explain the Range Safety Rules:

   (1) Three safety rules when on the shooting line

   (2) Three safety rules when retrieving arrows

   (3) The four whistle commands used on a range and their related verbal commands

   (b) State and explain the general safety rules for archery. Demonstrate how to safely carry arrows in your hands.

   (c) Tell about your local and state laws for owning and using archery equipment.

2. Do the following:

   (a) Name and point to the parts of an arrow.

   (b) Describe three or more different types of arrows.

   (c) Name the four principal materials for making arrow shafts.

   (d) Do ONE of the following

   (1) Make a complete arrow from a bare shaft using appropriate equipment available to you.

   OR

   (2) To demonstrate arrow repair, inspect the shafts and prepare and replace at least three vanes, one point, and one nock. You may use as many arrows as necessary to accomplish this. The repairs can be done on wood, fiberglass, or aluminum arrows.

   (e) Explain how to properly care for and store arrows.

3. Do the following:

   (a) Explain the proper use, care, and storage of, as well as the reasons for using tabs, arm guards, shooting gloves, and quivers.

(b) Explain the following terms: cast, draw weight, string height, aiming, spine, mechanical release, and barebow.

(c) Make a bowstring using appropriate materials.

4. Explain the following:

(a) The importance of obedience to a range officer or other person in charge of a range

(b) The difference between an end and a round

(c) The differences among field, target, and 3-D archery

(d) How the five-color World Archery Federation target is scored

(e) How the National Field Archery Association (NFAA) black-and-white field targets and blue indoor targets are scored

5. Do ONE of the following options.

Option A—Using a Recurve Bow or Longbow

(a) Name and point to the parts of the recurve or longbow you are shooting.

(b) Explain how to properly care for and store recurve bows and longbows.

(c) Show the 10 steps of good shooting for the bow you are shooting.

(d) Demonstrate the proper way to string a recurve bow or longbow.

(e) Using a bow square, locate and mark with dental floss, crimp-on, or other method, the nocking point on the bowstring of the bow that you are using.

(f) Do ONE of the following:

(1) Using a recurve or longbow and arrows with a finger release, shoot a single round of one of the following BSA, USA Archery, or NFAA rounds:

(a) An NFAA field round of 14 targets and make a score of 60 points

(b) A BSA Scout field round of 14 targets and make a score of 80 points

(c) A Junior 900 round and make a score of 180 points

(d) A World Archery/USA Archery indoor* round I and make a score of 80 points

(e) An NFAA indoor* round and make a score of 50 points

(2) Shooting 30 arrows in five-arrow ends at an 80-centimeter (32-inch) five-color target at 10 yards and using the 10 scoring regions, make a score of 150.

(3) As a member of the USA Archery Junior Olympic Archery Development program (JOAD), earn your indoor or outdoor green, purple, and gray achievement award pins using a recurve bow or longbow.

(4) As a member of the NFAA's Junior Division, earn a Cub or Youth 100-score Progression Patch.

*The indoor rounds can be shot outdoors if this is more convenient.

Option B—Using a Compound Bow

(a) Name and point to the parts of the compound bow you are shooting.

(b) Explain how to properly care for and store compound bows.

(c) Show the 10 steps of good shooting for the compound bow you are shooting.

(d) Explain why it is necessary to have the string or cable on a compound bow replaced at an archery shop.

(e) Locate and mark with dental floss, crimp-on, or other method, the nocking point on the bowstring of the bow that you are using.

(f) Do ONE of the following:

(1) Using a compound bow and arrows with a finger release, shoot a single round of one of the following BSA, USA Archery, or NFAA rounds:

(a) An NFAA field round of 14 targets and make a score of 70 points

(b) A BSA Scout field round of 14 targets and make a score of 90 points

(c) A Junior 900 round and make a score of 200 points

(d) A World Archery/USA Archery indoor* round I and make a score of 90 points

(e) An NFAA indoor* round and make a score of 60 points

(2) Shooting at an 80-centimeter (32-inch) five-color target using the 10 scoring regions, make a minimum score of 160. Accomplish this in the following manner:

Shoot 15 arrows in five-arrow ends, at a distance of 10 yards

AND

Shoot 15 arrows in five-arrow ends, at a distance of 15 yards.

(3) As a member of the USA Archery Junior Olympic Archery Development program (JOAD), earn your indoor or outdoor green, purple, and gray achievement award pins using a compound bow.

(4) As a member of the NFAA's Junior Division, earn a Cub or Youth 100-score Progression Patch.

---

*The indoor rounds can be shot outdoors if this is more convenient.

 **Architecture**

1. Do the following:

(a) Tour your community and list the different types of buildings you see. Try to identify buildings that can be associated with a specific period of history or style of architecture. Make a sketch of the building you most admire.

(b) Select an architectural achievement that has had a major impact on society. Using resources such as the internet (with your parent's permission), books, and magazines, find out how this achievement has influenced the world today. Tell your counselor what you learned.

2. In the Outdoor Code, a Scout pledges to "be conservation-minded." Discuss the following with your counselor:

(a) The term *sustainable architecture.* Identify three features typical of green buildings.

(b) The difference between renewable building materials and recycled building materials, and how each can be used in construction.

(c) The relationship of architecture with its surrounding environment and the community.

(d) How entire buildings can be reused rather than torn down when they no longer serve their original purpose.

3. Do ONE of the following:

(a) With your parent's and counselor's permission and approval, arrange to meet with an architect. Ask to see the scale model of a building and the drawings that a builder would use to construct this building. Discuss why the different building materials were selected. Look at the details in the drawings and the model to see how the materials and components are attached to each other during construction.

(b) With your parent's and counselor's permission and approval, arrange to meet with an architect at a construction site. Ask the architect to bring drawings that the builder uses to construct the building. While at the site, discuss why the different building materials being used were selected. Discuss how the different building materials and components are attached to each other during construction.

Note: To visit a construction site will require advance planning. You will need permission from your parents, counselor, the architect, and the construction site manager. A construction site is a very dangerous place. While there, you will need to closely follow the site manager's directions and comply with all the safety procedures, including wearing a hard hat, protective eyewear, and proper footwear. Be aware of the changing conditions at the site, and stay with the architect or site manager.

(c) Interview someone who might be your client (such as a prospective home-owner or business owner) if you were an architect. Find out what your client's requirements would be for designing a new home or business building. Write a short program including a list of requirements for the project, the functions of the building and site, how the functions relate to one another, and the goals of the project.

4. Measure a room such as one where you live or where your troop meets. Make an accurately scaled drawing of the room's floor plan showing walls, doors, closets, windows, and any built-in furniture or cabinets. Neatly label your drawing with the following: your name, the date, what room you drew, and the scale of the drawing. (Drawing scale: ¼ inch = 1 foot)

5. Find out about three career opportunities in architecture. Pick one and find out the education, training, and experience required for this profession. Discuss this with your counselor, and explain why this profession might interest you.

 **Art**

1. Discuss the following with your counselor:

   (a) What art is and what some of the different forms of art are

   (b) The importance of art to humankind

   (c) What art means to you and how art can make you feel

2. Discuss with your counselor the following terms and elements of art: line, value, shape, form, space, color, and texture. Show examples of each element.

3. Discuss with your counselor the six principles of design: rhythm, balance, proportion, variety, emphasis, and unity.

4. Render a subject of your choice in FOUR of these ways:

   (a) Pen and ink   (f) Tempera

   (b) Watercolors   (g) Acrylics

   (c) Pencil   (h) Charcoal

   (d) Pastels   (i) Computer drawing or painting

   (e) Oil paints

5. Do ONE of the following:

   (a) Design something useful. Make a sketch or model of your design. With your counselor's approval, create a promotional piece for the item using a picture or pictures.

   (b) Tell a story with a picture or pictures or using a 3-D rendering.

   (c) Design a logo. Share your design with your counselor and explain the significance of your logo. Then, with your parent's permission and your counselor's approval, put your logo on Scout equipment, furniture, ceramics, or fabric.

6. With your parent's permission and your counselor's approval, visit a museum, art exhibit, art gallery, artists' co-op, or artist's workshop. Find out about the art displayed or created there. Discuss what you learn with your counselor.

7. Find out about three career opportunities in art. Pick one and find out the education, training, and experience required for this profession. Discuss this with your counselor, and explain why this profession might interest you.

Astronomy

1. Do the following:

    (a) Explain to your counselor the most likely hazards you may encounter while participating in astronomy activities, and what you should do to anticipate, help prevent, mitigate, and respond to these hazards.

    (b) Explain first aid for injuries or illnesses such as heat and cold reactions, dehydration, bites and stings, and damage to your eyes that could occur during observation.

    (c) Describe the proper clothing and other precautions for safely making observations at night and in cold weather. Then explain how to safely observe the Sun, objects near the Sun, and the Moon.

2. Explain what light pollution is and how it and air pollution affect astronomy.

3. With the aid of diagrams (or real telescopes if available), do each of the following:

    (a) Explain why binoculars and telescopes are important astronomical tools. Demonstrate or explain how these tools are used.

    (b) Describe the similarities and differences of several types of astronomical telescopes, including at least one that observes light beyond the visible part of the spectrum (i.e., radio, X-ray, ultraviolet, or infrared).

    (c) Explain the purposes of at least three instruments used with astronomical telescopes.

    (d) Describe the proper care and storage of telescopes and binoculars both at home and in the field.

4. Do the following*:

    (a) Identify in the sky at least 10 constellations, at least four of which are in the zodiac.

    (b) Identify in the sky at least eight conspicuous stars, five of which are of magnitude 1 or brighter.

    (c) Make two sketches of the Big Dipper. In one sketch, show the Big Dipper's orientation in the early evening sky. In another sketch, show its position several hours later. In both sketches, show the North Star and the horizon. Record the date and time each sketch was made.

    (d) Explain what we see when we look at the Milky Way.

---

*If instruction is done in a planetarium, Scouts must still identify the required stars and constellations outside under the natural night sky.

5. Do the following:

(a) List the names of the five most visible planets. Explain which ones can appear in phases similar to lunar phases and which ones cannot, and explain why.

(b) Using the internet (with your parent's permission) and other resources, find out when each of the five most visible planets that you identified in requirement 5a will be observable in the evening sky during the next 12 months, then compile this information in the form of a chart or table.

(c) Describe the motion of the planets across the sky.

(d) Observe a planet and describe what you saw.

6. Do the following:

(a) Sketch the face of the Moon and indicate at least five seas and five craters. Label these landmarks.

(b) Sketch the phase and position of the Moon, at the same hour and place, for four nights within a one-week period. Include landmarks on the horizon such as hills, trees, and buildings. Explain the changes you observe.

(c) List the factors that keep the Moon in orbit around Earth.

(d) With the aid of diagrams, explain the relative positions of the Sun, Earth, and the Moon at the times of lunar and solar eclipses, and at the times of new, first-quarter, full, and last-quarter phases of the Moon.

7. Do the following:

(a) Describe the composition of the Sun, its relationship to other stars, and some effects of its radiation on Earth's weather and communications.

(b) Define sunspots and describe some of the effects they may have on solar radiation.

(c) Identify at least one red star, one blue star, and one yellow star (other than the Sun). Explain the meaning of these colors.

8. With your counselor's approval and guidance, do ONE of the following:

(a) Visit a planetarium or astronomical observatory. Submit a written report, a scrapbook, or a video presentation afterward to your counselor that includes the following information:

(1) Activities occurring there

(2) Exhibits and displays you saw

(3) Telescopes and other instruments being used

(4) Celestial objects you observed

(b) Plan and participate in a three-hour observation session that includes using binoculars or a telescope. List the celestial objects you want to observe, and find each on a star chart or in a guidebook. Prepare a log or notebook. Discuss with your counselor what you hope to observe prior to your observation session. Review your log or notebook with your counselor afterward.*

(c) Plan and host a star party for your Scout troop or other group such as your class at school. Use binoculars or a telescope to show and explain celestial objects to the group.

---

*To complete this requirement, you may use the Scout Planning Worksheet at http://troopleader.org/wp-content/uploads/2016/03/512-505_16_Wksht_WEB.pdf.

(d) Help an astronomy club in your community hold a star party that is open to the public.

(e) Personally take a series of photographs or digital images of the movement of the Moon, a planet, an asteroid, meteor, or a comet. In your visual display, label each image and include the date and time it was taken. Show all positions on a star chart or map. Show your display at school or at a troop meeting. Explain the changes you observed.

9. Find out about three career opportunities in astronomy. Pick one and find out the education, training, and experience required for this profession. Discuss this with your counselor, and explain why this profession might interest you.

 Athletics

If meeting any of the requirements for this merit badge is against the Scout's religious convictions, the requirement does not have to be done if the Scout's parents and the proper religious advisors state in writing that to do so would be against religious convictions. The Scout's parents must also accept full responsibility for anything that might happen because of this exemption.

Requirement 2a is being added for health and safety, and to provide consistency with the Personal Fitness merit badge.

1. Do the following:

(a) Explain to your counselor the most likely hazards you may encounter during athletics activities, and what you should do to anticipate, help prevent, mitigate, and respond to these hazards.

(b) Show that you know first aid for injuries or illnesses that could occur while participating in athletics events, including sprains, strains, contusions, abrasions, blisters, dehydration, and heat reactions.

2. Do the following:

(a) Before completing requirements 3 and 5, have your health-care practitioner give you a physical examination, using the Scout medical examination form.

(b) Explain the importance of a physical exam.

(c) Explain the importance of maintaining good health habits, especially during training—and how the use of tobacco products, alcohol, and other harmful substances can negatively affect your health and your performance in athletic activities.

(d) Explain the importance of maintaining a healthy diet.

3. Select an athletic activity that interests you, then do the following:

(a) With guidance from your counselor, establish a personal training program suited to the activity you have chosen. Follow this training program for three months.

(b) Create a chart to monitor your progress during this time.

(c) Explain to your counselor the equipment necessary to participate in this activity and the appropriate clothing for the time of year.

(d) At the end of four months, review the chart you created for requirement 3b, and discuss with your counselor what progress you have made during training. Tell how your development has affected you mentally and physically.

4. Do the following:

(a) Give the rules for two athletic activities, one of which is the activity you chose for requirement 3.

(b) Discuss the importance of warming up and cooling down.

(c) Explain to your counselor what an amateur athlete is and the differences between an amateur and a professional athlete.

(d) Discuss the traits and importance of good sportsmanship. Tell what role sportsmanship plays in both individual and group athletic activities.

5. Complete the activities in FOUR of the following groups and show improvement over a three-month period:

Group 1: Sprinting
(a) 100-meter dash
(b) 200-meter dash

Group 2: Long-Distance Running
(a) 3k run
(b) 5k run

Group 3: Long Jump OR High Jump
(a) Running long jump OR running high jump (best of three tries)
(b) Standing long jump OR standing high jump (best of three tries)

Group 4: Swimming
(a) 100-meter swim
(b) 200-meter swim

Group 5: Pull-Ups AND Push-Ups
(a) Pull-ups in two minutes
(b) Push-ups in two minutes

Group 6: Baseball Throw
(a) Baseball throw for accuracy, 10 throws at a target (distance to be determined by age): ages 11 to 12, 20 feet; ages 13 to 15, 30 feet; ages 16 to 17, 40 feet
(b) Baseball throw for distance, five throws (total distance)

Group 7: Basketball Shooting
(a) Basketball shot for accuracy, 10 free-throw shots
(b) Basketball throw for skill and agility, the following shots as shown on the diagram:
　　(1) Left-side layup
　　(2) Right-side layup

(3) Left side of hoop, along the key line

(4) Right side of hoop, along the key line

(5) Where key line and free-throw line meet, left side

(6) Where key line and free-throw line meet, right side

(7) Top of the key

(8) Anywhere along the three-point line

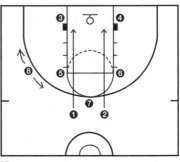

Group 8: Football Kick OR Soccer Kick

(a) Goals from the 10-yard line, eight kicks

(b) Football kick or soccer kick for distance, five kicks (total distance)

Group 9: Weight Training

(a) Chest/bench press, two sets of 15 repetitions each

(b) Leg curls, two sets of 15 repetitions each

6. Do the following:

(a) Prepare plans for conducting a sports meet or field day that includes 10 activities, at least five of which must come from the groups mentioned in requirement 5. Outline the duties of each official needed and list the equipment the meet will require.

(b) With your parent's and counselor's approval, serve as an official or volunteer at a sports meet to observe officials in action. Tell your counselor about your responsibilities at the meet and discuss what you learned.

 Automotive Maintenance

You will need access to a car or truck and its owner's manual to meet some requirements for this merit badge. If you do not have your own vehicle, you should work with your merit badge counselor or other trusted adult to obtain access to a vehicle and the owner's manual for that vehicle.

1. Do the following:

(a) Explain to your counselor the hazards you are most likely to encounter during automotive maintenance activities, and what you should do to anticipate, help prevent, mitigate, or lessen these hazards.

(b) Discuss with your counselor the safety equipment, tools, and clothing used while checking or repairing a motor vehicle. Use this equipment, tools, and/or clothing (when needed or called for) in meeting the requirements for this merit badge.

2. **General Maintenance, Safety, and Registration.** Do the following:

(a) Review the maintenance chart in the owner's manual. Explain the requirements and time limits.

(b) Demonstrate how to check the following:

(1) Brake fluid	(5) Windshield washer fluid
(2) Engine oil	(6) Transmission fluid
(3) Coolant	(7) Battery fluid (if possible) and condition of the battery terminals
(4) Power steering fluid	

(c) Locate the fuse boxes; determine the type and size of fuses. Demonstrate the proper replacement of burned-out fuses.

(d) Demonstrate how to check the condition and tension of belts and hoses.

(e) Check the vehicle for proper operation of its lights, including the interior overhead lights, instrument lights, warning lights, and exterior bulbs.

(f) Locate and check the air filter(s).

(g) Explain the purpose, importance, and limitations of safety belts and passive restraints.

(h) Find out the requirements for your state's emissions and safety inspections (as applicable), including how often a vehicle needs to be inspected.

(i) Explain the importance of registering a vehicle and find out the annual registration fee for renewing your family car's registration.

3. **Dashboard.** Do the following:

(a) Explain the function of the fuel gauge, speedometer, tachometer, oil pressure, and engine temperature gauge. Point each one out on the instrument cluster.

(b) Explain the symbols that light up on the dashboard and the difference between the yellow and red symbols. Explain each of the indicators on the dashboard, using the owner's manual if necessary.

4. **Tires.** Do the following:

(a) Explain the difference between tire manufacturer's and vehicle manufacturer's specifications and show where to find them.

(b) Demonstrate how to check tire pressure and properly inflate a tire. Check the spare tire and make sure it is ready for use.

(c) Explain why wheel alignment is important to the life of a tire. Explain caster, camber, and toe-in adjustments on wheel alignment.

(d) Explain the purpose of the lateral-wear bar indicator.

(e) Explain how to dispose of old tires in accordance with local laws and regulations.

5. **Engine.** Do the following:

(a) Explain how an internal combustion engine operates. Tell the differences between gasoline and diesel engines. Explain how a gasoline-electric hybrid vehicle is powered.

(b) Discuss the purpose of engine oil. Explain the API service code, the SAE number, and the viscosity rating.

(c) Explain where to find the recommended oil type and the amount of oil to be used in the vehicle engine.

6. **Cooling System.** Do the following:

(a) Explain the need for coolant in the cooling system, and the importance of selecting the correct coolant type for a given vehicle.

(b) Explain how to flush and change the engine coolant in the vehicle, and how to properly dispose of the used coolant.

7. **Fuel System.** Do the following:

(a) Explain how the air and fuel systems work together and why it is necessary to have an air filter and fuel filter.

(b) Explain how a fuel injection system works and how an onboard computer works with the fuel injection system.

8. **Ignition and Electrical Systems.** Do the following:

(a) Diagram and explain the parts of the electrical system.

(b) Explain the engine's firing order.

(c) Explain the purpose of the spark gap.

(d) Demonstrate how to safely connect jumper cables to your car battery.

9. **Drive Train.** Do the following:

(a) Diagram the drive train and explain the different parts.

(b) Explain the difference between automatic and standard transmissions.

(c) Explain the types of automatic transmission fluid.

(d) Explain the types of lubricants used in a standard transmission, and in the differential and transfer case.

(e) Explain the difference between front-wheel, rear-wheel, and four-wheel drive.

10. **Brake System.** Do the following:

(a) Explain the brake system (including antilock systems) and how it operates.

(b) Explain the differences between disc and drum systems.

(c) Demonstrate how to check the condition of a vehicle's brake system. After checking, make recommendations for repairs (if necessary).

11. Do TWO of the following:

(a) Determine the value of three different vehicles you are interested in purchasing. One must be new and one must be used; the third vehicle can be new or used. For each vehicle, find out the requirements and cost of automobile insurance to include basic liability and options for collision, comprehensive, towing, and rental car. Using the three vehicles you chose and with your merit badge counselor's assistance, complete the operation/maintenance chart provided in the merit badge pamphlet. Use this information to determine the operating cost per mile for each vehicle, and discuss what you learn with your counselor.

(b) Choose a car cleaner and wax product for a vehicle you want to clean. Explain clear-coat paint and the precautions necessary for care. Clean the vehicle, both inside and out, and wax the exterior. Use a vinyl and rubber protectant (on vinyl tops, rubber door seals, sidewalls, etc.) and explain the importance of this protectant.

(c) Locate the manufacturer's jack. Use the jack to demonstrate how to engage the jack correctly on the vehicle, then change a tire correctly.

(d) Perform an oil filter and oil change on a vehicle. Explain how to properly dispose of the used oil and filter.

12. Find out about three career opportunities in the automotive industry. Pick one and find out the education, training, and experience required for this profession. Discuss this with your counselor, and explain why this profession might interest you.

 # Aviation

1. Do the following:

(a) Define "aircraft." Describe some kinds and uses of aircraft today. Explain the operation of piston, turboprop, and jet engines.

(b) Point out on a model airplane the forces that act on an airplane in flight.

(c) Explain how an airfoil generates lift, how the primary control surfaces (ailerons, elevators, and rudder) affect the airplane's attitude, and how a propeller produces thrust.

(d) Demonstrate how the control surfaces of an airplane are used for takeoff, straight climb, level turn, climbing turn, descending turn, straight descent, and landing.

(e) Explain the following: the sport pilot, the recreational pilot, and the private pilot certificates; the instrument rating.

2. Do TWO of the following:

(a) Take a flight in an aircraft, with your parent's permission. Record the date, place, type of aircraft, and duration of flight, and report on your impressions of the flight.

(b) Under supervision, perform a preflight inspection of a light airplane.

(c) Obtain and learn how to read an aeronautical chart. Measure a true course on the chart. Correct it for magnetic variation, compass deviation, and wind drift to determine a compass heading.

(d) Using one of many flight simulator software packages available for computers, "fly" the course and heading you established in requirement 2c or another course you have plotted.

(e) Explain the purposes and functions of the various instruments found in a typical single-engine aircraft: attitude indicator, heading indicator, altimeter, airspeed indicator, turn and bank indicator, vertical speed indicator, compass, navigation (GPS and VOR) and communication radios, tachometer, oil pressure gauge, and oil temperature gauge.

(f)   Create an original poster of an aircraft instrument panel. Include and identify the instruments and radios discussed in requirement 2e.

3. Do ONE of the following:

(a)   Build and fly a fuel-driven or battery-powered electric model airplane. Describe safety rules for building and flying model airplanes. Tell safety rules for use of glue, paint, dope, plastics, fuel, and battery pack.

(b)   Build a model FPG-9. Get others in your troop or patrol to make their own model, then organize a competition to test the precision of flight and landing of the models.

4. Do ONE of the following:

(a)   Visit an airport. After the visit, report on how the facilities are used, how runways are numbered, and how runways are determined to be "active."

(b)   Visit a Federal Aviation Administration facility—a control tower, terminal radar control facility, air route traffic control center, or Flight Standards District Office. (Phone directory listings are under U.S. Government Offices, Transportation Department, Federal Aviation Administration. Call in advance.) Report on the operation and your impressions of the facility.

(c)   Visit an aviation museum or attend an air show. Report on your impressions of the museum or show.

5. Find out about three career opportunities in aviation. Pick one and find out the education, training, and experience required for this profession. Discuss this with your counselor, and explain why this profession might interest you.

Backpacking

1. Discuss the prevention of and treatment for the health concerns that could occur while backpacking, including hypothermia, heat reactions, frostbite, dehydration, insect stings, tick bites, snakebite, and blisters.

2. Do the following:

   (a) List 10 items that are essential to be carried on any backpacking trek and explain why each item is necessary.

   (b) Describe 10 ways you can limit the weight and bulk to be carried in your pack without jeopardizing your health or safety.

3. Do the following:

   (a) Define limits on the number of backpackers appropriate for a trek crew.

   (b) Describe how a trek crew should be organized.

   (c) Tell how you would minimize risk on a backpacking trek.

   (d) Explain the purpose of an emergency response plan.

4. Do the following:

   (a) Describe the importance of using Leave No Trace principles while backpacking, and at least five ways you can lessen the crew's impact on the environment.

   (b) Describe proper methods of handling human and other wastes while on a backpacking trek. Describe the importance of and means to assure personal cleanliness while on a backpacking trek.

   (c) Tell what factors are important in choosing a campsite.

5. Do the following:

   (a) Demonstrate two ways to treat water and tell why water treatment is essential.

   (b) Explain to your counselor the importance of staying well-hydrated during a trek.

6. Do the following:

   (a) Demonstrate that you can read topographic maps.

   (b) While on a trek, use a map and compass to establish your position on the ground at three different locations, OR use a GPS receiver to establish your position on a topographic map and on the ground at three different locations.

   (c) Explain how to stay found, and what to do if you get lost.

7. Tell how to prepare properly for and deal with inclement weather.

8. Do the following:

(a) Explain the advantages and disadvantages of the different types of back-packing stoves using at least three different types of fuel.

(b) Demonstrate that you know how to operate a backpacking stove safely and to handle liquid fuel safely.

(c) Prepare at least three meals using a stove and fuel you can carry in a backpack.

(d) Demonstrate that you know how to keep cooking and eating gear clean and sanitary, and that you practice proper methods for food storage while on a backpacking trek.

9. Do the following:

(a) Write a plan that includes a schedule for a patrol/crew backpacking hike of at least 2 miles.

(b) Conduct a prehike inspection of the patrol and its equipment.

(c) Show that you know how to properly pack your personal gear and your share of the crew's gear and food.

(d) Show you can properly shoulder your pack and adjust it for proper wear.

(e) While using the plan you developed for requirement 9a, carry your fully loaded pack to complete a hike of at least 2 miles.

10. Using Leave No Trace principles, participate in at least three backpacking treks of at least three days each and at least 15 miles each, and using at least two different campsites on each trek. Carry everything you will need throughout the trek.

11. Do the following:

(a) Write a plan for a backpacking trek of at least five days using at least three different campsites and covering at least 30 miles. Your plan must include a description of and route to the trek area, a schedule (including a daily schedule), a list of food and equipment needs, a safety and emergency plan, and a budget.

(b) Using Leave No Trace principles, take the trek you have planned and, while on the trek, complete at least one service project approved by your merit badge counselor.

(c) Keep a daily journal during the trek that includes a day-by-day description of your activities, including notes about what worked well and thoughts about improvements that could be made for the next trek.

Basketry

1. Do the following:

   (a) Explain to your counselor the hazards you are most likely to encounter while using basketry tools and materials, and what you should do to anticipate, help prevent, mitigate, and respond to these hazards.

   (b) Discuss the prevention of and first-aid treatment for injuries, including cuts, scratches, and scrapes, that could occur while working with basketry tools and materials.

2. Do the following:

   (a) Show your counselor that you are able to identify each of the following types of baskets: plaited, coiled, ribbed, and wicker.

   (b) Describe three different types of weaves to your counselor.

3. Plan and weave EACH of the following projects:

   (a) a square basket

   (b) a round basket

   (c) a campstool seat

 # Bird Study

1. Explain the need for bird study and why birds are useful indicators of the quality of the environment. Describe how birds are part of the ecosystem.

2. Show that you are familiar with the terms used to describe birds by sketching or tracing a perched bird and then labeling 15 different parts of the bird. Sketch or trace an extended wing and label six types of wing feathers.

3. Demonstrate that you know how to properly use and care for binoculars, a spotting scope, or a monocular.

   (a) Explain what the specification numbers mean on binoculars, a spotting scope, or a monocular.

   (b) Show how to adjust the eyepiece and how to focus for proper viewing.

   (c) Show how to properly care for and clean the lenses.

   (d) Describe when and where each type of viewing device would be most effective.

4. Demonstrate that you know how to use a bird field guide. Show your counselor that you are able to understand a range map by locating in the book and pointing out the wintering range, the breeding range, and/or the year-round range of one species of each of the following types of birds:

(a) Seabird

(b) Plover

(c) Falcon or hawk

(d) Warbler or vireo

(e) Heron or egret

(f) Sparrow

(g) Nonnative bird (introduced to North America from a foreign country since 1800)

5. Observe and be able to identify at least 20 species of wild birds. Prepare a field notebook, making a separate entry for each species, and record the following information from your field observations and other references.

(a) Note the date and time.

(b) Note the location and habitat.

(c) Describe the bird's main feeding habitat and list two types of food that the bird is likely to eat.

(d) Note whether the bird is a migrant or a summer, winter, or year-round resident of your area.

6. Describe to your counselor how certain orders of birds are uniquely adapted to a specific habitat. In your description, include characteristics such as the size and shape of the following:

(a) Beak

(b) Body

(c) Leg and foot

(d) Feathers/plumage

7. Explain the function of a bird's song. Be able to identify five of the 20 species in your field notebook by song or call alone. For each of these five species, enter a description of the song or call, and note the behavior of the bird making the sound. Note why you think the bird was making the call or song that you heard.

8. Do ONE of the following:

(a) Go on a field trip with a local club or with others who are knowledgeable about birds in your area.

(1) Keep a list or fill out a checklist of all the birds your group observed during the field trip.

(2) Tell your counselor which birds your group saw and why some species were common and some were present in small numbers.

(3) Tell your counselor what makes the area you visited good for finding birds.

(b) By using a public library, the internet, or contacting the National Audubon Society, find the name and location of the Christmas Bird Count nearest your home and obtain the results of a recent count.

(1) Explain what kinds of information are collected during the annual event.

(2) Tell your counselor which species are most common, and explain why these birds are abundant.

(3) Tell your counselor which species are uncommon, and explain why these were present in small numbers. If the number of birds of these species is decreasing, explain why, and what, if anything, could be done to reverse their decline.

9. Do ONE of the following. For the option you choose, describe what birds you hope to attract, and why.

(a) Build a bird feeder and put it in an appropriate place in your yard or another location.

(b) Build a birdbath and put it in an appropriate place.

(c) Build a backyard sanctuary for birds by planting trees and shrubs for food and cover.

10. Do the following:

(a) Explain the differences between extinct, endangered, and threatened.

(b) Identify a bird species that is on the endangered or threatened list. Explain what caused their decline. Discuss with your counselor what can be done to reverse this trend and what can be done to help remove the species from the endangered or threatened list.

11. Identify three career opportunities connected to the study of birds. Pick one and find out the education, training, and experience required for this profession. Discuss with your counselor if this profession might interest you.

 **Bugling**

1. Give a brief history of the bugle.

2. Do the following:

(a) Explain and demonstrate how the bugle makes sound, and explain how the bugle is related to other brass wind instruments.

(b) Compose a bugle call for your troop or patrol to signal a common group activity, such as assembling for mealtime or striking a campsite. Play the call that you have composed before your unit or patrol.

3. Sound the following bugle calls: "First Call," "Reveille," "Assembly," "Mess," "Drill," "Fatigue," "Officers," "Recall," "Church," "Swimming," "Fire," "Retreat," "To the Colors," "Call to Quarters," and "Taps."

4. Explain when each of the calls in requirement 3 is used.

5. Explain how to care for, clean, and maintain a bugle.

6. Serve as bugler in your troop for three months.*

*NOTE: A bugle, trumpet, or cornet may be used to meet these requirements.

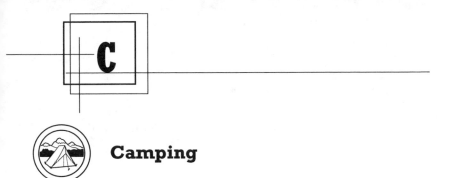

Camping

1. Do the following:

    (a) Explain to your counselor the most likely hazards you may encounter while participating in camping activities and what you should do to anticipate, help prevent, mitigate, and respond to these hazards.

    (b) Discuss with your counselor why it is important to be aware of weather conditions before and during your camping activities. Tell how you can prepare should the weather turn bad during your campouts.

    (c) Show that you know first aid for and how to prevent injuries or illnesses that could occur while camping, including hypothermia, frostbite, heat reactions, dehydration, altitude sickness, insect stings, tick bites, snakebite, blisters, and hyperventilation.

2. Learn the Leave No Trace principles and the Outdoor Code and explain what they mean. Write a personal and group plan for implementing these principles on your next outing.

3. Make a written plan* for an overnight trek and show how to get to your camping spot by using a topographical map and one of the following:

    (a) A compass

    (b) A GPS receiver**

    (c) A smartphone with a GPS app*

4. Do the following:

    (a) Make a duty roster showing how your patrol is organized for an actual overnight campout. List assignments for each member.

    (b) Help a Scout patrol or a Webelos Scout unit in your area prepare for an actual campout, including creating the duty roster, menu planning, equipment needs, general planning, and setting up camp.

5. Do the following:

    (a) Prepare a list of clothing you would need for overnight campouts in both warm and cold weather. Explain the term "layering."

    (b) Discuss footwear for different kinds of weather and how the right footwear is important for protecting your feet.

    (c) Explain the proper care and storage of camping equipment (clothing, footwear, bedding).

---

*To complete this requirement, you may use the Scout Planning Worksheet at http://troopleader.org/wp-content/uploads/2016/03/512-505_16_Wksht_WEB.pdf.

**If a GPS-equipped device is not available, explain how to use one to get to your camping spot.

(d) List the outdoor essentials necessary for any campout, and explain why each item is needed.

(e) Present yourself to your Scoutmaster with your pack for inspection. Be correctly clothed and equipped for an overnight campout.

6. Do the following:

(a) Describe the features of four types of tents, when and where they could be used, and how to care for tents. Working with another Scout, pitch a tent.

(b) Discuss the importance of camp sanitation and tell why water treatment is essential. Then demonstrate two ways to treat water.

(c) Describe the factors to be considered in deciding where to pitch your tent.

(d) Tell the difference between internal- and external-frame packs. Discuss the advantages and disadvantages of each.

(e) Discuss the types of sleeping bags and what kind would be suitable for different conditions. Explain the proper care of your sleeping bag and how to keep it dry. Make a comfortable ground bed.

7. Prepare for an overnight campout with your patrol by doing the following:

(a) Make a checklist of personal and patrol gear that will be needed.

(b) Pack your own gear and your share of the patrol equipment and food for proper carrying. Show that your pack is right for quickly getting what is needed first, and that it has been assembled properly for comfort, weight, balance, size, and neatness.

8. Do the following:

(a) Explain the safety procedures for

(1) Using a propane or butane/propane stove

(2) Using a liquid fuel stove

(3) Proper storage of extra fuel

(b) Discuss the advantages and disadvantages of different types of lightweight cooking stoves.

(c) Prepare a camp menu. Explain how the menu would differ from a menu for a backpacking or float trip. Give recipes and make a food list for your patrol. Plan two breakfasts, three lunches, and two suppers. Discuss how to protect your food against bad weather, animals, and contamination.

(d) While camping in the outdoors, cook at least one breakfast, one lunch, and one dinner for your patrol from the meals you have planned for requirement 8c. At least one of those meals must be a trail meal requiring the use of a lightweight stove.

9. Show experience in camping by doing the following:

(a) Camp a total of at least 20 nights at designated Scouting activities or events. One long-term camping experience of up to six consecutive nights may be applied toward this requirement. Sleep each night under the sky or in a tent you have pitched. If the camp provides a tent that has already been pitched, you need not pitch your own tent.

(b) On any of these camping experiences, you must do TWO of the following, only with proper preparation and under qualified supervision.

    (1) Hike up a mountain, gaining at least 1,000 vertical feet.

    (2) Backpack, snowshoe, or cross-country ski for at least 4 miles.

    (3) Take a bike trip of at least 15 miles or at least four hours.

    (4) Take a nonmotorized trip on the water of at least four hours or 5 miles.

    (5) Plan and carry out an overnight snow camping experience.

    (6) Rappel down a rappel route of 30 feet or more.

(c) Perform a conservation project approved by the landowner or land managing agency. This can be done alone or with others.

10. Discuss how the things you did to earn this badge have taught you about personal health and safety, survival, public health, conservation, and good citizenship. In your discussion, tell how Scout spirit and the Scout Oath and Scout Law apply to camping and outdoor ethics.

Canoeing

1. Do the following:

(a) Explain to your counselor the most likely hazards you may encounter while participating in canoeing activities and what you should do to anticipate, help prevent, mitigate, and respond to these hazards.

(b) Review prevention, symptoms, and first-aid treatment for the following injuries or illnesses that could occur while canoeing: blisters, cold-water shock and hypothermia, dehydration, heat-related illnesses, sunburn, sprains, and strains.

(c) Discuss the BSA Safety Afloat policy. Tell how it applies to canoeing activities.

2. Before doing the following requirements, successfully complete the BSA swimmer test: Jump feetfirst into water over the head in depth. Level off and swim 75 yards in a strong manner using one or more of the following strokes: sidestroke, breaststroke, trudgen, or crawl; then swim 25 yards using an easy, resting backstroke. The 100 yards must be completed in one swim without stops and must include at least one sharp turn. After completing the swim, rest by floating.

3. Do the following:

(a) Name and point out the major parts of a canoe.

(b) Describe how the length and shape of a canoe affect its performance.

(c) Discuss the advantages and disadvantages of the different materials used to make canoes.

4. Do the following:

(a) Name and point out the parts of a paddle. Explain the difference between a straight and bent-shaft paddle and when each is best used.

(b) Demonstrate how to size correctly a paddle for a paddler in a sitting position and a kneeling position.

5. Do the following:

(a) Discuss with your counselor the characteristics of life jackets most appropriate for canoeing and tell why a life jacket must always be worn while paddling.

(b) Demonstrate how to select and properly fit the correct size life jacket.

6. Discuss with your counselor the general care and maintenance of canoes, paddles, and other canoeing equipment.

7. Do the following:

(a) Discuss what personal and group equipment would be appropriate for a canoe camping trip. Describe how personal and group equipment can be packed and protected from water.

(b) Using the containers and packs from requirement 7a, demonstrate how to load and secure the containers and other equipment in the canoe.

(c) Using appropriate knots, including a trucker's hitch, taut-line hitch, and bowline, demonstrate how to secure a canoe to a vehicle or a trailer, or if these are not available, a rack on land.

8. With a companion, use a properly equipped canoe to demonstrate the following:

(a) Safely carry and launch the canoe from a dock or shore (both, if possible).

(b) Safely land the canoe on a dock or shore (both, if possible) and return it to its proper storage location.

(c) Demonstrate kneeling and sitting positions in a canoe and explain the proper use for each position.

(d) Change places while afloat in the canoe.

9. With a companion, use a properly equipped canoe to demonstrate the following:

(a) In deep water, exit the canoe and get back in without capsizing.

(b) Safely perform a controlled capsize of the canoe and demonstrate how staying with a capsized canoe will support both paddlers.

(c) Swim, tow, or push a swamped canoe 50 feet to shallow water. In the shallow water, empty the swamped canoe and reenter it.

(d) In deep water, rescue a swamped canoe and its paddlers by emptying the swamped canoe and helping the paddlers safely reenter their boat without capsizing.

10. With a companion, use a properly equipped canoe to demonstrate the following paddling strokes as both a bow and stern paddler:

(a) Forward stroke

(b) Backstroke

(c) Draw

For stern paddling only:

(d) J-stroke

(e) Pushaway

(f) Forward sweep

(g) Reverse sweep

(h) Rudder stroke

(i) Stern pry

11. Using the strokes in requirement 10, and in an order determined by your counselor, use a properly equipped canoe to demonstrate the following tandem maneuvers while paddling on opposite sides and without changing sides. Each paddler must demonstrate these maneuvers in both the bow and stern and on opposite paddling sides:

(a) Pivot or spin the canoe in either direction.

(b) Move the canoe sideways or abeam in either direction.

(c) Stop the canoe.

(d) Move the canoe in a straight line for 50 yards.

12. Use a properly equipped canoe to demonstrate solo canoe handling:

(a) Launch from shore or a pier (both, if possible).

(b) Using a single-blade paddle and paddling only on one side, demonstrate proper form and use of the forward stroke, backstroke, draw stroke, pushaway stroke, forward sweep, reverse sweep, J-stroke, and rudder stroke. Repeat while paddling on the other side.

(c) Using a single-blade paddle and paddling only on one side, demonstrate proper form and use of a combination of a forward stroke, rudder stroke, and stern pry by canoeing to a target 50 yards away. Repeat while paddling on the other side.

(d) Make a proper landing at a dock or shore (both, if possible). Store canoe properly (with assistance, if needed).

13. Discuss the following types of canoeing:

(a) Olympic canoe sprint

(b) Flatwater and river touring

(c) Outrigger

(d) Marathon

(e) Freestyle

(f) Whitewater

(g) Canoe poling

Chemistry

1. Do EACH of the following:

   (a) Describe three examples of safety equipment used in a chemistry laboratory and the reason each one is used.

   (b) Describe what a safety data sheet (SDS) is and tell why it is used.

   (c) Obtain an SDS for both a paint and an insecticide. Compare and discuss the toxicity, disposal, and safe-handling sections for these two common household products.

   (d) Discuss the safe storage of chemicals. How does the safe storage of chemicals apply to your home, your school, your community, and the environment?

2. Do EACH of the following:

   (a) Predict what would happen if you placed an iron nail in a copper sulfate solution. Then, put an iron nail in a copper sulfate solution. Describe your observations and make a conclusion based on your observations. Compare your prediction and original conclusion with what actually happened. Write the formula for the reaction that you described.

   (b) Describe how you would separate sand from water, table salt from water, oil from water, and gasoline from motor oil. Name the practical processes that require these kinds of separations.

   (c) Describe the difference between a chemical reaction and a physical change.

3. Construct a Cartesian diver. Describe its function in terms of how gases in general behave under different pressures and different temperatures. Describe how the behavior of gases affects a backpacker at high altitudes and a scuba diver underwater.

4. Do EACH of the following:

   (a) Cut a round onion into small chunks. Separate the onion chunks into three equal portions. Leave the first portion raw. Cook the second portion of onion chunks until the pieces are translucent. Cook the third portion until the onions are caramelized, or brown in color. Taste each type of onion. Describe the taste of raw onion versus partially cooked onion versus caramelized onion. Explain what happens to molecules in the onion during the cooking process.

   (b) Describe the chemical similarities and differences between toothpaste and an abrasive household cleanser. Explain how the end use or purpose of a product affects its chemical formulation.

   (c) In a clear container, mix a half-cup of water with a tablespoon of oil. Explain why the oil and water do not mix. Find a substance that will help the two combine, and add it to the mixture. Describe what happened, and explain how that substance worked to combine the oil and water.

5. List the five classical divisions of chemistry. Briefly describe each one, and tell how it applies to your everyday life.

6. Do EACH of the following:

   (a) Name two government agencies that are responsible for tracking the use of chemicals for commercial or industrial use. Pick one agency and briefly describe its responsibilities to the public and the environment.

   (b) Define pollution. Explain the chemical effects of ozone and global climate change. Pick a current environmental problem as an example. Briefly describe what people are doing to resolve this hazard and to increase understanding of the problem.

   (c) Using reasons from chemistry, describe the effect on the environment of ONE of the following:

   (1) The production of aluminum cans or plastic milk cartons

   (2) Burning fossil fuels

   (3) Used motor oil

   (4) Newspaper

   (d) Briefly describe the purpose of phosphates in fertilizer and in laundry detergent. Explain how the use of phosphates in fertilizers affects the environment. Also, explain why phosphates have been removed from laundry detergents.

7. Do ONE of the following activities:

   (a) Visit a laboratory and talk to a practicing chemist. Ask what the chemist does and what training and education are needed to work as a chemist.

   (b) Using resources found at the library and in periodicals, books, and the internet (with your parent's permission), learn about two different kinds of work done by chemists, chemical engineers, chemical technicians, or industrial chemists. For each of the four positions, find out the education and training requirements.

   (c) Visit an industrial plant that makes chemical products or uses chemical processes and describe the processes used. What, if any, pollutants are produced and how are they handled?

   (d) Visit a county farm agency or similar governmental agency and learn how chemistry is used to meet the needs of agriculture in your county.

Chess

1. Discuss with your merit badge counselor the history of the game of chess. Explain why it is considered a game of planning and strategy.

2. Discuss with your merit badge counselor the following:

   (a) The benefits of playing chess, including developing critical thinking skills, concentration skills, and decision-making skills, and how these skills can help you in other areas of your life

   (b) Sportsmanship and chess etiquette

3. Demonstrate to your counselor that you know each of the following. Then, using Scouting's Teaching EDGE*, teach someone (preferably another Scout) who does not know how to play chess:

   (a) The name of each chess piece

   (b) How to set up a chessboard

   (c) How each chess piece moves, including castling and en passant captures

4. Do the following:

   (a) Demonstrate scorekeeping using the algebraic system of chess notation.

   (b) Discuss the differences between the opening, the middle game, and the endgame.

   (c) Explain four opening principles.

   (d) Explain the four rules for castling.

   (e) On a chessboard, demonstrate a "scholar's mate" and a "fool's mate."

   (f) Demonstrate on a chessboard four ways a chess game can end in a draw.

5. Do the following:

   (a) Explain four of the following elements of chess strategy: exploiting weaknesses, force, king safety, pawn structure, space, tempo, time.

   (b) Explain any five of these chess tactics: clearance sacrifice, decoy, discovered attack, double attack, fork, interposing, overloading, overprotecting, pin, remove the defender, skewer, zwischenzug.

   (c) Set up a chessboard with the white king on *e1*, the white rooks on *a1* and *h1*, and the black king on *e5*. With White to move first, demonstrate how to force checkmate on the black king.

   (d) Set up and solve five direct-mate problems provided by your merit badge counselor.

---

*You may learn about Scouting's Teaching EDGE from your unit leader, another Scout, or by attending training.

6. Do ONE of the following:

(a) Play at least three games of chess with other Scouts and/or your merit badge counselor. Replay the games from your score sheets and discuss with your counselor how you might have played each game differently.

(b) Play in a scholastic (youth) chess tournament and use your score sheets from that tournament to replay your games with your merit badge counselor. Discuss with your counselor how you might have played each game differently.

(c) Organize and run a chess tournament with at least four players, plus you. Have each competitor play at least two games.

 # Citizenship in the Community

1. Discuss with your counselor what citizenship in the community means and what it takes to be a good citizen in your community. Discuss the rights, duties, and obligations of citizenship, and explain how you can demonstrate good citizenship in your community, Scouting unit, place of worship, or school.

2. Do the following:

(a) On a map of your community or using an electronic device, locate and point out the following:

(1) Chief government buildings such as your city hall, county courthouse, and public works/services facilities

(2) Fire station, police station, and hospital nearest your home

(3) Parks, playgrounds, recreation areas, and trails

(4) Historical or other interesting points of interest

(b) Chart the organization of your local or state government. Show the top offices and tell whether they are elected or appointed.

3. Do the following:

(a) Attend a meeting of your city, town, or county council or school board; OR attend a municipal, county, or state court session.

(b) Choose one of the issues discussed at the meeting where a difference of opinions was expressed, and explain to your counselor why you agree with one opinion more than you do another one.

4. Choose an issue that is important to the citizens of your community; then do the following:

(a) Find out which branch of local government is responsible for this issue.

(b) With your counselor's and a parent's approval, interview one person from the branch of government you identified in requirement 4a. Ask what is being done about this issue and how young people can help.

(c) Share what you have learned with your counselor.

5. With the approval of your counselor and a parent, watch a movie that shows how the actions of one individual or group of individuals can have a positive effect on a community. Discuss with your counselor what you learned from the movie about what it means to be a valuable and concerned member of the community.

6. List some of the services (such as the library, recreation center, public transportation, and public safety) your community provides that are funded by taxpayers. Tell your counselor why these services are important to your community.

7. Do the following:

    (a) Identify three charitable organizations outside of Scouting that interest you and bring people in your community together to work for the good of your community.

    (b) Pick ONE of the organizations you chose for requirement 7a. Using a variety of resources (including newspapers, fliers and other literature, the internet, volunteers, and employees of the organization), find out more about this organization.

    (c) With your counselor's and your parent's approval, contact the organization you chose for requirement 7b, and find out what young people can do to help. While working on this merit badge, volunteer at least eight hours of your time for the organization. After your volunteer experience is over, discuss what you have learned with your counselor.

8. Develop a public presentation (such as a video, slide show, speech, digital presentation, or photo exhibit) about important and unique aspects of your community. Include information about the history, cultures, and ethnic groups of your community; its best features and popular places where people gather; and the challenges it faces. Stage your presentation in front of your merit badge counselor or a group, such as your patrol or a class at school.

 # Citizenship in the Nation

1. Explain what citizenship in the nation means and what it takes to be a good citizen of this country. Discuss the rights, duties, and obligations of a responsible and active American citizen.

2. Do TWO of the following:

    (a) Visit a place that is listed as a National Historic Landmark or that is on the National Register of Historic Places. Tell your counselor what you learned about the landmark or site and what you found interesting about it.

    (b) Tour your state capitol building or the U.S. Capitol. Tell your counselor what you learned about the capitol, its function, and the history.

(c) Tour a federal facility. Explain to your counselor what you saw there and what you learned about its function in the local community and how it serves this nation.

(d) Choose a national monument that interests you. Using books, brochures, the internet (with your parent's permission), and other resources, find out more about the monument. Tell your counselor what you learned, and explain why the monument is important to this country's citizens.

3. Watch the national evening news five days in a row OR read the front page of a major daily newspaper five days in a row. Discuss the national issues you learned about with your counselor. Choose one of the issues and explain how it affects you and your family.

4. Discuss each of the following documents with your counselor. Tell your counselor how you feel life in the United States might be different without each one.
(a) Declaration of Independence
(b) Preamble to the Constitution
(c) The Constitution
(d) Bill of Rights
(e) Amendments to the Constitution

5. List the six functions of government as noted in the preamble to the Constitution. Discuss with your counselor how these functions affect your family and local community.

6. With your counselor's approval, choose a speech of national historical importance. Find out about the author, and tell your counselor about the person who gave the speech. Explain the importance of the speech at the time it was given, and tell how it applies to American citizens today. Choose a sentence or two from the speech that has significant meaning to you, and tell your counselor why.

7. Name the three branches of our federal government and explain to your counselor their functions. Explain how citizens are involved in each branch. For each branch of government, explain the importance of the system of checks and balances.

8. Name your two senators and the member of Congress from your congressional district. Write a letter about a national issue and send it to one of these elected officials, sharing your view with him or her. Show your letter and any response you receive to your counselor.

Citizenship in the World

1. Explain what citizenship in the world means to you and what you think it takes to be a good world citizen.

2. Explain how one becomes a citizen in the United States, and explain the rights, duties, and obligations of U.S. citizenship. Discuss the similarities and differences between the rights, duties, and obligations of U.S. citizens and the citizens of two other countries.

3. Do the following:

   (a) Pick a current world event. In relation to this current event, discuss with your counselor how a country's national interest and its relationship with other countries might affect areas such as its security, its economy, its values, and the health of its citizens.

   (b) Select a foreign country and discuss with your counselor how its geography, natural resources, and climate influence its economy and its global partnerships with other countries.

4. Do TWO of the following:

   (a) Explain international law and how it differs from national law. Explain the role of international law and how international law can be used as a tool for conflict resolution.

   (b) Using resources such as major daily newspapers, the internet (with your parent's permission), and news magazines, observe a current issue that involves international trade, foreign exchange, balance of payments, tariffs, and free trade. Explain what you have learned. Include in your discussion an explanation of why countries must cooperate in order for world trade and global competition to thrive.

   (c) Select TWO of the following organizations and describe their role in the world.

      (1) The United Nations and UNICEF
      (2) The World Court
      (3) Interpol
      (4) World Organization of the Scout Movement
      (5) The World Health Organization
      (6) Amnesty International
      (7) The International Committee of the Red Cross
      (8) CARE (Cooperative for American Relief Everywhere)
      (9) European Union

5. Do the following:

   (a) Discuss the differences between constitutional and nonconstitutional governments.

(b) Name at least five different types of governments currently in power in the world.

(c) Show on a world map countries that use each of these five different forms of government.

6. Do the following:

(a) Explain how a government is represented abroad and how the United States government is accredited to international organizations.

(b) Describe the roles of the following in the conduct of foreign relations.

    (1) Ambassador

    (2) Consul

    (3) Bureau of International Information Programs

    (4) Agency for International Development

    (5) United States and Foreign Commercial Service

(c) Explain the purpose of a passport and visa for international travel.

7. Do TWO of the following (with your parent's permission) and share with your counselor what you have learned:

(a) Visit the website of the U.S. State Department. Learn more about an issue you find interesting that is discussed on this website.

(b) Visit the website of an international news organization or foreign government, OR examine a foreign newspaper available at your local library, bookstore, or newsstand. Find a news story about a human right realized in the United States that is not recognized in another country.

(c) Visit with a student or Scout from another country and discuss the typical values, holidays, ethnic foods, and traditions practiced or enjoyed there.

(d) Attend a world Scout jamboree.

(e) Participate in or attend an international event in your area, such as an ethnic festival, concert, or play.

 # Climbing

1. Do the following:

(a) Explain to your counselor the most likely hazards you may encounter while participating in climbing and rappelling activities and what you should do to anticipate, help prevent, mitigate, and respond to these hazards.

(b) Show that you know first aid for and how to prevent injuries or illnesses that could occur during climbing activities, including heat and cold reactions, dehydration, stopped breathing, sprains, abrasions, fractures, rope burns, blisters, snakebite, and insect bites or stings.

(c) Identify the conditions that must exist before performing CPR on a person.

2. Learn the Leave No Trace principles and Outdoor Code, and explain what they mean.

3. Present yourself properly dressed for belaying, climbing, and rappelling (i.e., appropriate clothing, footwear, and a helmet; rappellers can also wear gloves).

4. **Location.** Do the following:

   (a) Explain how the difficulty of climbs is classified, and apply classifications to the rock faces or walls where you will demonstrate your climbing skills.

   (b) Explain the following: top-rope climbing, lead climbing, and bouldering.

   (c) Evaluate the safety of a particular climbing area. Consider weather, visibility, the condition of the climbing surface, and any other environmental hazards.

   (d) Determine how to summon aid to the climbing area in case of an emergency.

5. **Verbal signals.** Explain the importance of using verbal signals during every climb and rappel, and while bouldering. With the help of the merit badge counselor or another Scout, demonstrate the verbal signals used by each of the following:

   (a) Climbers

   (b) Rappellers

   (c) Belayers

   (d) Boulderers and their spotters

6. **Rope.** Do the following:

   (a) Describe the kinds of rope acceptable for use in climbing and rappelling.

   (b) Show how to examine a rope for signs of wear or damage.

   (c) Discuss ways to prevent a rope from being damaged.

   (d) Explain when and how a rope should be retired.

   (e) Properly coil a rope.

7. **Knots.** Demonstrate the ability to tie each of the following knots. Give at least one example of how each knot is used in belaying, climbing, or rappelling.

   (a) Figure eight on a bight

   (b) Figure eight follow-through

   (c) Water knot

   (d) Double fisherman's knot (grapevine knot)

   (e) Safety knot

8. **Harnesses.** Correctly put on a commercially made climbing harness.

9. **Belaying.** Do the following:

   (a) Explain the importance of belaying climbers and rappellers and when it is necessary.

   (b) Belay three different climbers ascending a rock face or climbing wall.

(c) Belay three different rappellers descending a rock face or climbing wall using a top rope.

10. **Climbing.** Do the following:

(a) Show the correct way to directly tie into a belay rope.

(b) Climb at least three different routes on a rock face or climbing wall, demonstrating good technique and using verbal signals with a belayer.

11. **Rappelling.** Do the following:

(a) Using a carabiner and a rappel device, secure your climbing harness to a rappel rope.

(b) Tie in to a belay rope set up to protect rappellers.

(c) Rappel down three different rock faces or three rappel routes on a climbing wall. Use verbal signals to communicate with a belayer, and demonstrate good rappelling technique.

12. Demonstrate ways to store rope, hardware, and other gear used for climbing, rappelling, and belaying.

 # Coin Collecting

1. Understand how coins are made and where the active U.S. Mint facilities are located.

2. Explain these collecting terms:

(a) Obverse

(b) Reverse

(c) Reeding

(d) Clad

(e) Type set

(f) Date set

3. Explain the grading terms Uncirculated, Extremely Fine, Very Fine, Fine, Very Good, Good, and Poor. Show five different grade examples of the same coin type. Explain the term *proof* and why it is not a grade. Tell what encapsulated coins are.

4. Know three different ways to store a collection, and describe the benefits, drawbacks, and expense of each method. Pick one to use when completing requirements.

5. Do ONE of the following:

(a) Demonstrate to your counselor that you know how to use two U.S. or world coin reference catalogs.

(b) Read a numismatic magazine or newspaper and tell your counselor about what you learned.

6. Describe the 1999–2008 50 State Quarters® program or the America the Beautiful Quarters® program. Collect and show your counselor five different quarters from circulation you have acquired from one of these programs.

7. Collect from circulation a set of current U.S. coins. Include one coin of each denomination (cent, nickel, dime, quarter, half dollar, dollar). For each coin, locate the mint marks, if any, and the designer's initials, if any.

8. Do the following:

    (a) Identify the people depicted on the following denominations of current U.S. paper money: $1, $2, $5, $10, $20, $50, and $100.

    (b) Explain "legal tender."

    (c) Describe the role the Federal Reserve System plays in the distribution of currency.

9. Do ONE of the following:

    (a) Collect and identify 50 foreign coins from at least 10 different countries.

    (b) Collect and identify 20 bank notes from at least five different countries.

    (c) Collect and identify 15 different tokens or medals.

    (d) For each year since the year of your birth, collect a date set of a single type of coin.

10. Do ONE of the following:

    (a) Tour a U.S. Mint facility, a Bureau of Engraving and Printing facility, a Federal Reserve bank, or a numismatic museum or exhibit, and describe what you learned to your counselor.

    (b) With your parent's permission, attend a coin show or coin club meeting, or view the website of the U.S. Mint or a coin dealer, and report what you learned.

    (c) Give a talk about coin collecting to a group such as your troop, a Cub Scout pack, or your class at school.

    (d) Do drawings of five Colonial-era U.S. coins.

Collections

1. Prepare a short written report or outline for your counselor, giving a detailed description of your collection*, including a short history. Be sure to include why you chose that particular type of collecting and what you enjoy and have learned from your collection.*

2. Explain the growth and development of your collection.

3. Demonstrate your knowledge of preserving and displaying your collection.

   (a) Explain the precautions you need to take to preserve your collection, including

      (1) Handling

      (2) Cleaning

      (3) Storage

   (b) Explain how best to display your collection, keeping in mind preserving as discussed above.

   (c) Explain to your counselor the events available for a hobbyist of this collection, including shows, seminars, conventions, contests, and museum programs or exhibits.

4. Demonstrate your knowledge of collecting and investing. Discuss with your counselor:

   (a) How investing and speculation would apply to your collection

   (b) What you would look for in purchasing other collections similar to yours

   (c) What you would expect in return value if you decided to sell all or part of the collection

5. Do the following:

   (a) Discuss with your counselor at least 10 terms commonly used in your collection and be prepared to discuss the definition of each.

   (b) Show your counselor any two groups from your collection. Explain how you organized your collection and why you chose that method. (Note: If your collection is too large to transport and your counselor is unable to view your collection directly, photographs should be available to share.)

   (c) Explain how your collection is valued by other collectors, and display to your counselor any price guides that may be available.

   (d) Explain how your collection is graded for value, physical defects, size, and age. Show the various classifications or ratings used in your collection.

---

*Stamp and coin collecting are excluded from eligibility for this merit badge.

(e) List the national, state, or local association responsive to your collection.

(f) Show the location of and explain to your counselor the identification number (if applicable), series, brand name (if any), and any other special identification marks.

6. Discuss with your counselor the plans you have to continue with the collection in the future.

7. Discuss with your counselor why and how collecting has changed and how this applies to your collection.

8. Find out about career opportunities in collecting. Pick one and find out the education, training, and experience required for this profession. Discuss this with your counselor, and explain why this profession might interest you.

 # Communication

1. Do ONE of the following:

(a) For one day, keep a log in which you describe your communication activities. Keep track of the time and different ways you spend communicating, such as talking person-to-person, listening to teachers, listening to the radio or podcasts, watching television, using social media, reading books and other print media, and using any electronic communication device. Discuss with your counselor what your log reveals about the importance of communication in your life. Think of ways to improve your communication skills.

(b) For three days, keep a journal of your listening experiences. Identify one example of each of the following, and discuss with your counselor when you have listened to:

    (1) Obtain information

    (2) Be persuaded

    (3) Appreciate or enjoy something

    (4) Understand someone's feelings

(c) In a small-group setting, meet with other Scouts or with friends. Have them share personal stories about significant events in their lives that affected them in some way. Take note of how each Scout participates in the group discussion and how effectively each Scout communicates their story. Report what you have learned to your counselor about the differences you observed in effective communication.

(d) List as many ways as you can think of to communicate with others (face-to-face, by telephone, letter, email, text messages, social media, and so on). For each type of communication, discuss with your counselor an instance when that method might not be appropriate or effective.

2. Do ONE of the following:

   (a) Think of a creative way to describe yourself using, for example, a collage, short story or autobiography, drawing or series of photographs, or a song or skit. Using the aid you created, make a presentation to your counselor about yourself.

   (b) Choose a concept, product, or service in which you have great confidence. Build a sales plan based on its good points. Try to persuade the counselor to agree with, use, or buy your concept, product, or service. After your sales talk, discuss with your counselor how persuasive you were.

3. Write a five-minute speech. Give it at a meeting of a group.

4. Interview someone you know fairly well, like, or respect because of his or her position, talent, career, or life experiences. Listen actively to learn as much as you can about the person. Then prepare and deliver to your counselor an introduction of the person as though this person were to be a guest speaker, and include reasons why the audience would want to hear this person speak. Show how you would call to invite this person to speak.

5. Attend a public meeting (city council, school board, debate) approved by your counselor where several points of view are given on a single issue. Practice active listening skills and take careful notes of each point of view. Prepare an objective report that includes all points of view that were expressed, and share this with your counselor.

6. With your counselor's approval, develop a plan to teach a skill or inform someone about something. Prepare teaching aids for your plan. Carry out your plan. With your counselor, determine whether the person has learned what you intended.

7. Do ONE of the following:

   (a) Write to the editor of a magazine or your local newspaper to express your opinion or share information on any subject you choose. Send your message by fax, email, or regular mail.

   (b) Create a webpage or blog of special interest to you (for instance, your troop or crew, a hobby, or a sport). Include at least three articles or entries and one photograph or illustration, and one link to some other webpage or blog that would be helpful to someone who visits the webpage or blog you have created. *It is not necessary to post your webpage or blog to the internet, but if you decide to do so, you must first share it with your parents and counselor and get their permission.*

   (c) Use desktop publishing to produce a newsletter, brochure, flier, or other printed material for your troop or crew, class at school, or other group. Include at least one article and one photograph or illustration.

8. Plan a troop or crew court of honor, campfire program, or interfaith worship service. Have the patrol leaders' council approve it, then write the script and prepare the program. Serve as master of ceremonies.

9. Find out about three career opportunities in communication. Pick one and find out the education, training, and experience required for this profession. Discuss this with your counselor, and explain why this profession might interest you.

Composite Materials

1. Do the following:

   (a) Explain to your counselor the most likely hazards you may encounter while working with composite materials and what you should do to anticipate, mitigate and prevent, and respond to these hazards. Describe the appropriate safety gear and clothing that should be used when working with composite materials.

   (b) Explain the precautions that must be taken when handling, storing, and disposing of resins, reinforcements, and other materials used in composites. Include in your discussion the importance of health, safety, and environmental responsibility and awareness.

   (c) Describe what a material safety data sheet (MSDS) is and tell why it is used.

2. Do the following:

   (a) Explain what composite materials are. Include a brief history of composites and how they have developed.

   (b) Compare the similarities and differences between composites and wood, aluminum, copper, and steel. Describe the physical, electrical, mechanical, corrosive, flammability, cost, and other such properties. For each of these raw materials, give one example of how it can be shaped and used for a specific application.

3. Describe how composite materials are made. Then do the following:

   (a) Discuss three different composite reinforcement materials, their positive and negative characteristics, and their uses. Obtain the MSDS for each one and discuss the toxicity, disposal, and safe-handling sections for these materials.

   (b) Discuss three different resins used in composites, their positive and negative characteristics, and their uses. Obtain the MSDS for each one and discuss the toxicity, disposal, and safe-handling sections for these materials. Include thermoset resins and thermoplastic resins in your discussion.

   (c) For each of the three resins you chose for requirement 3b, think of a new application that might be worth developing.

4. With your parent's permission and your counselor's approval do ONE of the following:

   (a) Visit a company that manufactures or repairs products made with composites. Discuss what you learn with your counselor.

   (b) Find three composites-related websites. Share and discuss what you learn with your counselor.

5. Do the following:

   (a) Use composite materials to complete two projects, at least one of which must come from the *Composite Materials* merit badge pamphlet. The second project may come from the pamphlet OR may be one you select on your own that has been approved by your counselor in advance.

(b) With your counselor's assistance, find an appropriate site where the projects can be safely completed under your counselor's supervision and/or the supervision of an adult approved by your counselor who is knowledgeable about composites.

(c) With your counselor, determine how the finished projects will be evaluated. Using those guidelines, evaluate the completed projects with your counselor.

6. Find out about three career opportunities in composite materials. Pick one and find out the education, training, and experience required for this profession. Discuss this with your counselor, and explain why this profession might interest you.

 **Cooking**

1. **Health and safety.** Do the following:

(a) Explain to your counselor the most likely hazards you may encounter while participating in cooking activities and what you should do to anticipate, help prevent, mitigate, and respond to these hazards.

(b) Show that you know first aid for and how to prevent injuries or illnesses that could occur while preparing meals and eating, including burns and scalds, cuts, choking, and allergic reactions.

(c) Describe how meat, fish, chicken, eggs, dairy products, and fresh vegetables should be stored, transported, and properly prepared for cooking. Explain how to prevent cross-contamination.

(d) Discuss with your counselor food allergies, food intolerance, and food-related illnesses and diseases. Explain why someone who handles or prepares food needs to be aware of these concerns.

(e) Discuss with your counselor why reading food labels is important. Explain how to identify common allergens such as peanuts, tree nuts, milk, eggs, wheat, soy, and shellfish.

2. **Nutrition.** Do the following:

(a) Using the MyPlate food guide or the current USDA nutrition model, give five examples for EACH of the following food groups, the recommended number of daily servings, and the recommended serving size:

    (1) Fruits

    (2) Vegetables

    (3) Grains

    (4) Proteins

    (5) Dairy

(b) Explain why you should limit your intake of oils and sugars.

(c) Determine your daily level of activity and your caloric need based on your activity level. Then, based on the MyPlate food guide, discuss with your counselor an appropriate meal plan for yourself for one day.

(d) Discuss your current eating habits with your counselor and what you can do to eat healthier, based on the MyPlate food guide.

(e) Discuss the following food label terms: calorie, fat, saturated fat, trans fat, cholesterol, sodium, carbohydrate, dietary fiber, sugar, protein. Explain how to calculate total carbohydrates and nutritional values for two servings, based on the serving size specified on the label.

3. **Cooking basics.** Do the following:

(a) Discuss EACH of the following cooking methods. For each one, describe the equipment needed, how temperature control is maintained, and name at least one food that can be cooked using that method: baking, boiling, broiling, pan frying, simmering, steaming, microwaving, grilling, foil cooking, and use of a Dutch oven.

(b) Discuss the benefits of using a camp stove on an outing vs. a charcoal or wood fire.

(c) Describe for your counselor how to manage your time when preparing a meal so components for each course are ready to serve at the correct time.

Note: The meals prepared for Cooking merit badge requirements 4, 5, and 6 will count only toward fulfilling those requirements and will not count toward rank advancement or other merit badges. Meals prepared for rank advancement or other merit badges may not count toward the Cooking merit badge. You must not repeat any menus for meals actually prepared or cooked in requirements 4, 5, and 6.

4. **Cooking at home.** Using the MyPlate food guide or the current USDA nutrition model, plan menus for three full days of meals (three breakfasts, three lunches, and three dinners) plus one dessert. Your menus should include enough to feed yourself and at least one adult, keeping in mind any special needs (such as food allergies) and how you kept your foods safe and free from cross-contamination. List the equipment and utensils needed to prepare and serve these meals.

Then do the following:

(a) Create a shopping list for your meals showing the amount of food needed to prepare and serve each meal, and the cost for each meal.

(b) Share and discuss your meal plan and shopping list with your counselor.

(c) Using at least five of the 10 cooking methods from requirement 3, prepare and serve yourself and at least one adult (parent, family member, guardian, or other responsible adult) one breakfast, one lunch, one dinner, and one dessert from the meals you planned.*

---

*The meals for requirement 4 may be prepared on different days, and they need not be prepared consecutively. The requirement calls for Scouts to plan, prepare, and serve one breakfast, one lunch, and one dinner to at least one adult; those served need not be the same for all meals.

(d) Time your cooking to have each meal ready to serve at the proper time. Have an adult verify the preparation of the meal to your counselor.

(e) After each meal, ask a person you served to evaluate the meal on presentation and taste, then evaluate your own meal. Discuss what you learned with your counselor, including any adjustments that could have improved or enhanced your meals. Tell how better planning and preparation help ensure a successful meal.

5. **Camp cooking.** Do the following:

(a) Using the MyPlate food guide or the current USDA nutrition model, plan five meals for your patrol (or a similar size group of up to eight youth, including you) for a camping trip. Your menus should include enough food for each person, keeping in mind any special needs (such as food allergies) and how you keep your foods safe and free from cross-contamination. These five meals must include at least one breakfast, one lunch, one dinner, AND at least one snack OR one dessert. List the equipment and utensils needed to prepare and serve these meals.

(b) Create a shopping list for your meals showing the amount of food needed to prepare and serve each meal, and the cost for each meal.

(c) Share and discuss your meal plan and shopping list with your counselor.

(d) In the outdoors, using your menu plans for this requirement, cook two of the five meals you planned using either a lightweight stove or a low-impact fire. Use a different cooking method from requirement 3 for each meal. You must also cook a third meal using either a Dutch oven OR a foil pack OR kabobs. Serve all of these meals to your patrol or a group of youth.**

(e) In the outdoors, prepare a dessert OR a snack and serve it to your patrol or a group of youth.**

(f) After each meal, have those you served evaluate the meal on presentation and taste, and then evaluate your own meal. Discuss what you learned with your counselor, including any adjustments that could have improved or enhanced your meals. Tell how planning and preparation help ensure successful outdoor cooking.

(g) Explain to your counselor how you cleaned the equipment, utensils, and the cooking site thoroughly after each meal. Explain how you properly disposed of dishwater and of all garbage.

(h) Discuss how you followed the Outdoor Code and no-trace principles when preparing your meals.

**Where local regulations do not allow you to build a fire, the counselor may adjust the requirement to meet the law. The meals in requirements 5 and 6 may be prepared for different trips and need not be prepared consecutively. Scouts working on this badge in summer camp should take into consideration foods that can be obtained at the camp commissary.

6. **Trail and backpacking meals.** Do the following:

(a) Using the MyPlate food guide or the current USDA nutrition model, plan a menu for trail hiking or backpacking that includes one breakfast, one lunch, one dinner, and one snack. These meals must not require refrigeration and are to be consumed by three to five people (including you). Be sure to keep in mind any special needs (such as food allergies) and how you will keep your foods safe and free from cross-contamination. List the equipment and utensils needed to prepare and serve these meals.

(b) Create a shopping list for your meals, showing the amount of food needed to prepare and serve each meal, and the cost for each meal.

(c) Share and discuss your meal plan and shopping list with your counselor. Your plan must include how to repackage foods for your hike or backpacking trip to eliminate as much bulk, weight, and garbage as possible.

(d) While on a trail hike or backpacking trip, prepare and serve two meals and a snack from the menu planned for this requirement. At least one of those meals must be cooked over a fire, or an approved trail stove (with proper supervision).**

(e) After each meal, have those you served evaluate the meal on presentation and taste, then evaluate your own meal. Discuss what you learned with your counselor, including any adjustments that could have improved or enhanced your meals. Tell how planning and preparation help ensure successful trail hiking or backpacking meals.

(f) Discuss how you followed the Outdoor Code and no-trace principles during your outing. Explain to your counselor how you cleaned any equipment, utensils, and the cooking site after each meal. Explain how you properly disposed of any dishwater and packed out all garbage.

7. **Food-related careers.** Find out about three career opportunities in cooking. Select one and find out the education, training, and experience required for this profession. Discuss this with your counselor, and explain why this profession might interest you.

**Where local regulations do not allow you to build a fire, the counselor may adjust the requirement to meet the law. The meals in requirements 5 and 6 may be prepared for different trips and need not be prepared consecutively. Scouts working on this badge in summer camp should take into consideration foods that can be obtained at the camp commissary.

Crime Prevention

1. Discuss the role and value of laws in society with regard to crime and crime prevention. Include in your discussion the definitions of "crime" and "crime prevention."

2. Prepare a journal from various sources that address crime and crime prevention efforts in your community.

3. Discuss the following with your counselor:

   (a) The role of citizens, including youth, in crime prevention.

   (b) Gangs and their impact on the community.

   (c) When and how to report a crime.

4. After doing EACH of the following, discuss with your counselor what you have learned.

   (a) Inspect your neighborhood for opportunities that may lead to crime. Learn how to do a crime prevention survey.

   (b) Using the checklist in this pamphlet, conduct a security survey of your home and discuss the results with your family.

5. Teach your family or patrol members how to protect themselves from crime at home, at school, in your community, and while traveling.

6. Help raise awareness about one school safety issue facing students by doing ONE of the following:

   (a) Create a poster for display on a school bulletin board.

   (b) With permission from school officials, create a pagelong public service announcement that could be read over the public address system at school or posted on the school's website.

   (c) Make a presentation to a group such as a Cub Scout den that addresses the issue.

7. Do ONE of the following:

   (a) Assist in the planning and organization of a crime prevention program in your community such as Neighborhood Watch, Community Watch, or Crime Stoppers. Explain how this program can benefit your neighborhood.

   (b) With your parent's and counselor's approval, visit a jail or detention facility or a criminal court hearing. Discuss your experience with your counselor.

8. Discuss the following with your counselor:

   (a) How drug abuse awareness programs such as "Drugs: A Deadly Game" help prevent crime.

(b) Why alcohol, tobacco, and marijuana are sometimes called "gateway drugs" and how gateway drugs can lead to the use of other drugs.

(c) The potential consequences from the misuse of prescription drugs.

(d) How the illegal sale and use of drugs lead to other crimes.

(e) Three resources in your city where a person with a drug problem or drug-related problem can go for help.

(f) How to recognize child abuse.

(g) The three R's of Youth Protection.

9. Discuss the following with your counselor:

(a) The role of a sheriff's or police department in crime prevention.

(b) The purpose and operation of agencies in your community that help law enforcement personnel prevent crime, and how those agencies function during emergency situations.

(c) Explain the role private security plays in crime prevention.

(d) Choose a career in the crime prevention or security industry that interests you. Describe the level of education required and responsibilities of a person in that position. Tell why this position interests you.

 # Cycling

1. Do the following:

(a) Explain to your counselor the most likely hazards you may encounter while participating in cycling activities and what you should do to anticipate, help prevent, mitigate, and respond to these hazards.

(b) Show that you know first aid for injuries or illnesses that could occur while cycling, including cuts, scratches, blisters, sunburn, heat exhaustion, heatstroke, hypothermia, frostbite, dehydration, insect stings, tick bites, and snakebite. Explain to your counselor why you should be able to identify the poisonous plants and poisonous animals that are found in your area.

(c) Explain the importance of wearing a properly sized and fitted helmet while cycling, and of wearing the right clothing for the weather. Know the BSA Bike Safety Guidelines.

2. Clean and adjust a bicycle. Prepare it for inspection using a bicycle safety checklist. Be sure the bicycle meets local laws.

3. Show your bicycle to your counselor for inspection. Point out the adjustments or repairs you have made. Do the following:

(a) Show all points that need regular lubrication.

(b) Show points that should be checked regularly to make sure the bicycle is safe to ride.

(c) Show how to adjust brakes, seat level and height, and steering tube.

4. Describe how to brake safely with foot brakes and with hand brakes.

5. Show how to repair a flat by removing the tire, replacing or patching the tube, and remounting the tire.

6. Describe your state and local traffic laws for bicycles. Compare them with motor-vehicle laws.

7. Using the BSA buddy system, complete all of the requirements for ONE of the following options: road biking OR mountain biking.*

Option A: Road Biking

(a) Take a road test with your counselor and demonstrate the following:

(1) Properly mount, pedal, and brake, including emergency stops.

(2) On an urban street with light traffic, properly execute a left turn from the center of the street; also demonstrate an alternate left-turn technique used during periods of heavy traffic.

(3) Properly execute a right turn.

(4) Demonstrate appropriate actions at a right-turn-only lane when you are continuing straight.

(5) Show proper curbside and road-edge riding. Show how to ride safely along a row of parked cars.

(6) Cross railroad tracks properly.

(b) Avoiding main highways, take two rides of 10 miles each, two rides of 15 miles each, and two rides of 25 miles each. You must make a report of the rides taken. List dates for the routes traveled, and interesting things seen.

(c) After completing requirement b for the road biking option, do ONE of the following:

(1) Lay out on a road map a 50-mile trip. Stay away from main highways. Using your map, make this ride in eight hours.

(2) Participate in an organized bike tour of at least 50 miles. Make this ride in eight hours. Afterward, use the tour's cue sheet to make a map of the ride.

Option B: Mountain Biking

(a) Take a trail ride with your counselor and demonstrate the following:

(1) Properly mount, pedal, and brake, including emergency stops.

(2) Show shifting skills as applicable to climbs and obstacles.

(3) Show proper trail etiquette to hikers and other cyclists, including when to yield the right-of-way.

(4) Show proper technique for riding up and down hills.

---

*The bicycle used for fulfilling these requirements must have all required safety features and must be registered as required by your local traffic laws.

(5) Demonstrate how to correctly cross an obstacle by either going over the obstacle on your bike or dismounting your bike and crossing over or around the obstacle.

(6) Cross rocks, gravel, and roots properly.

(b) Describe the rules of trail riding, including how to know when a trail is unsuitable for riding.

(c) On trails approved by your counselor, take two rides of 2 miles each, two rides of 5 miles each, and two rides of 8 miles each. You must make a report of the rides taken. List dates for the routes traveled, and interesting things seen.

(d) After fulfilling the previous requirement, lay out on a trail map a 22-mile trip. You may include multiple trail systems, if needed. Stay away from main highways. Using your map, make this ride in six hours.

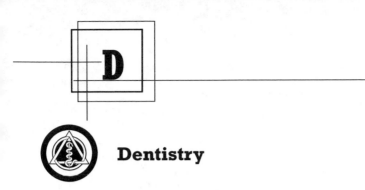

Dentistry

1. Using X-ray (radiographic) films and with your counselor's guidance, study the tooth structure and look for decay. Then do the following:

   (a) Using the radiographs as a guide, draw a lower molar. Label its parts and surfaces. Show surrounding structures such as bone and gum tissues.

   (b) Show on your drawing where the nerves and blood vessels enter the tooth.

   (c) Show on your drawing where bacterial plaque is most likely to be found.

2. Do the following:

   (a) Tell or write about what causes dental decay and gum disease. Tell how each of the following contributes to dental decay and gum disease: bacterial plaque, sugars, and acid.

   (b) Tell the possible causes for traumatic tooth loss, describe the types of mouth guards used to help prevent tooth trauma, and list the athletic activities during which a person should wear a mouth guard.

   (c) Explain the first-aid procedure for saving a tooth that has been knocked out.

   (d) Discuss how the use of tobacco products can negatively affect your oral health.

3. Arrange for a visit with a dentist. Before you go, ask whether your visit can include a dental examination and a plaque-control demonstration. Afterward, ask questions about things you want to know. Then tell your counselor what the dentist does during a checkup examination.

4. Do TWO of the following:

   (a) Name at least five instruments and five pieces of equipment a dentist uses.

   (b) With the help of a dentist, prepare a dental stone cast using a vibrator, a mixing bowl, a water measure, a plastic measure, model stone, and a spatula.

   (c) Keep a record of everything you eat for three days. Circle those items that may provide the sugars that bacterial plaque needs to make acid. List snacks that you should avoid to help maintain the best oral health.

5. Discuss with your merit badge counselor the following:

   (a) How fluorides help prevent tooth decay and the ways fluorides can be provided to the teeth.

   (b) How the mouth is related to the rest of the body. Topics might include chewing, saliva, enzymes, nutrition, and speech.

6. Do TWO of the following:

(a) Make a model tooth out of soap, clay, papier-mâché, or wax. Using a string and a large hand brush, show your troop or a school class proper tooth-brushing and flossing procedures.

(b) Make a poster on the prevention of dental disease. Show the importance of good oral health.

(c) Collect at least five advertisements for different toothpastes. List the claims that each one makes. Tell about the accuracy of the advertisements.

(d) Write a feature story for your school newspaper on the proper care of teeth and gums. Include in your story how the use of tobacco products can negatively affect a person's oral health.

(e) Make drawings and write about the progress of dental decay. Describe the types of dental filling and treatments a dentist can use to repair dental decay problems.

7. Learn about career opportunities for both Doctor of Dental Surgery (D.D.S.) and auxiliary dental professions. Pick either general dentistry OR a dental specialty, plus one auxiliary dental profession. Find out about the education, training, and experience required for these two professions. Discuss these with your counselor, and explain why these professions interest you.

 # Digital Technology

1. Show your counselor your current, up-to-date Cyber Chip.

2. Do the following:

(a) Give a brief history of the changes in digital technology over time. Discuss with your counselor how digital technology in your lifetime compares with that of your parent's, grandparent's, or other adult's lifetime.

(b) Describe what kinds of computers or devices you imagine might be available when you are an adult.

3. Do the following:

(a) Explain to your counselor how text, sound, pictures, and videos are digitized for storage.

(b) Describe the difference between lossy and lossless data compression, and give an example where each might be used.

(c) Describe two digital devices and how they are made more useful by their programming.

(d) Discuss the similarities and differences between computers, mobile devices, and gaming consoles.

(e) Explain what a computer network is and describe the network's purpose.

4. Do the following:

(a) Explain what a program or software application or "app" is and how it is created.

(b) Name four software programs or mobile apps you or your family use, and explain how each one helps you.

(c) Describe what malware is, and explain how to protect your digital devices and the information stored on them.

5. Do the following:

(a) Describe how digital devices are connected to the internet.

(b) Using an internet search engine (with your parent's permission), find ideas about how to conduct a troop court of honor or campfire program. Print out a copy of the ideas from at least three different websites. Share what you found with your counselor, and explain how you used the search engine to find this information.

(c) Use a web browser to connect to an HTTPS (secure) website (with your parent's permission). Explain to your counselor how to tell whether the site's security certificate can be trusted, and what it means to use this kind of connection.

6. Do THREE of the following. For each project you complete, copy the files to a backup device and share the finished projects with your counselor.

(a) Using a spreadsheet or database program, develop a food budget for a patrol weekend campout OR create a troop roster that includes the name, rank, patrol, and telephone number of each Scout. Show your counselor that you can sort the roster by each of the following categories: rank, patrol, and alphabetically by name.

(b) Using a word processor, write a draft letter to the parents of your troop's Scouts, inviting them to a troop event.

(c) Using a graphics program, design and draw a campsite plan for your troop OR create a flier for an upcoming troop event, incorporating text and some type of visual such as a photograph or an illustration.

(d) Using a presentation software program, develop a report about a topic approved by your counselor. For your presentation, create at least five slides, with each one incorporating text and some type of visual such as a photograph or an illustration.

(e) Using a digital device, take a picture of a troop activity. Send or transfer this image to a device where it can be shared with your counselor.

(f) Make a digital recording of your voice, transfer the file to a different device, and have your counselor play back the recording.

(g) Create a blog and use it as an online journal of your Scouting activities, including group discussions and meetings, campouts, and other events. Include at least five entries and two photographs or illustrations.

Share your blog with your counselor. You need not post the blog to the internet; however, if you choose to go live with your blog, you must first share it with your parents AND counselor AND get their approval.

(h) Create a webpage for your troop, patrol, school, or place of worship. Include at least three articles and two photographs or illustrations. Include at least one link to a website of interest to your audience. You need not post the page to the internet; however, if you decide to do so, you must first share the webpage with your parents AND counselor AND get their approval.

7. Do the following:

(a) Explain to your counselor each of these protections and why they exist: copyright, patents, trademarks, trade secrets.

(b) Explain when it is permissible to accept a free copy of a program from a friend.

(c) Discuss with your counselor an article or a news report about a recent legal case involving an intellectual property dispute.

8. Do TWO of the following:

(a) Describe why it is important to properly dispose of digital technology. List at least three dangerous chemicals that could be used to create digital devices or used inside a digital device.

(b) Explain to your counselor what is required to become a certified recycler of digital technology hardware or devices.

(c) Do an internet search for an organization that collects discarded digital technology hardware or devices for repurposing or recycling. Find out what happens to that waste. Share with your counselor what you found.

(d) Visit a recycling center that disposes of digital technology hardware or devices. Find out what happens to that waste. Share what you learned with your counselor.

(e) Find a battery recycling center near you and find out what it does to recycle batteries. Share what you have learned with your counselor about the proper methods for recycling batteries.

9. Do ONE of the following:

(a) Investigate three career opportunities that involve digital technology. Pick one and find out the education, training, and experience required for this profession. Discuss this with your counselor, and explain why this profession might interest you.

(b) Visit a business or an industrial facility that uses digital technology. Describe four ways digital technology is being used there. Share what you learned with your counselor.

 Disabilities Awareness

1. Do the following:

(a) Define and discuss with your counselor the following disabilities awareness terms: disability, accessibility, adaptation, accommodation, invisible disability, and person-first language.

(b) Explain why proper disability etiquette is important, and how it may differ depending on the specific disability.

2. Visit an agency that works with people with physical, mental, emotional, or educational disabilities. Collect and read information about the agency's activities. Learn about opportunities its members have for training, employment, and education. Discuss what you have learned with your counselor.

3. Do TWO of the following:

(a) Talk with a Scout who has a disability and learn about the Scout's experiences taking part in Scouting activities and earning different merit badges. Discuss what you have learned with your counselor.

(b) Talk with an individual who has a disability and learn about this person's experiences and the activities in which this person likes to participate. Discuss what you have learned with your counselor.

(c) Learn how people with disabilities take part in a particular adaptive sport or recreational activity. Discuss what you have learned with your counselor.

(d) Learn about independent living aids such as service animals, canes, and augmentative communication devices such as captioned telephones and videophones. Discuss with your counselor how people use such aids.

(e) Plan or participate in an activity that helps others understand what a person with a visible or invisible disability experiences. Discuss what you have learned with your counselor.

4. Do EITHER option A or option B:

Option A. Visit TWO of the following locations and take notes about the accessibility to people with disabilities. In your notes, give examples of five things that could be done to improve upon the site and five things about the site that make it friendly to people with disabilities. Discuss your observations with your counselor.

(a) Your school

(b) Your place of worship

(c) A Scouting event or campsite

(d) A public exhibit or attraction (such as a theater, museum, or park)

Option B. Visit TWO of the following locations and take notes while observing features and methods that are used to accommodate people with invisible disabilities. While there, ask staff members to explain any accommodation features that may not be obvious. Note anything you think could be done to better accommodate people who have invisible disabilities. Discuss your observations with your counselor.

(a) Your school

(b) Your place of worship

(c) A Scouting event or campsite

(d) A public exhibit or attraction (such as a theater, museum, or park)

5. Explain what advocacy is. Do ONE of the following advocacy activities:

    (a) Present a counselor-approved disabilities awareness program to a Cub Scout pack or other group. During your presentation, explain and use person-first language.

    (b) Find out about disability awareness education programs in your school or school system, or contact a disability advocacy agency. Volunteer with a program or agency for eight hours.

    (c) Using resources such as disability advocacy agencies, government agencies, the internet (with your parent's permission), and news magazines, learn about myths and misconceptions that influence the general public's understanding of people with disabilities. List 10 myths and misconceptions about people with disabilities and learn the facts about each myth. Share your list with your counselor, then use it to make a presentation to a Cub Scout pack or other group.

6. Make a commitment to your merit badge counselor describing what you will do to show a positive attitude about people with disabilities and to encourage positive attitudes among others. Discuss how your awareness has changed as a result of what you have learned.

7. Name five professions that provide services to people with disabilities. Pick one that interests you and find out the education, training, and experience required for this profession. Discuss what you learn with your counselor, and tell why this profession interests you.

 # Dog Care

1. Do the following:

    (a) Briefly discuss the historical origin and domestication of the dog.

    (b) Describe some common characteristics of the dogs that make up each of the seven major dog groups.

    (c) Tell some specific characteristics of seven breeds of dogs (one from each major group), OR give a short history of one breed.

2. Point out on a dog or a sketch at least 10 body parts. Give the correct name of each one.

3. Do the following:

    (a) Explain the importance of house-training, obedience training, and socialization training for your dog.

    (b) Explain what "responsible pet ownership" means.

    (c) Explain what issues (including temperament) must be considered when deciding on what breed of dog to get as a family pet.

4. For two months, keep and care for your dog.* Maintain a log of your activities during this period that includes these items: feeding schedule, types of food used, amount fed, exercise periods, training schedule, a weekly body

---

*The activities used to fulfill the requirements for the Dog Care merit badge may not be used to help fulfill requirements for other merit badges.

weight record, grooming and bathing schedules, veterinary care, if necessary, and costs. Also include a brief description of the type of housing/shelter arrangements you have for your dog.

5. Explain the correct way to obedience train a dog and what equipment you would need. Show with your dog any three of these commands: "come," "sit," "down," "heel," "stay," "fetch" or "get it," and "drop it."

6. Do the following:

   (a) Discuss the proper vaccination schedule for a dog in your area from puppyhood through adulthood.

   (b) Discuss the control methods for preventing fleas, ticks, heartworms, and intestinal parasites (worms) for a dog in your area from puppyhood through adulthood.

   (c) Explain the importance of dental care and tooth brushing to your pet's health.

   (d) Discuss the benefits of grooming your dog's coat and nails on a regular basis.

   (e) Discuss with your counselor any seasonal conditions (like hot summers, cold winters, or extreme humidity) where you live that need to be considered for your dog.

   (f) Discuss with your counselor the considerations and advantages of spaying or neutering your dog.

7. Do the following:

   (a) Explain precautions to take in handling a hurt dog.

   (b) Show how to put on an emergency muzzle.

   (c) Explain how to treat wounds. Explain first aid for a dog bite.

   (d) Show how to put on a simple dressing and bandage the foot, body, or head of your dog.

   (e) Explain what to do if a dog is hit by a car.

   (f) List the things needed in every dog owner's first-aid kit.

   (g) Tell the dangers of home treatment of a serious ailment.

   (h) Briefly discuss the cause and method of spread, the signs and symptoms and the methods of prevention of rabies, parvovirus, distemper, and heartworms in dogs.

8. Visit a veterinary hospital or an animal shelter and give a report about your visit to your counselor.

9. Know the laws and ordinances involving dogs that are in force in your community.

10. Learn about three career opportunities for working with dogs. Pick one and find out about the education, training, and experience required for this career, and discuss this with your counselor. Tell why this profession interests you.

Drafting

1. Format TWO sheets of drawing paper with proper borders and title blocks—one for your manual project (see requirement 2) and one for your lettering project (see requirement 5).

   (a) Make a rough sketch for each of your project drawings to determine the correct size of paper to format.

   (b) Using either single-stroke vertical or slant Gothic lettering, fill in all important information in the title block sections of the formatted paper.

2. Using the formatted sheet of paper you prepared for your manual project, produce a pencil drawing as it would be used for manufacturing. Fill in all title block information. The manual drawing may be any one of the following drawing types:

   (a) **Architectural:** Make a scale drawing of an architectural project. The architectural drawing may be a floor plan; electrical, plumbing, or mechanical service plan; elevation plan; or landscaping plan. Use an architect's scale and show dimensions to communicate the actual size of features. Include any important sectional drawings, notes, and considerations necessary for construction.

   (b) **Mechanical:** Make a scale drawing of some mechanical device or interesting object. The mechanical drawing may be of the orthographic or isometric style. Use an engineer's scale and show dimensions to communicate the actual size of features. Include any important sectional drawings, notes, and manufacturing considerations.

   (c) **Electrical:** Draw a simple schematic of a radio or electronic circuit. Properly print a bill of materials including all of the major electrical components used in the circuit. Use standard drawing symbols to represent the electronic components.

3. Produce a computer-aided design (CAD) drawing as it would be used in manufacturing. Fill in all title block information. The CAD drawing may be any one of the following drawing types:

   (a) **Architectural:** Make a scale drawing of an architectural project. The architectural drawing may be a floor plan; electrical, plumbing, or mechanical service plan; elevation plan; or landscaping plan. Use an architect's scale and show dimensions to communicate the actual size of features. Include any important sectional drawings, notes, and considerations necessary for construction.

   (b) **Mechanical:** Make a scale drawing of some mechanical device or interesting object. The mechanical drawing may be of the orthographic or isometric style. Use an engineer's scale and show dimensions to communicate the actual size of features. Include any important sectional drawings, notes, and manufacturing considerations.

   (c) **Electrical:** Draw a simple schematic of a radio or electronic circuit. Properly print a bill of materials including all of the major electrical components used in the circuit. Use standard drawing symbols to represent the electronic components.

4. Discuss with your counselor how fulfilling requirements 2 and 3 differed from each other. Tell about the benefits derived from using CAD for requirement 3. Include in your discussion the software you used as well as other software options that are available.

5. Using single-stroke slant or vertical Gothic lettering (without the aid of a template or lettering guide), write a brief explanation of what you consider to be the most important benefit in using CAD in a particular industry (aerospace, electronics, manufacturing, architectural, or other). Use the experience gained in fulfilling requirements 2, 3, and 4 to support your opinion. Use the formatted sheet of paper you prepared in requirement 1 for your lettering project.

6. Do ONE of the following (a or b):

(a) Visit a facility or industry workplace where drafting is part of the business. Ask to see an example of the work that is done there, the different drafting facilities, and the tools used.

(1) Find out how much of the drafting done there is manual and how much is done using CAD. If CAD is used, find out what software is used and how and why it was chosen.

(2) Ask about the drafting services provided. Ask who uses the designs produced in the drafting area and how those designs are used. Discuss how the professionals who perform drafting cooperate with other individuals in the drafting area and other areas of the business.

(3) Ask how important the role of drafting is to producing the end product or service that this business supplies. Find out how drafting contributes to the company's end product or service.

(b) Using resources you find on your own such as at the library and on the internet (with your parent's permission), learn more about the drafting trade and discuss the following with your counselor.

(1) The drafting tools used in the past—why and how they were used. Explain which tools are still used today and how their use has changed with the advent of new tools. Discuss which tools are being made obsolete by newer tools in the industry.

(2) Tell what media types were used in the past and how drawings were used, stored, and reproduced. Tell how the advent of CAD has changed the media used, and discuss how these changes affect the storage or reproduction of drawings.

(3) Discuss whether the types of media have changed such that there are new uses the drawings, or other outputs, produced by designers. Briefly discuss how new media types are used in the industry today.

7. Find out about three career opportunities in drafting. Pick one and find out the education, training, and experience required for this profession. Discuss this with your counselor, and explain why this profession might interest you.

Electricity

1. Demonstrate that you know how to respond to electrical emergencies by doing the following:

   (a) Show how to rescue a person touching a live wire in the home.

   (b) Show how to render first aid to a person who is unconscious from electrical shock.

   (c) Show how to treat an electrical burn.

   (d) Explain what to do in an electrical storm.

   (e) Explain what to do in the event of an electrical fire.

2. Complete an electrical home safety inspection of your home, using the checklist found in the *Electricity* merit badge pamphlet or one approved by your counselor. Discuss what you find with your counselor.

3. Make a simple electromagnet and use it to show magnetic attraction and repulsion.

4. Explain the difference between direct current and alternating current.

5. Make a simple drawing to show how a battery and an electric bell work.

6. Explain why a fuse blows or a circuit breaker trips. Tell how to find a blown fuse or tripped circuit breaker in your home. Show how to safely reset the circuit breaker.

7. Explain what overloading an electric circuit means. Tell what you have done to make sure your home circuits are not overloaded.

8. Make a floor plan wiring diagram of the lights, switches, and outlets for a room in your home. Show which fuse or circuit breaker protects each one.

9. Do the following:

   (a) Read an electric meter and, using your family's electric bill, determine the energy cost from the meter readings.

   (b) Discuss with your counselor five ways in which your family can conserve energy.

10. Explain the following electrical terms: volt, ampere, watt, ohm, resistance, potential difference, rectifier, rheostat, conductor, ground, circuit, and short circuit.

11. Do any TWO of the following:

    (a) Connect a buzzer, bell, or light with a battery. Have a key or switch in the line.

(b) Make and run a simple electric motor (not from a kit).

(c) Build a simple rheostat. Show that it works.

(d) Build a single-pole, double-throw switch. Show that it works.

(e) Hook a model electric train layout to a house circuit. Tell how it works.

Electronics

1. Describe the safety precautions you must exercise when using, building, altering, or repairing electronic devices.

2. Do the following:

   (a) Draw a simple schematic diagram. It must show resistors, capacitors, and transistors or integrated circuits. Use the correct symbols. Label all parts.

   (b) Tell the purpose of each part.

3. Do the following:

   (a) Show the right way to solder and desolder.

   (b) Show how to avoid heat damage to electronic components.

   (c) Tell about the function of a printed circuit board. Tell what precautions should be observed when soldering printed circuit boards.

4. Do the following:

   (a) Discuss each of the following with your merit badge counselor:

   (i) How to use electronics for a control purpose

   (ii) The basic principles of digital techniques

   (iii) How to use electronics for three different audio applications

   (b) Show how to change three decimal numbers into binary numbers and three binary numbers into decimal numbers.

   (c) Choose ONE of the following three projects. For your project, find or create a schematic diagram. To the best of your ability, explain to your counselor how the circuit you built operates.

   (i) A control device

   (ii) A digital circuit

   (iii) An audio circuit

5. Do the following:

   (a) Show how to solve a simple problem involving current, voltage, and resistance using Ohm's law.

   (b) Tell about the need for and the use of test equipment in electronics. Name three types of test equipment. Tell how they operate.

6. Find out about three career opportunities in electronics that interest you. Discuss with and explain to your counselor what training and education are needed for each position.

 # Emergency Preparedness

1. Earn the First Aid merit badge.
2. Do the following:
   (a) Discuss with your counselor the aspects of emergency preparedness:
      (1) Prevention
      (2) Protection
      (3) Mitigation
      (4) Response
      (5) Recovery

      Include in your discussion the kinds of questions that are important to ask yourself as you consider each of these.

   (b) Using a chart, graph, spreadsheet, or another method approved by your counselor, demonstrate your understanding of each aspect of emergency preparedness listed in requirement 2a (prevention, protection, mitigation, response, and recovery) for 10 emergency situations from the list below. **You must use the first five situations listed below in boldface,** plus any other five of your choice. Discuss your findings with your counselor.
      (1) Home kitchen fire
      (2) Home basement/storage room/garage fire
      (3) Explosion in the home
      (4) Automobile crash
      (5) Food-borne disease (food poisoning)
      (6) Fire or explosion in a public place
      (7) Vehicle stalled in the desert
      (8) Vehicle trapped in a blizzard
      (9) Earthquake or tsunami
      (10) Mountain/backcountry accident
      (11) Boating or water accident
      (12) Gas leak in a home or a building
      (13) Tornado or hurricane
      (14) Major flooding or a flash flood
      (15) Toxic chemical spills and releases

(16) Nuclear power plant emergency

(17) Avalanche (snowslide or rockslide)

(18) Violence in a public place

(c) Meet with and teach your family how to get or build a kit, make a plan, and be informed for the situations on the chart you created for requirement 2b. Complete a family plan. Then meet with your counselor and report on your family meeting, discuss their responses, and share your family plan.

3. Show how you could safely save a person from the following:

(a) Touching a live household electric wire

(b) A structure filled with carbon monoxide

(c) Clothes on fire

(d) Drowning, using nonswimming rescues (including accidents on ice)

4. Show three ways of attracting and communicating with rescue planes/aircraft.

5. With another person, show a good way to transport an injured person out of a remote and/or rugged area, conserving the energy of rescuers while ensuring the well-being and protection of the injured person.

6. Do the following:

(a) Describe the National Incident Management System (NIMS)/Incident and the Incident Command System (ICS).

(b) Identify the local government or community agencies that normally handle and prepare for emergency services similar to those of the NIMS or ICS. Explain to your counselor ONE of the following:

(1) How the NIMS/ICS can assist a Scout troop when responding in a disaster

(2) How a group of Scouts could volunteer to help in the event of these types of emergencies

(c) Find out who is your community's emergency management director and learn what this person does to **prevent, protect, mitigate, respond to, and recover from** emergency situations in your community. Discuss this information with your counselor, utilizing the information you learned from requirement 2b.

7. Do the following:

(a) Take part in an emergency service project, either a real one or a practice drill, with a Scouting unit or a community agency.

(b) Prepare a written plan for mobilizing your troop when needed to do emergency service. If there is already a plan, explain it. Tell your part in making it work.

8. Do the following:

(a) Tell the things a group of Scouts should be prepared to do, the training they need, and the safety precautions they should take for the following emergency services:

(1) Crowd and traffic control

(2) Messenger service and communication

(3) Collection and distribution services

(4) Group feeding, shelter, and sanitation

(b) Prepare a personal emergency service pack for a mobilization call. Prepare a family emergency kit (suitcase or waterproof box) for use by your family in case an emergency evacuation is needed. Explain the needs and uses of the contents.

9. Do ONE of the following:

(a) Using a safety checklist approved by your counselor, inspect your home for potential hazards. Explain the hazards you find and how they can be corrected.

(b) Review or develop a plan of escape for your family in case of fire in your home.

(c) Develop an accident prevention program for five family activities outside the home (such as taking a picnic or seeing a movie) that includes an analysis of possible hazards, a proposed plan to correct those hazards, and the reasons for the corrections you propose.

 **Energy**

1. Do the following:

(a) With your parent's permission, use the internet to find a blog, podcast, website, or an article on the use or conservation of energy. Discuss with your counselor what details in the article were interesting to you, the questions it raises, and what ideas it addresses that you do not understand.

(b) After you have completed requirements 2 through 8, revisit your source for requirement 1a. Explain to your counselor what you have learned in completing the requirements that helps you better understand the article.

2. Show you understand energy forms and conversions by doing the following:

(a) Explain how THREE of the following devices use energy, and explain their energy conversions: toaster, greenhouse, lightbulb, bow drill, cell phone, nuclear reactor, sweat lodge.

(b) Construct a system that makes at least two energy conversions and explain this to your counselor.

3. Show you understand energy efficiency by explaining to your counselor a common example of a situation where energy moves through a system to produce a useful result. Do the following:

(a) Identify the parts of the system that are affected by the energy movement.

(b) Name the system's primary source of energy.

(c) Identify the useful outcomes of the system.

(d) Identify the energy losses of the system.

4. Conduct an energy audit of your home. Keep a 14-day log that records what you and your family did to reduce energy use. Include the following in your report and, after the 14-day period, discuss what you have learned with your counselor.

(a) List the types of energy used in your home such as electricity, wood, oil, liquid petroleum, and natural gas, and tell how each is delivered and measured, and the current cost; OR record the transportation fuel used, miles driven, miles per gallon, and trips using your family car or another vehicle.

(b) Describe ways you and your family can use energy resources more wisely. In preparing your discussion, consider the energy required for the things you do and use on a daily basis (cooking, showering, using lights, driving, watching TV, using the computer). Explain what is meant by sustainable energy sources. Explain how you can change your energy use through reuse and recycling.

5. In a notebook, identify and describe five examples of energy waste in your school or community. Suggest in each case possible ways to reduce this waste. Describe the idea of trade-offs in energy use. In your response, do the following:

(a) Explain how the changes you suggest would lower costs, reduce pollution, or otherwise improve your community.

(b) Explain what changes to routines, habits, or convenience are necessary to reduce energy waste. Tell why people might resist the changes you suggest.

6. Prepare pie charts showing the following information, and explain to your counselor the important ideas each chart reveals. Tell where you got your information. Explain how cost affects the use of a nonrenewable energy resource and makes alternatives practical.

(a) The energy resources that supply the United States with most of its energy

(b) The share of energy resources used by the United States that comes from other countries

(c) The proportion of energy resources used by homes, businesses, industry, and transportation

(d) The fuels used to generate America's electricity

(e) The world's known and estimated primary energy resource reserves

7. Tell what is being done to make FIVE of the following energy systems produce more usable energy. In your explanation, describe the technology, cost, environmental impacts, and safety concerns.

- Biomass digesters or waste-to-energy plants
- Cogeneration plants
- Fossil fuel power plants
- Fuel cells
- Geothermal power plants
- Nuclear power plants

- Solar power systems
- Tidal energy, wave energy, or ocean thermal energy conversion devices
- Wind turbines

8. Find out what opportunities are available for a career in energy. Choose one position that interests you and describe the education and training required.

 # Engineering

1. Select a manufactured item in your home (such as a toy or an appliance) and, under adult supervision and with the approval of your counselor, investigate how and why it works as it does. Find out what sort of engineering activities were needed to create it. Discuss with your counselor what you learned and how you got the information.

2. Select an engineering achievement that has had a major impact on society. Using resources such as the internet (with your parent's permission), books, and magazines, find out about the engineers who made this engineering feat possible, the special obstacles they had to overcome, and how this achievement has influenced the world today. Tell your counselor what you learned.

3. Explain the work of six types of engineers. Pick two of the six and explain how their work is related.

4. Visit with an engineer (who may be your counselor or parent) and do the following:

   (a) Discuss the work this engineer does and the tools the engineer uses.

   (b) Discuss with the engineer a current project and the engineer's particular role in it.

   (c) Find out how the engineer's work is done and how results are achieved.

   (d) Ask to see the reports that the engineer writes concerning the project.

   (e) Discuss with your counselor what you learned about engineering from this visit.

5. Do ONE of the following:

   (a) Use the systems engineering approach to make step-by-step plans for your next campout. List alternative ideas for such items as program schedule, campsites, transportation, and costs. Tell why you made the choices you did and what improvements were made.

   (b) Make an original design for a piece of patrol equipment. Use the systems engineering approach to help you decide how it should work and look. Draw plans for it. Show the plans to your counselor, explain why you designed it the way you did, and explain how you would make it.

6. Do TWO of the following:

   (a) *Transforming motion.* Using common materials or a construction set, make a simple model that will demonstrate motion. Explain how the model uses basic mechanical elements like levers and inclined planes to demonstrate motion. Describe an example where this mechanism is used in a real product.

(b) *Using electricity.* Make a list of 10 electrical appliances in your home. Find out approximately how much electricity each uses in one month. Learn how to find out the amount and cost of electricity used in your home during periods of light and heavy use. List five ways to conserve electricity.

(c) *Understanding electronics.* Using an electronic device such as a mobile telephone or portable digital media player, find out how sound travels from one location to another. Explain how the device was designed for ease of use, function, and durability.

(d) *Using materials.* Do experiments to show the differences in strength and heat conductivity in wood, metal, and plastic. Discuss with your counselor what you have learned.

(e) *Converting energy.* Do an experiment to show how mechanical, heat, chemical, solar, and/or electrical energy may be converted from one or more types of energy to another. Explain your results. Describe to your counselor what energy is and how energy is converted and used in your surroundings.

(f) *Moving people.* Find out the different ways people in your community get to work. Make a study of traffic flow (number of vehicles and relative speed) in both heavy and light traffic periods. Discuss with your counselor what might be improved to make it easier for people in your community to get where they need to go.

(g) *Building an engineering project.* Enter a project in a science or engineering fair or similar competition. (This requirement may be met by participation on an engineering competition project team.) Discuss with your counselor what your project demonstrates, the kinds of questions visitors to the fair asked you, and how well you were able to answer their questions.

7. Explain what it means to be a registered Professional Engineer (P.E.). Name the types of engineering work for which registration is most important.

8. Study the Engineer's Code of Ethics. Explain how it is like the Scout Oath and Scout Law.

9. Find out about three career opportunities in engineering. Pick one and research the education, training, and experience required for this profession. Discuss this with your counselor, and explain why this profession might interest you.

 # Entrepreneurship

1. In your own words, define *entrepreneurship*. Explain to your merit badge counselor how entrepreneurs impact the U.S. economy.

2. Explain to your counselor why having good skills in the following areas is important for an entrepreneur: communication, planning, organization, problem solving, decision making, basic math, adaptability, technical and social skills, teamwork, and leadership.

3. Identify and interview an individual who has started a business. Learn about this person's educational background, early work experiences, where the idea for the business came from, and what was involved in starting the business. Find out how the entrepreneur raised the capital (money) to start the business, examples of successes and challenges faced, and how the business is currently doing (if applicable). Discuss with your counselor what you have learned.

4. Think of as many ideas for a business as you can, and write them down. From your list, select three ideas you believe represent the best opportunities. Choose one of these and explain to your counselor why you selected it and why you feel it can be successful.

5. Create a written business plan for your idea that includes all of the following:

   (a) Product or Service

      (1) Describe the product or service to be offered.

      (2) Identify goals for your business.

      (3) Explain how you can make enough of the product or perform the service to meet your goals.

      (4) Identify and describe the potential liability risks for your product or service.

      (5) Determine what type of license, if any, you might need in order to sell or make your product or service.

   (b) Market Analysis

      (1) Identify the types of people who would buy your product or service.

      (2) Identify your business's competitors, and describe their strengths and weaknesses.

      (3) Describe what makes your product or service unique.

   (c) Financial

      (1) Determine how much money you will need to start your business, and identify how you will obtain the money.

      (2) Determine the cost of offering your product or service and the price you will charge in order to make a profit.

      (3) Describe what will happen with the money you make from the sales of your product or service.

   (d) Personnel

      (1) Determine what parts of the business you will handle yourself, and describe your qualifications.

      (2) Determine whether you will need additional help to operate your business. If you will need help, describe the responsibilities and qualifications needed for the personnel who will fill each role.

   (e) Promotion and Marketing

      (1) Describe the methods you will use to promote your business to potential customers.

      (2) Explain how you will utilize the internet and social media to increase awareness of your product or service.

(3) Design a promotional flier or poster for your product or service.

6. When you believe your business idea is feasible, imagine your business idea is now up and running. What successes and problems might you experience? How would you overcome any failures? Discuss with your counselor any ethical questions you might face and how you would deal with them.

 # Environmental Science

1. Make a time line of the history of environmental science in America. Identify the contribution made by the Boy Scouts of America to environmental science. Include dates, names of people or organizations, and important events.

2. Define the following terms: population, community, ecosystem, biosphere, symbiosis, niche, habitat, conservation, threatened species, endangered species, extinction, pollution prevention, brownfield, ozone, watershed, airshed, nonpoint source, hybrid vehicle, fuel cell.

3. Do ONE activity from EACH of the following categories (using the activities in this pamphlet as the basis for planning and projects):

(a) Ecology

(1) Conduct an experiment to find out how living things respond to changes in their environments. Discuss your observations with your counselor.

(2) Conduct an experiment illustrating the greenhouse effect. Keep a journal of your data and observations. Discuss your conclusions with your counselor.

(3) Discuss what is an ecosystem. Tell how it is maintained in nature and how it survives.

(b) Air Pollution

(1) Perform an experiment to test for particulates that contribute to air pollution. Discuss your findings with your counselor.

(2) Record the trips taken, mileage, and fuel consumption of a family car for seven days, and calculate how many miles per gallon the car gets. Determine whether any trips could have been combined ("chained") rather than taken out and back. Using the idea of trip chaining, determine how many miles and gallons of gas could have been saved in those seven days.

(3) Explain what is acid rain. In your explanation, tell how it affects plants and the environment and the steps society can take to help reduce its effects.

(c) Water Pollution

(1) Conduct an experiment to show how living things react to thermal pollution. Discuss your observations with your counselor.

(2) Conduct an experiment to identify the methods that could be used to mediate (reduce) the effects of an oil spill on waterfowl. Discuss your results with your counselor.

(3) Describe the impact of a waterborne pollutant on an aquatic community. Write a 100-word report on how that pollutant affected aquatic life, what the effect was, and whether the effect is linked to biomagnification.

(d) Land Pollution

(1) Conduct an experiment to illustrate soil erosion by water. Take photographs or make a drawing of the soil before and after your experiment, and make a poster showing your results. Present your poster to your counselor.

(2) Perform an experiment to determine the effect of an oil spill on land. Discuss your conclusions with your counselor.

(3) Photograph an area affected by erosion. Share your photographs with your counselor and discuss why the area has eroded and what might be done to help alleviate the erosion.

(e) Endangered Species

(1) Do research on one endangered species found in your state. Find out what its natural habitat is, why it is endangered, what is being done to preserve it, and how many individual organisms are left in the wild. Prepare a 100-word report about the organism, including a drawing. Present your report to your patrol or troop.

(2) Do research on one species that was endangered or threatened but that has now recovered. Find out how the organism recovered, and what its new status is. Write a 100-word report on the species and discuss it with your counselor.

(3) With your parent's and counselor's approval, work with a natural resource professional to identify two projects that have been approved to improve the habitat for a threatened or endangered species in your area. Visit the site of one of these projects and report on what you saw.

(f) Pollution Prevention, Resource Recovery, and Conservation

(1) Look around your home and determine 10 ways your family can help reduce pollution. Practice at least two of these methods for seven days and discuss with your counselor what you have learned.

(2) Determine 10 ways to conserve resources or use resources more efficiently in your home, at school, or at camp. Practice at least two of these methods for seven days and discuss with your counselor what you have learned.

(3) Perform an experiment on packaging materials to find out which ones are biodegradable. Discuss your conclusion with your counselor.

(g) Pollination

(1) Using photographs or illustrations, point out the differences between a drone and a worker bee. Discuss the stages of bee development (eggs, larvae, pupae). Explain the pollination process, and what propolis is and how it is used by honey bees. Tell how bees make honey and beeswax,

and how both are harvested. Explain the part played in the life of the hive by the queen, the drones, and the workers.

(2) Present to your counselor a one-page report on how and why honey bees are used in pollinating food crops. In your report, discuss the problems faced by the bee population today, and the impact to humanity if there were no pollinators. Share your report with your troop or patrol, your class at school, or another group approved by your counselor.

Before you choose requirement 3g(3), you will need to first find out whether you are allergic to bee stings. Visit an allergist or your family physician to find out. If you are allergic to bee stings, you should choose another option within requirement 3. In completing requirement 3g(3), your counselor can help you find an established beekeeper to meet with you and your buddy. Ask whether you can help hive a swarm or divide a colony of honey bees. Before your visit, be sure your buddy is not allergic to bee stings. For help with locating a beekeeper in your state, visit www.beeculture.com and click on "Bee Resources," then "Find a Local Beekeeper."

(3) Hive a swarm OR divide at least one colony of honey bees. Explain how a hive is constructed.

4. Choose two outdoor study areas that are very different from one another (e.g., hilltop vs. bottom of a hill; field vs. forest; swamp vs. dry land). For BOTH study areas, do ONE of the following:

(a) Mark off a plot of 4 square yards in each study area, and count the number of species found there. Estimate how much space is occupied by each plant species and the type and number of nonplant species you find. Write a report that adequately discusses the biodiversity and population density of these study areas. Discuss your report with your counselor.

(b) Make at least three visits to each of the two study areas (for a total of six visits), staying for at least 20 minutes each time, to observe the living and non-living parts of the ecosystem. Space each visit far enough apart that there are readily apparent differences in the observations. Keep a journal that includes the differences you observe. Then, write a short report that adequately addresses your observations, including how the differences of the study areas might relate to the differences noted, and discuss this with your counselor.

5. Using the construction project provided or a plan you create on your own, identify the items that would need to be included in an environmental impact statement for the project planned.

6. Find out about three career opportunities in environmental science. Pick one and find out the education, training, and experience required for this profession. Discuss this with your counselor, and explain why this profession might interest you.

Exploration

1. **General Knowledge.** Do the following:

   (a) Define exploration and explain how it differs from adventure travel, trekking or hiking, tour-group trips, or recreational outdoor adventure trips.

   (b) Explain how approaches to exploration may differ if it occurs in the ocean, in space, in a jungle, or in a science lab in a city.

2. **History of Exploration.** Discuss with your counselor the history of exploration. Select a field of study with a history of exploration to illustrate the importance of exploration in the development of that field (for example, aerospace, oil industry, paleontology, oceanography, etc.).

3. **Importance of Exploration.** Explain to your counselor why it is important to explore. Discuss the following:

   (a) Why it is important for exploration to have a scientific basis

   (b) How explorers have aided in our understanding of our world

   (c) What you think it takes to be an explorer

4. **Real-Life Exploration.** Do ONE of the following:

   (a) Learn about a living explorer. Create a short report or presentation (verbal, written, or multimedia slide presentation) on this individual's objectives and the achievements of one of the explorer's expeditions. Share what you have learned with your counselor and unit.

   (b) Learn about an actual scientific exploration expedition. Gather information about the mission objectives and the expedition's most interesting or important discoveries. Share what you have learned with your counselor and unit. Tell how the information gained from this expedition helped scientists answer important questions.

   (c) Learn about types of exploration that may take place in a laboratory or scientific research facility (medicine, biology, chemistry, physics, astronomy, etc.). Explain to your counselor how laboratory research and exploration are similar to field research and exploration.

5. **Exploration in Lab and Field.** Do ONE of the following, and share what you learn with your counselor:

   (a) With your parent's permission and counselor's approval, visit either in person or via the internet an exploration sponsoring organization (such as The Explorers Club, National Geographic Society, Smithsonian Institution, Alpine Club, World Wildlife Fund, or similar organization). Find out what type(s) of exploration the organization supports.

   (b) With permission and approval, visit either in person or via the internet a science lab, astronomical observatory, medical research facility, or similar site. Learn what exploration is done in this facility.

As you work on the Exploration merit badge, remember to always use the buddy system. Whether you are out in the field or meeting with your merit badge counselor, having a buddy will help ensure everyone's safety. You and your buddy can watch out for each other wherever you may be or whatever you may be doing.

6. **Expedition Planning.** Discuss with your counselor each of the following steps for conducting a successful exploration activity. Explain the need for each step.

   (a) Identify the objectives (establish goals).

   (b) Plan the mission. Create an expedition agenda or schedule. List potential documents or permits needed.

   (c) Budget and plan for adequate financial resources. Estimate costs for travel, equipment, accommodations, meals, permits or licenses, and other expedition expenses.

   (d) Determine equipment and supplies required for personal and mission needs for the length of the expedition.

   (e) Determine communication and transportation needs. Plan how to keep in contact with your base or the outside world, and determine how you will communicate with each other on-site.

   (f) Establish safety and first-aid procedures (including planning for medical evacuation). Identify the hazards that explorers could encounter on the expedition, and establish procedures to prevent or avoid those hazards.

   (g) Determine team selection. Identify who is essential for the expedition to be successful and what skills are required by the expedition leader.

   (h) Establish detailed recordkeeping (documentation) procedures. Plan the interpretation and sharing of information at the conclusion of the expedition.

7. **Prepare for an Expedition.** With your parent's permission and counselor's approval, prepare for an actual expedition to an area you have not previously explored; the place may be nearby or far away. Do the following:

   (a) Make your preparations under the supervision of a trained expedition leader, expedition planner, or other qualified adult experienced in exploration (such as a school science teacher, museum representative, or qualified instructor).

   (b) Use the steps listed in requirement 6 to guide your preparations. List the items of equipment and supplies you will need. Discuss with your counselor why you chose each item and how it will be of value on the expedition. Determine who should go on the expedition.

   (c) Conduct a pre-expedition check, covering the steps in requirement 6, and share the results with your counselor. With your counselor, walk through the Sweet Sixteen of BSA Safety for your expedition. Ensure that all foreseeable hazards for your expedition are adequately addressed.

8. **Go on an Expedition.** Complete the following:

(a) With your parent's permission and under the supervision of your merit badge counselor or a counselor-approved qualified person, use the planning steps you learned in requirement 6 and the preparations you completed in requirement 7 to personally undertake an actual expedition to an area you have not previously explored.

(b) Discuss with your counselor what is outdoor ethics and its role in exploration and enjoying the outdoors responsibly.

(c) After you return, compile a report on the results of your expedition and how you accomplished your objective(s). Include a statement of the objectives, note your findings and observations, include photos, note any discoveries, report any problems or adverse events, and have a conclusion (whether you reached your objective or not). The post-expedition report must be at least one page and no more than three; one page can be photos, graphs, or figures.

9. **Career Opportunities.** Identify three career opportunities in exploration. Pick one and explain to your counselor how to prepare for such a career. Discuss what education and training are required, and why this profession might interest you.

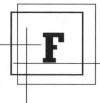

 Family Life

Note to the Counselor

Some of the issues surrounding requirement 6 for the family meeting could be considered of a personal nature. Use discretion when reviewing this requirement with the Scout.

1. Prepare an outline on what a family is and discuss this with your merit badge counselor. Tell why families are important to individuals and to society. Discuss how the actions of one member can affect other members.

2. List several reasons why you are important to your family and discuss this with your parents or guardians and with your merit badge counselor.

3. Prepare a list of your regular home duties or chores (at least five) and do them for 90 days. Keep a record of how often you do each of them. Discuss with your counselor the effect your chores had on your family.

4. With the approval of your parents or guardians and your merit badge counselor, decide on and carry out a project that you would do around the home that would benefit your family. Submit a report to your merit badge counselor outlining how the project benefited your family.

5. Plan and carry out a project that involves the participation of your family. After completing the project, discuss the following with your merit badge counselor:

   (a) The objective or goal of the project

   (b) How individual members of your family participated

   (c) The results of the project

6. Do the following:

   (a) Discuss with your merit badge counselor how to plan and carry out a family meeting.

   (b) After this discussion, plan and carry out a family meeting to include the following subjects:

      (1) Avoiding substance abuse, including tobacco, alcohol, and drugs, all of which negatively affect your health and well-being

(2) Understanding the growing-up process and how the body changes, and making responsible decisions dealing with sex*

(3) How your chores in requirement 3 contributed to your role in the family

(4) Personal and family finances

(5) A crisis situation within your family

(6) The effect of technology on your family

(7) Good etiquette and manners

Discussion of each of these subjects will very likely carry over to more than one family meeting.

7. Discuss with your counselor your understanding of what makes an effective parent and why, and your thoughts on the parent's role and responsibilities in the family.

---

*This conversation may take place with only one or both of your parents or guardians.

 # Farm Mechanics

1. Do the following:

(a) Discuss with your counselor the safety equipment, tools, and clothing used while checking or repairing farm equipment. Use this equipment, tools, and/or clothing (when needed or called for) in meeting the requirements for this merit badge.

(b) Draw a plan showing a well-equipped farm shop. Point out the shop's mandatory safety devices and features.

(c) Find all the universal warning and safety symbols on a piece of equipment and explain what they mean.

(d) Describe what a material safety data sheet (MSDS) is and tell why it is used. Obtain the MSDS for any engine coolant, oil, grease, fuel, hydraulic or transmission fluid, or other flammable or hazardous materials you use in meeting the requirements for this merit badge.

2. Explain how power is produced or transferred in a:

(a) Diesel engine

(b) Hydraulic system

(c) Transmission or any other power system

3. Do TWO of the following:

(a) Replace the handle of any tool found on the farm.

(b) Organize a tool rack or a storage system for nails, bolts, nuts, and washers.

(c) Using a hand file, properly dress the mushroomed head of a chisel or punch.

(d) Using a hand file, correctly dress a screwdriver tip.

4. Do ONE of the following:

(a) On an engine-powered machine: Grease all fittings, change the oil and oil filter, clean the air filter, clean the radiator fins, and replace the fuel filters.

(b) For any engine-powered machine, create a preoperational checklist; include checking the engine coolant, engine oil, hydraulic and/or transmission fluid, and battery voltage (using a voltmeter). Using your checklist, conduct a preoperational check of that machinery or equipment.

(c) Prepare any farm machine for winter storage.

5. Visit an implement dealer. Interview the dealer technician or service manager for hints on good preventive maintenance. Ask why it is important, the costs, and what causes wear or damage. Report what you learn.

6. Explain each step in ONE of the following maintenance procedures:

(a) Tightening hydraulic fittings

(b) Checking the air filter

(c) Cleaning a work piece with a wire-brush wheel

7. Find out about three career opportunities in farm mechanics. Pick one and find out the education, training, and experience required for this profession. Discuss this with your counselor, and explain why this profession might interest you.

 # Fingerprinting

1. Give a short history of fingerprinting. Tell the difference between civil and criminal identification.

2. Explain the difference between the automated fingerprint identification systems (AFIS) now used by law enforcement agencies and the biometric fingerprint systems used to control access to computers and places like buildings and airports.

3. Do the following:

(a) Name the surfaces of the body where friction or papillary ridges are found.

(b) Name the two basic principles supporting the science of fingerprints and give a brief explanation of each principle.

(c) Explain what it takes to positively identify a person using fingerprints.

4. Take a clear set of prints using ONE of the following methods.

(a) Make both rolled and plain impressions. Make these on an 8-by-8-inch fingerprint identification card, available from your local police department or your counselor.

(b) Using clear adhesive tape, a pencil, and plain paper, record your own fingerprints or those of another person.

5. Show your merit badge counselor you can identify the three basic types of fingerprint patterns and their subcategories. Using your own hand, identify the types of patterns you see.

 **Fire Safety**

1. Do the following:

(a) Demonstrate the technique of stop, drop, cover, roll, cover your face, and cool. Explain how burn injuries can be prevented.

(b) List the most frequent causes of burn injuries.

(c) Explain how to safely discard and store flammable liquids.

2. Explain the chemistry and physics of fire. Name the parts of the fire tetrahedron. Explain why vapors are important to the burning process. Name the products of combustion. Give an example of how fire grows and what happens.

3. Name the most frequent causes of fire in the home, and give examples of ways they can be prevented. Include a discussion about fires caused by smoking in the home, cooking, candles, fireplaces, and electrical appliances.

4. Explain the role of human behavior in the arson problem in this country.

5. List the actions and common circumstances that cause seasonal and holiday-related fires. Explain how these fires can be prevented.

6. Conduct a home safety survey with the help of an adult. Then do the following:

(a) Draw a home fire-escape plan, create a home fire-drill schedule, and conduct a home fire drill.

(b) Test a smoke alarm and demonstrate regular maintenance of a smoke alarm.

(c) Explain what to do when you smell gas and when you smell smoke.

(d) Explain how you would report a fire alarm.

(e) Explain what fire safety equipment can be found in public buildings.

(f) Explain who should use fire extinguishers and when these devices can be used.

(g) Explain how to extinguish a grease pan fire.

(h) Explain what fire safety precautions you should take when you are in a public building.

7. Do the following:

    (a) Demonstrate lighting a match safely.

    (b) Demonstrate the safe way to start a charcoal fire.

    (c) Demonstrate how to safely light a candle. Discuss with your counselor how to safely use candles.

8. Explain the difference between combustible and noncombustible liquids and between combustible and noncombustible fabrics.

9. Do the following:

    (a) Describe for your counselor the safe way to refuel a liquid fuel engine, such as a lawn mower, weed eater, an outboard motor, farm machine, or an automobile with gas from an approved gas can.

    (b) Demonstrate the safety factors, such as proper ventilation, for auxiliary heating devices and the proper way to fuel those devices.

10. Do the following:

    (a) Explain the cost of outdoor and wildland fires and how to prevent them.

    (b) Demonstrate setting up and putting out a cooking fire.

    (c) Demonstrate using a camp stove and lantern.

    (d) Explain how to set up a campsite safe from fire.

11. Visit a fire station. Identify the types of fire trucks. Find out about the fire prevention activities in your community.

12. Determine if smoke detectors are required in all dwellings within your municipality. If so, explain which specific types are required. Tell your counselor what type of smoke detectors your house has or needs.

13. Choose a fire safety–related career that interests you and describe the level of education required and responsibilities of a person in that position. Tell why this position interests you.

 First Aid

1. Demonstrate to your counselor that you have current knowledge of all first-aid requirements for Tenderfoot, Second Class, and First Class ranks.

2. Explain how you would obtain emergency medical assistance from:

    (a) Your home

    (b) A remote location on a wilderness camping trip

    (c) An activity on open water

3. Define the term *triage*. Explain the steps necessary to assess and handle a medical emergency until help arrives.

4. Explain the universal precautions as applied to the transmission of infections. Discuss the ways you should protect yourself and the victim while administering first aid.

5. Do the following:

   (a) Prepare a first-aid kit for your home. Display and discuss its contents with your counselor.

   (b) With an adult leader, inspect your troop's first-aid kit. Evaluate it for completeness. Report your findings to your counselor and Scout leader.

6. Describe the early signs and symptoms of each of the following and explain what actions you should take:

   (a) Shock

   (b) Heart attack

   (c) Stroke

7. Do the following:

   (a) Describe the conditions that must exist before performing CPR on a person. Then demonstrate proper CPR technique using a training device approved by your counselor.

   (b) Explain the use of an automated external defibrillator (AED). Identify the location of the AED at your school, place of worship, and troop meeting place, if one is present.

8. Do the following:

   (a) Show the steps that need to be taken for someone who has a large open wound or cut that is not bleeding severely.

   (b) Show the steps that need to be taken for someone who has a large open wound or cut that is severely bleeding.

   (c) Tell the dangers in the use of a tourniquet and the conditions under which its use is justified.

9. Explain when a bee sting could be life threatening and what action should be taken for prevention and for first aid.

10. Describe the signs and symptoms and demonstrate the proper procedures for handling and immobilizing suspected closed and open fractures or dislocations of the

    (a) Forearm

    (b) Wrist

    (c) Upper leg

    (d) Lower leg

    (e) Ankle

11. Describe the signs, symptoms, and possible complications and demonstrate care for someone with a suspected injury to the head, neck, or back.

12. Describe the symptoms, proper first-aid procedures, and possible prevention measures for the following conditions:

(a) Anaphylaxis/allergic reactions

(b) Bruises

(c) Sprains or strains

(d) Hypothermia

(e) Frostbite

(f) Burns—first, second, and third degree

(g) Convulsions/seizures

(h) Dehydration

(i) Muscle cramps

(j) Heat exhaustion

(k) Heat stroke

(l) Abdominal pain

(m) Broken, chipped, or loosened tooth

13. Do the following:

(a) Describe the conditions under which an injured person should be moved.

(b) If a sick or an injured person must be moved, tell how you would determine the best method. Demonstrate this method.

(c) With helpers under your supervision, improvise a stretcher and move a presumably unconscious person.

14. Teach another Scout a first-aid skill selected by your counselor.

Fish and Wildlife Management

1. Describe the meaning and purposes of fish and wildlife conservation and management.

2. List and discuss at least three major problems that continue to threaten your state's fish and wildlife resources.

3. Describe some practical ways in which everyone can help with the fish and wildlife conservation effort.

4. List and describe five major fish and wildlife management practices used by managers in your state.

5. Do ONE of the following:

(a) Construct, erect, and check regularly at least two artificial nest boxes (wood duck, bluebird, squirrel, etc.) and keep written records for one nesting season.

(b) Construct, erect, and check regularly bird feeders and keep written records of the kinds of birds visiting the feeders.

(c) Develop and implement a fishery improvement project or a backyard wildlife habitat improvement project. Share the results with your counselor.

(d) Design and construct a wildlife blind near a game trail, water hole, salt lick, bird feeder, or birdbath and take good photographs or make sketches from the blind of any combination of 10 wild birds, mammals, reptiles, or amphibians.

6. Do ONE of the following:

(a) Observe and record 25 species of wildlife. Your list may include mammals, birds, reptiles, amphibians, and fish. Write down when and where each animal was seen.

(b) List the wildlife species in your state that are classified as endangered, threatened, exotic, non-native, game species, furbearers, or migratory game birds. Discuss with your counselor management practices in place or being developed for at least three of these species.

(c) Start a scrapbook of North American fish and wildlife. Insert markers to divide the book into separate parts for mammals, birds, reptiles, amphibians, and fish. Collect articles on such subjects as life histories, habitat, behavior, and feeding habits on all of the five categories and place them in your notebook accordingly. Articles and pictures may be taken from newspapers or science, nature, and outdoor magazines, or from other sources including the internet (with your parent's permission). Enter at least five articles on mammals, five on birds, five on reptiles, five on amphibians, and five on fish. Put each animal on a separate sheet in alphabetical order. Include pictures whenever possible.

7. Do ONE of the following:

(a) Determine the age of five species of fish from scale samples or identify various age classes of one species in a lake and report the results.

(b) Conduct a creel census on a small lake to estimate catch per unit effort.

(c) Examine the stomach contents of three fish and record the findings. It is not necessary to catch any fish for this option. You must visit a cleaning station set up for fishermen or find another, similar alternative.

(d) Make a freshwater aquarium. Include at least four species of native plants and four species of animal life, such as whirligig beetles, freshwater shrimp, tadpoles, water snails, and golden shiners. After 60 days of observation, discuss with your counselor the life cycles, food chains, and management needs you have recognized. After completing requirement 7d to your counselor's satisfaction, with your counselor's assistance, check local laws to determine what you should do with the specimens you have collected.

8. Using resources found at the library and in periodicals, books, and the internet (with your parent's permission), learn about three different positions held by fisheries and/or wildlife professionals. Find out the education and training requirements for each position.

Fishing

1. Do the following:

    (a) Explain to your counselor the most likely hazards you may encounter while participating in fishing activities, and what you should do to anticipate, help prevent, mitigate, and respond to these hazards.

    (b) Discuss the prevention of and treatment for the following health concerns that could occur while fishing, including cuts and scratches, puncture wounds, insect bites, hypothermia, dehydration, heat exhaustion, heatstroke, and sunburn.

    (c) Explain how to remove a hook that has lodged in your arm.

    (d) Name and explain five safety practices you should always follow while fishing.

2. Discuss the differences between two types of fishing outfits. Point out and identify the parts of several types of rods and reels. Explain how and when each would be used. Review with your counselor how to care for this equipment.

3. Demonstrate the proper use of two different types of fishing equipment.

4. Demonstrate how to tie the following knots: improved clinch knot, Palomar knot, uni knot, uni to uni knot, and arbor knot. Explain how and when each knot is used.

5. Name and identify five basic artificial lures and five natural baits and explain how to fish with them. Explain why baitfish are not to be released.

6. Do the following:

    (a) Explain the importance of practicing Leave No Trace techniques. Discuss the positive effects of Leave No Trace on fishing resources.

    (b) Discuss the meaning and importance of catch and release. Describe how to properly release a fish safely to the water.

7. Obtain and review the regulations affecting game fishing where you live. Explain why they were adopted and what is accomplished by following them.

> Scouts should obey all local fishing regulations and property laws.

8. Explain what good outdoor sportsmanlike behavior is and how it relates to anglers. Tell how the Outdoor Code of the Boy Scouts of America relates to a fishing sports enthusiast, including the aspects of littering, trespassing, courteous behavior, and obeying fishing regulations.

9. Catch at least one fish and identify it.

10. If regulations and health concerns permit, clean and cook a fish you have caught. Otherwise, acquire a fish and cook it. (You do not need to eat your fish.)

Fly-Fishing

1. Do the following:

    (a) Explain to your counselor the most likely hazards you may encounter while participating in fly-fishing activities and what you should do to anticipate, help prevent, mitigate, and respond to these hazards. Name and explain five safety practices you should always follow while fly-fishing.

    (b) Discuss the prevention of and treatment for health concerns that could occur while fly-fishing, including cuts and scratches, puncture wounds, insect bites, hypothermia, dehydration, heat exhaustion, heatstroke, and sunburn.

    (c) Explain how to remove a hook that has lodged in your arm.

2. Demonstrate how to match a fly rod, line, and leader to achieve a balanced system. Discuss several types of fly lines, and explain how and when each would be used. Review with your counselor how to care for this equipment.

3. Demonstrate how to tie proper knots to prepare a fly rod for fishing:

    (a) Tie backing to the arbor of a fly reel spool using an arbor knot.

    (b) Tie backing to the fly line using a nail knot.

    (c) Attach a leader to the fly line using a nail knot or a loop-to-loop connection.

    (d) Add a tippet to a leader using a surgeon's knot or a loop-to-loop connection.

    (e) Tie a fly onto the terminal end of the leader using an improved clinch knot.

4. Explain how and when each of the following types of flies is used: dry flies, wet flies, nymphs, streamers, bass bugs, poppers, and saltwater flies. Tell what each one imitates. Tie at least two types of the flies mentioned in this requirement.

5. Demonstrate the ability to cast a fly 30 feet consistently and accurately using both overhead and roll cast techniques.

6. Go to a suitable fishing location and observe what fish may be eating both above and beneath the water's surface. Explain the importance of matching the hatch.

7. Do the following:

    (a) Explain the importance of practicing Leave No Trace techniques. Discuss the positive effects of Leave No Trace on fly-fishing resources.

    (b) Discuss the meaning and importance of catch and release. Describe how to properly release a fish safely to the water.

8. Obtain and review a copy of the regulations affecting game fishing where you live or where you plan to fish. Explain why they were adopted and what is accomplished by following them.

9. Discuss what good sportsmanlike behavior is and how it relates to anglers. Tell how the Outdoor Code of the Boy Scouts of America relates to a fishing enthusiast, including the aspects of littering, trespassing, courteous behavior, "catch and release," and obeying fishing regulations.

10. Catch at least one fish and identify it.

11. If regulations and health concerns permit, clean and cook a fish you have caught. Otherwise, acquire a fish and cook it. (You do not need to eat your fish.)

 **Forestry**

1. Prepare a field notebook, make a collection, and identify 15 species of trees, wild shrubs, or vines in a local forested area. Write a description in which you identify and discuss the following:

   (a) The characteristics of leaf, twig, cone, or fruiting bodies

   (b) The habitat in which these trees, shrubs, or vines are found

   (c) The important ways each tree, shrub, or vine is used by humans or wild-life and whether the species is native or was introduced to the area. If it is not native, explain whether it is considered invasive or potentially invasive.

2. Do ONE of the following:

   (a) Collect and identify wood samples of 10 species of trees. List several ways the wood of each species can be used.

   (b) Find and examine three stumps, logs, or core samples that show variations in the growth rate of their ring patterns. In the field notebook you prepared for requirement 1, describe the location or origin of each example (including elevation, aspect, slope, and the position on the slope), and discuss possible reasons for the variations in growth rate. Photograph or sketch each example.

   (c) Find and examine two types of animal, insect, or disease damage to trees. In the field notebook you prepared for requirement 1, identify the damage, explain how the damage was caused, and describe the effects of the damage on the trees. Photograph or sketch each example.

3. Do the following:

   (a) Describe the contributions forests make to:

      (1) Our economy in the form of products

      (2) Our social well-being, including recreation

      (3) Soil protection and increased fertility

      (4) Clean water

      (5) Clean air (carbon cycling, sequestration)

      (6) Wildlife habitat

      (7) Fisheries habitat

      (8) Threatened and endangered species of plants and animals

   (b) Tell which watershed or other source your community relies on for its water supply.

4. Describe what forest management means, including the following:

    (a) Multiple-use management

    (b) Sustainable forest management

    (c) Even-aged and uneven-aged management and the silvicultural systems associated with each

    (d) Intermediate cuttings

    (e) The role of prescribed burning and related forest-management practices

5. With your parent's and counselor's approval, do ONE of the following:

    (a) Visit a managed public or private forest area with the manager or a forester who is familiar with it. Write a brief report describing the type of forest, the management objectives, and the forestry techniques used to achieve the objectives.

    (b) With a knowledgeable individual, visit a logging operation or wood-using manufacturing plant. Write a brief report describing the following:

    (1) The species and size of trees being harvested or used and the location of the harvest area or manufacturer

    (2) The origin of the forest or stands of trees being utilized (e.g., planted or natural)

    (3) The forest's successional stage. What is its future?

    (4) Where the trees are coming from (land ownership) or where they are going (type of mill or processing plant)

    (5) The products that are made from the trees

    (6) How the products are made and used

    (7) How waste materials from the logging operation or manufacturing plant are disposed of or utilized

    (c) Take part in a forest-fire prevention campaign in cooperation with your local fire warden, state wildfire agency, forester, or counselor. Write a brief report describing the campaign, how it will help prevent wildfires, and your part in it.

6. In your camp, local recreation area (park or equivalent), or neighborhood, inventory the trees that may be a hazard to structures or people. Make a list by area (campsite, road, trail, street, etc.). Note the species and hazardous condition, and suggest a remedy (removal or trimming). Make your list available to the proper authority or agency.

7. Do the following:

    (a) Describe the consequences to forests that result from FIVE of the following elements: wildfire, absence of fire, destructive insects, loss of pollinating insect population, tree diseases, air pollution, overgrazing, deer or other wildlife over-population, improper harvest, and urbanization.

    (b) Explain what can be done to reduce the consequences you discussed in 7a.

    (c) Describe what you should do if you discover a forest fire and how a professional firefighting crew might control it. Name your state or local wildfire control agency.

8. Visit one or more local foresters and write a brief report about the person (or persons). Or, write about a forester's occupation including the education, qualifications, career opportunities, and duties related to forestry.

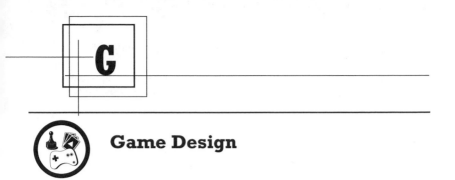

Game Design

1. Do the following:

    (a) Analyze four games you have played, each from a different medium. Identify the medium, player format, objectives, rules, resources, and theme (if relevant). Discuss with your counselor the play experience, what you enjoy in each game, and what you dislike. Make a chart to compare and contrast the games.

    (b) Describe four types of play value and provide an example of a game built around each concept. Discuss with your counselor other reasons people play games.

2. Discuss with your counselor five of the following 17 game design terms. For each term that you pick, describe how it relates to a specific game.

    Thematic game elements: *story, setting, characters*

    Gameplay elements: *play sequence, level design, interface design*

    Game analysis: *difficulty, balance, depth, pace, replay value, age appropriateness*

    Related terms: *single-player vs. multiplayer, cooperative vs. competitive, turn-based vs. real-time, strategy vs. reflex vs. chance, abstract vs. thematic*

3. Define the term *intellectual property*. Describe the types of intellectual property associated with the game design industry. Describe how intellectual property is protected and why protection is necessary. Define and give an example of a licensed property.

4. Do the following:

    (a) Pick a game where the players can change the rules or objectives (examples: basketball, hearts, chess, kickball). Briefly summarize the standard rules and objectives and play through the game normally.

    (b) Propose changes to several rules or objectives. Predict how each change will affect gameplay.

    (c) Play the game with one rule or objective change, observing how the players' actions and emotional experiences are affected by the rule change. Repeat this process with two other changes.

    (d) Explain to your counselor how the changes affected the actions and experience of the players. Discuss the accuracy of your predictions.

5. Design a new game. Any game medium or combination of mediums is acceptable. Record your work in a game design notebook.

(a) Write a vision statement for your game. Identify the medium, player format, objectives, and theme of the game. If suitable, describe the setting, story, and characters.

(b) Describe the play value.

(c) Make a preliminary list of the rules of the game. Define the resources.

(d) Draw the game elements.

You must have your merit badge counselor's approval of your concept before you begin creating the prototype.

6. Do the following:

(a) Prototype your game from requirement 5. If applicable, demonstrate to your counselor that you have addressed player safety through the rules and equipment. Record your work in your game design notebook.

(b) Test your prototype with as many other people as you need to meet the player format. Compare the play experience to your descriptions from requirement 5b. Correct unclear rules, holes in the rules, dead ends, and obvious rule exploits. Change at least one rule, mechanic, or objective from your first version of the game, and describe why you are making the change. Play the game again. Record in your game design notebook whether or not your change had the expected effect.

(c) Repeat 6b at least two more times and record the results in your game design notebook.

7. Blind test your game. Do the following:

(a) Write an instruction sheet that includes all of the information needed to play the game. Clearly describe how to set up the game, play the game, and end the game. List the game objectives.

(b) Share your prototype from requirement 6 with a group of players that has not played it or witnessed a previous playtest. Provide them with your instruction sheet(s) and any physical components. Watch them play the game, but do not provide them with instruction. Record their feedback in your game design notebook.

(c) Share your game design notebook with your counselor. Discuss the player reactions to your project and what you learned about the game design process. Based on your testing, determine what you like most about your game and suggest one or more changes.

8. Do ONE of the following:

(a) With your parent's permission and your counselor's approval, visit with a professional in the game development industry and ask him or her about his or her job and how it fits into the overall development process. Alternately, meet with a professional in game development education and discuss the skills he or she emphasizes in the classroom.

(b) List three career opportunities in game development. Pick one and find out about the education, training, and experience required for the profession. Discuss this with your counselor. Explain why this profession might interest you.

 # Gardening

1. Do the following:
   (a) Explain to your counselor the most likely hazards associated with gardening and what you should do to anticipate, help prevent, mitigate, and respond to these hazards.
   (b) Discuss the prevention of and treatment for health concerns that could occur while gardening, including cuts, scratches, puncture wounds, insect bites, anaphylactic shock, heat reactions, and reactions from exposure to pesticides and fertilizers.
2. Do the following, and discuss your observations throughout the process with your counselor:
   (a) Grow six vegetables, three from seeds and three from seedlings, through harvest.
   (b) Grow six flowers, three from seeds and three from seedlings, through flowering.
3. Give the nutritional value of the following:
   (a) Three root or tuber crops
   (b) Three vegetables that bear above the ground
   (c) Three fruits
4. Test 100 seeds for germination. Determine the percentage of seeds that germinate. Explain why you think some did not germinate.
5. Visit your county extension agent's office, local university agricultural college, nursery, or a botanical garden or arboretum. Report on what you learned.
6. Explain to your counselor how and why honeybees are used in pollinating food crops and the problems that face the bee population today. Discuss what the impact to humanity would be if there were no pollinators.
7. Identify five garden pests (insects, diseased plants). Recommend two solutions for each pest. At least one of the two solutions must be an organic method.

8. Do ONE of the following and record weekly observations. Discuss the results of your project with your counselor.

(a) Build a compost bin and maintain it for 90 days.

(b) Build a vermipost bin (worm compost bin) and maintain it for 90 days.

(c) Build a hydroponic garden containing three vegetables or herbs, or three ornamental plants. Maintain this garden through harvest or flowering, or for 90 days.

(d) Build one water garden, either in a container (at least 12 by 6 inches and 6 inches deep), or in the ground as a small, decorative pond no larger than 6 by 3 feet and 24 inches deep. Maintain the water garden for 90 days.

(e) Prepare a honey super for use on a hive or colony. Remove a filled honey super from the hive or colony and prepare the honey for sale.

 # Genealogy

1. Explain to your counselor what the words *genealogy, ancestor,* and *descendant* mean.

2. Do ONE of the following:

(a) Create a time line for yourself or for a relative. Then write a short biography based on that time line.

(b) Keep a journal for six weeks. You must write in it at least once a week.

3. With your parent's help, choose a relative or a family acquaintance you can interview in person, by telephone, or by email or letter. Record the information you collect so you do not forget it.

4. Do the following:

(a) Name three types of genealogical resources and explain how these resources can help you chart your family tree.

(b) Obtain at least one genealogical document that supports an event that is or can be recorded on your pedigree chart or family group record. The document could be found at home or at a government office, religious organization, archive, or library.

(c) Tell how you would evaluate the genealogical information you found for requirement 4b.

5. Contact ONE of the following individuals or institutions. Ask what genealogical services, records, or activities this individual or institution provides, and report the results:

(a) A genealogical or lineage society

(b) A professional genealogist (someone who gets paid for doing genealogical research)

(c) A surname organization, such as your family's organization

(d) A genealogical educational facility or institution

(e) A genealogical record repository of any type (courthouse, genealogical library, state or national archive, state library, etc.)

6. Begin your family tree by listing yourself and include at least two additional generations. You may complete this requirement by using the chart provided in the *Genealogy* merit badge pamphlet or the genealogy software program of your choice.

7. Complete a family group record form, listing yourself and your brothers and sisters as the children. On another family group record form, show one of your parents and his or her brothers and sisters as the children. This requirement may be completed using the chart provided or the genealogy software program of your choice.

8. Do the following:

   (a) Explain the effect computers and the internet are having on the world of genealogy.

   (b) Explain how photography (including microfilming) has influenced genealogy.

9. Discuss what you have learned about your family and your family members through your genealogical research.

 # Geocaching

1. Do the following:

   (a) Explain to your counselor the most likely hazards you may encounter while participating in geocaching activities, and what you should do to anticipate, help prevent, mitigate, and respond to these hazards.

   (b) Discuss first aid and prevention for the types of injuries or illnesses that could occur while participating in geocaching activities, including cuts, scrapes, snakebite, insect stings, tick bites, exposure to poisonous plants, heat and cold reactions (sunburn, heatstroke, heat exhaustion, hypothermia), and dehydration.

   (c) Discuss how to properly plan an activity that uses GPS, including using the buddy system, sharing your plan with others, and considering the weather, route, and proper attire.

2. Discuss the following with your counselor:

   (a) Why you should never bury a cache

   (b) How to use proper geocaching etiquette when hiding or seeking a cache, and how to properly hide, post, maintain, and dismantle a geocache

   (c) The principles of Leave No Trace as they apply to geocaching

3. Explain the following terms used in geocaching: waypoint, log, cache, accuracy, difficulty and terrain ratings, attributes, trackable. Choose five additional terms to explain to your counselor.

4. Explain how the Global Positioning System (GPS) works. Then, using Scouting's Teaching EDGE, demonstrate to your counselor the use of a GPS unit. Include marking and editing a waypoint, changing field functions, and changing the coordinate system in the unit.

5. Do the following:

    (a) Show you know how to use a map and compass and explain why this is important for geocaching.

    (b) Explain the similarities and differences between GPS navigation and standard map-reading skills and describe the benefits of each.

6. Describe to your counselor the four steps to finding your first cache. Then mark and edit a waypoint.

7. With your parent's permission*, go to www.geocaching.com. Type in your city and state to locate public geocaches in your area. Share with your counselor the posted information about three of those geocaches. Then, pick one of the three and find the cache.

8. Do ONE of the following:

    (a) If a Cache to Eagle® series exists in your council, visit at least three of the locations in the series. Describe the projects that each cache you visit highlights, and explain how the Cache to Eagle® program helps share our Scouting service with the public.

    (b) Create a Scouting-related Travel Bug® that promotes one of the values of Scouting. "Release" your Travel Bug into a public geocache and, with your parent's permission, monitor its progress at www.geocaching.com for 30 days. Keep a log, and share this with your counselor at the end of the 30-day period.

    (c) Set up and hide a public geocache, following the guidelines in the *Geocaching* merit badge pamphlet. Before doing so, share with your counselor a three-month maintenance plan for the geocache where you are personally responsible for those three months. After setting up the geocache, with your parent's permission, follow the logs online for 30 days and share them with your counselor. You must archive the geocache when you are no longer maintaining it.

    (d) Explain what Cache In Trash Out (CITO) means, and describe how you have practiced CITO at public geocaches or at a CITO event. Then, either create CITO containers to leave at public caches, or host a CITO event for your unit or for the public.

9. Plan a geohunt for a youth group such as your troop or a neighboring pack, at school, or your place of worship. Choose a theme, set up a course with at least four waypoints, teach the players how to use a GPS unit, and play the game. Tell your counselor about your experience, and share the materials you used and developed for this event.

---

*To fulfill this requirement, you will need to set up a free user account with www.geocaching.com. Before doing so, ask your parent for permission and help.

Geology

1. Define geology. Discuss how geologists learn about rock formations. In geology, explain why the study of the present is important to understanding the past.

2. Pick three resources that can be extracted or mined from Earth for commercial use. Discuss with your counselor how each product is discovered and processed.

3. Review a geologic map of your area or an area selected by your counselor, and discuss the different rock types and estimated ages of rocks represented. Determine whether the rocks are horizontal, folded, or faulted, and explain how you arrived at your conclusion.

4. Do ONE of the following:

   (a) With your parent's and counselor's approval, visit with a geologist, land-use planner, or civil engineer. Discuss this professional's work and the tools required in this line of work. Learn about a project that this person is now working on, and ask to see reports and maps created for this project. Discuss with your counselor what you have learned.

   (b) Find out about three career opportunities available in geology. Pick one and find out the education, training, and experience required for this profession. Discuss this with your counselor, and explain why this profession might interest you.

5. Do ONE of the following (a OR b OR c OR d):

   (a) **Surface and Sedimentary Processes Option**

   (1) Conduct an experiment approved by your counselor that demonstrates how sediments settle from suspension in water. Explain to your counselor what the exercise shows and why it is important.

   (2) Using topographical maps provided by your counselor, plot the stream gradients (different elevations divided by distance) for four different stream types (straight, meandering, dendritic, trellis). Explain which ones flow fastest and why, and which ones will carry larger grains of sediment and why.

   (3) On a stream diagram, show areas where you will find the following features: cut bank, fill bank, point bar, medial channel bars, lake delta. Describe the relative sediment grain size found in each feature.

   (4) Conduct an experiment approved by your counselor that shows how some sedimentary material carried by water may be too small for you to see without a magnifier.

   (5) Visit a nearby stream. Find clues that show the direction of water flow, even if the water is missing. Record your observations in a notebook, and sketch those clues you observe. Discuss your observations with your counselor.

(b) **Energy Resources Option**

(1) List the top five Earth resources used to generate electricity in the United States.

(2) Discuss source rock, trap, and reservoir rock—the three components necessary for the occurrence of oil and gas underground.

(3) Explain how each of the following items is used in subsurface exploration to locate oil or gas: reflection seismic, electric well logs, stratigraphic correlation, offshore platform, geologic map, subsurface structure map, subsurface isopach map, and core samples and cutting samples.

(4) Using at least 20 data points provided by your counselor, create a subsurface structure map and use it to explain how subsurface geology maps are used to find oil, gas, or coal resources.

(5) Do ONE of the following activities:

(a) Make a display or presentation showing how oil and gas or coal is found, extracted, and processed. You may use maps, books, articles from periodicals, and research found on the internet (with your parent's permission). Share the display with your counselor or a small group (such as your class at school) in a five-minute presentation.

(b) With your parent's and counselor's permission and assistance, arrange for a visit to an operating drilling rig. While there, talk with a geologist and ask to see what the geologist does onsite. Ask to see cutting samples taken at the site.

(c) **Mineral Resources Option**

(1) Define rock. Discuss the three classes of rocks including their origin and characteristics.

(2) Define mineral. Discuss the origin of minerals and their chemical composition and identification properties, including hardness, specific gravity, color, streak, cleavage, luster, and crystal form.

(3) Do ONE of the following:

(a) Collect 10 different rocks or minerals. Record in a notebook where you obtained (found, bought, traded) each one. Label each specimen, identify its class and origin, determine its chemical composition, and list its physical properties. Share your collection with your counselor.

(b) With your counselor's assistance, identify 15 different rocks and minerals. List the name of each specimen, tell whether it is a rock or mineral, and give the name of its class (if it is a rock) or list its identifying physical properties (if it is a mineral).

(4) List three of the most common road-building materials used in your area. Explain how each material is produced and how each is used in road building.

(5) Do ONE of the following activities:

(a) With your parent's and counselor's approval, visit an active mining site, quarry, or sand and gravel pit. Tell your counselor what you learned about the resources extracted from this location and how these resources are used by society.

(b) With your counselor, choose two examples of rocks and two examples of minerals. Discuss the mining of these materials and describe how each is used by society.

(c) With your parent's and counselor's approval, visit the office of a civil engineer and learn how geology is used in construction. Discuss what you learned with your counselor.

(d) Earth History Option

(1) Create a chart showing suggested geological eras and periods. Determine which period the rocks in your region might have been formed.

(2) Explain to your counselor the processes of burial and fossilization, and discuss the concept of extinction.

(3) Explain to your counselor how fossils provide information about ancient life, environment, climate, and geography. Discuss the following terms and explain how animals from each habitat obtain food: benthonic, pelagic, littoral, lacustrine, open marine, brackish, fluvial, eolian, protected reef.

(4) Collect 10 different fossil plants or animals OR (with your counselor's assistance) identify 15 different fossil plants or animals. Record in a notebook where you obtained (found, bought, traded) each one. Classify each specimen to the best of your ability, and explain how each one might have survived and obtained food. Tell what else you can learn from these fossils.

(5) Do ONE of the following:

(a) Visit a science museum or the geology department of a local university that has fossils on display. With your parent's and counselor's approval, before you go, make an appointment with a curator or guide who can show you how the fossils are preserved and prepared for display.

(b) Visit a structure in your area that was built using fossiliferous rocks. Determine what kind of rock was used and tell your counselor the kinds of fossil evidence you found there.

(c) Visit a rock outcrop that contains fossils. Determine what kind of rock contains the fossils, and tell your counselor the kinds of fossil evidence you found at the outcrop.

(d) Prepare a display or presentation on your state fossil. Include an image of the fossil, the age of the fossil, and its classification. You may use maps, books, articles from periodicals, and research found on the internet (with your parent's permission). Share the display with your counselor or a small group (such as your class at school). If your state does not have a state fossil, you may select a state fossil from a neighboring state.

Golf

1. Discuss safety on the golf course. Show that you know first aid for injuries or illnesses that could occur while golfing, including lightning, heat reactions, dehydration, blisters, sprains, and strains.

2. Study the USGA "Rules of Golf" now in use.

    (a) Tell about the three categories of golf etiquette.

    (b) Demonstrate that you understand the definitions of golf terms.

    (c) Show that you understand the "Rules of Amateur Status."

3. Tell about your understanding of the USGA system of handicapping.

4. Do the following:

    (a) Tell about the early history of golf.

    (b) Describe golf's early years in the United States.

    (c) Tell about the accomplishments of a top golfer of your choice.

5. Discuss with your counselor vocational opportunities related to golf.

6. Do the following:

    (a) Tell how golf can contribute to a healthy lifestyle, mentally and physically.

    (b) Tell how a golf exercise plan can help you play better. Show two exercises that would help improve your game.

7. Show the following:

    (a) The proper grip, stance, posture, and key fundamentals of a good swing

    (b) Driver played from a tee

    (c) The fairway wood shot

    (d) The long iron shot

    (e) The short iron shot

    (f) The approach, chip-and-run, and pitch shots

    (g) The sand iron shot, bunker, or heavy rough recovery shots

    (h) A sound putting stroke

8. Play a minimum of two nine-hole rounds or one 18-hole round of golf with another golfer about your age and with your counselor, or an adult approved by your counselor. Do the following:

    (a) Follow the "Rules of Golf."

    (b) Practice good golf etiquette.

    (c) Show respect to fellow golfers, committee, sponsor, and gallery.

Graphic Arts

1. Review with your counselor the processes for producing printed communications: offset lithography, screen printing, electronic/digital, relief, and gravure. Collect samples of three products, each one produced using a different printing process, or draw diagrams to help you with your description.

2. Explain the differences between continuous tone, line, and halftone artwork. Describe how digital images can be created and/or stored in a computer.

3. Design a printed piece (flier, T-shirt, program, form, etc.) and produce it. Explain your decisions for the typeface or typefaces you use and the way you arrange the elements in your design. Explain which printing process is best suited for printing your design. If desktop publishing is available, identify what hardware and software would be appropriate for outputting your design.

4. Produce the design you created for requirement 3 using one of the following printing processes:

(a) Offset lithography

Make a layout, and produce a plate using a process approved by your counselor. Run the plate and print at least 50 copies.

(b) Screen printing

Make a hand-cut or photographic stencil and attach it to a screen that you have prepared. Mask the screen and print at least 20 copies.

(c) Electronic/digital printing

Create a layout in electronic form, download it to the press or printer, and run 50 copies. If no electronic interface to the press or printer is available, you may print and scan a paper copy of the layout.

(d) Relief printing

Prepare a layout or set the necessary type. Make a plate or lock up the form. Use this to print 50 copies.

5. Review the following postpress operations with your counselor:

(a) Discuss the finishing operations of padding, drilling, cutting, and trimming.

(b) Collect, describe, or identify examples of the following types of binding: perfect, spiral, plastic comb, saddle-stitched, and case.

6. Do ONE of the following, and then describe the highlights of your visit:

(a) Visit a newspaper printing plant: Follow a story from the editor to the press.

(b) Visit a retail, commercial, or in-plant printing facility. Follow a project from beginning to end.

(c) Visit a school's graphic arts program. Find out what courses are available and what the prerequisites are.

(d) Visit three websites (with your parent's permission) that belong to graphic arts professional organizations and/or printing-related companies (suppliers, manufacturers, printers). With permission from your parent or counselor, print out or download product or service information from two of the sites.

7. Find out about three career opportunities in graphic arts. Pick one and find out the education, training, and experience required for this profession. Discuss this with your counselor, and explain why this profession might interest you.

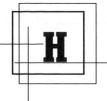

Hiking

1. Do the following:

   (a) Explain to your counselor the most likely hazards you may encounter while hiking, and what you should do to anticipate, help prevent, mitigate, and respond to these hazards.

   (b) Show that you know first aid for injuries or illnesses that could occur while hiking, including hypothermia, frostbite, dehydration, heat exhaustion, heatstroke, sunburn, hyperventilation, altitude sickness, sprained ankle, blisters, insect stings, tick bites, and snakebite.

2. Explain and, where possible, show the points of good hiking practices including proper outdoor ethics, hiking safety in the daytime and at night, courtesy to others, choice of footwear, and proper care of feet and footwear.

3. Explain how hiking is an aerobic activity. Develop a plan for conditioning yourself for 10-mile hikes, and describe how you will increase your fitness for longer hikes.

4. Take the five following hikes, each on a different day, and each of continuous miles. These hikes MUST be taken in the following order:

   One 5-mile hike

   Three 10-mile hikes

   One 15-mile hike

   You may stop for as many short rest periods as needed, as well as one meal, during each hike, but **not** for an extended period (example: overnight). Prepare a written hike plan before each hike and share it with your Scoutmaster or a designee. Include map routes, a clothing and equipment list, and a list of items for a trail lunch.*

5. Take a hike of 20 continuous miles in one day following a hike plan you have prepared. You may stop for as many short rest periods as needed, as well as one meal, but **not** for an extended period (example: overnight).*

6. After each of the hikes (or during each hike if on one continuous "trek") in requirements 4 and 5, write a short reflection of your experience. Give dates and descriptions of routes covered, the weather, and any interesting things you saw. It may include something you learned about yourself, about the outdoors, or about others you were hiking with. Share this with your merit badge counselor.

---

*The required hikes for this badge may be used in fulfilling hiking requirements for rank advancement. However, these hikes cannot be used to fulfill requirements of other merit badges.

Home Repairs

1. Do the following:

    (a) Explain to your counselor the most likely hazards you may encounter while working on home repairs and what you should do to anticipate, mitigate and prevent, and respond to these hazards. Describe the appropriate safety gear and clothing that should be used when working on home repairs.

    (b) Discuss general precautions related to home repairs. Name at least 10 safe practices that every home repairer should exercise.

2. Under the supervision of your merit badge counselor, do FOUR of the following:

    (a) Maintain or recondition a yard tool and show that you know how to clean up and properly store this equipment.

    (b) Weather-strip a window or door.

    (c) Caulk cracks or joints open to the weather.

    (d) Waterproof a basement.

    (e) Repair a break in a concrete or asphalt surface.

    (f) Repair the screen in a window or door.

    (g) Replace a pane of glass.

    (h) Solder a broken wire or metal object.

3. Under the supervision of your merit badge counselor, do THREE of the following:

    (a) Install or build equipment for storing tools.

    (b) Build a workbench.

    (c) Repair a piece of furniture.

    (d) Paint or varnish a piece of furniture, a door, or trim on a house.

    (e) Repair a sagging door or gate.

    (f) Repair a loose step or railing.

    (g) Repair a fence.

Either a parent or the merit badge counselor may supervise the Scout's work on any Home Repairs requirements.

---

4. Under the supervision of your merit badge counselor, do TWO of the following:

(a) Locate a main electrical switch box and know how to replace a fuse or reset a circuit breaker.

(b) Replace an electrical cord or repair a plug or lamp socket.

(c) Install a single-pole light switch.

(d) Replace an electrical wall outlet.

5. Under the supervision of your merit badge counselor, do TWO of the following:

(a) Clear a clogged drain or trap.

(b) Repair a leaky water faucet.

(c) Repair a flush toilet.

(d) Repair a leaky hose or connector.

(e) Clean or replace a sprinkler head.

6. Under the supervision of your merit badge counselor, do THREE of the following:

(a) Paint a wall or ceiling.

(b) Repair or replace damaged tile, linoleum, or vinyl flooring.

(c) Install drapery or curtain rods and then hang drapes or curtains.

(d) Replace window blind cords.

(e) Repair or replace a window sash cord.

(f) Reinforce a picture frame.

(g) Mend an object made of china, glass, or pottery.

 Horsemanship

1. Do the following:

(a) Describe the safety precautions you should take when handling and caring for a horse.

(b) Describe the fire safety precautions you should take in a barn and around horses.

2. Name the 15 main parts of a horse.

3. Name four breeds of horses. Explain the special features for which each breed is known.

4. Describe the symptoms of colic. Name and describe four other horse health problems.

5. Explain what conformation is and why it is important. Explain the difference between lameness and unsoundness.

6. Explain the importance of hoof care and why a horse might need to wear shoes.

7. Demonstrate how to groom a horse, including picking hooves and caring for a horse after a ride.

8. Explain how to determine what and how much to feed a horse and why the amount and kind of feed are changed according to the activity level and the breed of horse.

9. Do the following:

   (a) Name 10 parts of the saddle and bridle that you will use, and explain how to care for this equipment.

   (b) Show how to properly saddle and bridle a horse.

   (c) Demonstrate how to safely mount and dismount a horse.

10. Explain and demonstrate how to approach and lead a horse safely from a stall, corral, or field and how to tie the horse securely.

11. On level ground, continuously do the following movements after safely mounting the horse. Do them correctly, at ease, and in harmony with the horse.

    (a) Walk the horse in a straight line for 60 feet.

    (b) Walk the horse in a half-circle of not more than 16 feet in radius.

    (c) Trot or jog the horse in a straight line for 60 feet.

    (d) Trot or jog the horse in a half-circle of not more than 30 feet in radius.

    (e) Halt straight.

    (f) Back up straight four paces.

    (g) Halt and dismount.

Indian Lore

1. Identify the different American Indian cultural areas. Explain what makes them each unique.

2. Give the history of one American Indian tribe, group, or nation that lives or has lived near you. Visit it, if possible. Tell about traditional dwellings, way of life, tribal government, religious beliefs, family and clan relationships, language, clothing styles, arts and crafts, food preparation, means of getting around, games, customs in warfare, where members of the group now live, and how they live.

3. Do TWO of the following. Focus on a specific group or tribe.

   (a) Make an item of clothing worn by members of the tribe.

   (b) Make and decorate three items used by the tribe, as approved by your counselor.

   (c) Make an authentic model of a dwelling used by an Indian tribe, group, or nation.

   (d) Visit a museum to see Indian artifacts. Discuss them with your counselor. Identify at least 10 artifacts by tribe or nation, their shape, size, and use.

4. Do ONE of the following:

   (a) Learn three games played by a group or tribe. Teach and lead one game with a Scout group.

   (b) Learn and show how a tribe traditionally cooked or prepared food. Make three food items.

   (c) Give a demonstration showing how a specific Indian group traditionally hunted, fished, or trapped.

5. Do ONE of the following:

   (a) Write or briefly describe how life might have been different for the European settlers if there had been no native Americans to meet them when they came to this continent.

   (b) Sing two songs in an Indian language. Explain their meanings.

   (c) Learn in an Indian language at least 25 common terms and their meanings.

   (d) Show 25 signs in Indian sign language. Include those that will help you ask for water, for food, and where the path or road leads.

(e) Learn an Indian story of up to 300 words (or several shorter stories adding up to no more than 300 words). Tell the story or stories at a Scout gathering or campfire.

(f) Write or tell about eight things adopted by others from American Indians.

(g) Learn 25 Indian place names. Tell their origins and meanings.

(h) Name five well-known American Indian leaders, either from the past or people of today. Give their tribes or nations. Describe what they did or do now that makes them notable.

(i) Attend a contemporary American Indian gathering. Discuss with your counselor what you learned and observed. Include in your discussion any singing, dancing, drumming, and the various men's and women's dance styles you saw.

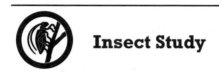 **Insect Study**

1. Do the following:

   (a) Explain to your counselor the most likely hazards associated with exposure to ants and bees and what you should do to anticipate, help prevent, mitigate, and respond to these hazards.

   (b) Discuss the prevention of and treatment for health concerns that could occur while working with ants and bees, including insect bites and anaphylactic shock.

2. Tell how insects are different from all other animals. Show how insects are different from centipedes and spiders.

3. Point out and name the main parts of an insect.

4. Describe the characteristics that distinguish the principal families and orders of insects.

5. Do the following:

   (a) Observe 20 different live species of insects in their habitat. In your observations, include at least four orders of insects.

   (b) Make a scrapbook of the 20 insects you observe in 5a. Include photographs, sketches, illustrations, and articles. Label each insect with its common and scientific names, where possible. Share your scrapbook with your merit badge counselor.

6. Do the following:

   (a) From your scrapbook collection, identify three species of insects helpful to humans and five species of insects harmful to humans.

   (b) Discuss the use of integrated pest management vs. chemical methods of insect control. What are the advantages and disadvantages of each?

7. Explain the symbiotic relationship between bees and humankind. Explain what colony collapse disorder (CCD) is and some of the possible causes. Discuss how CCD affects our food supply.

8. Compare the life histories of a butterfly and a grasshopper. Tell how they are different.

9. Raise an insect through complete metamorphosis from its larval stage to its adult stage (e.g., raise a butterfly or moth from a caterpillar).*

10. Do ONE of the following:

(a) Observe an ant colony in a formicarium (ant farm). Find the queen and worker ants. Explain to your counselor the different chambers found within an ant colony.

(b) Study a hive of bees. Remove the combs and find the queen. Estimate the amount of brood and count the number of queen cells. Explain how to determine the amount of honey in the hive.

11. Tell things that make social insects different from solitary insects.

12. Tell how insects fit in the food chains of other insects, fish, birds, and mammals.

13. Find out about three career opportunities in insect study. Pick one and find out the education, training, and experience required for this profession. Discuss this with your counselor, and explain why this profession might interest you.

---

*Some insects are endangered species and are protected by federal or state law. Every species is found *only* in its own special type of habitat. Be sure to check natural resources authorities in advance to be sure that you will not be collecting any species that is known to be protected or endangered, or in any habitat where collecting is prohibited. In most cases, all specimens should be returned at the location of capture after the requirement has been met. Check with your merit badge counselor for those instances where the return of these specimens would not be appropriate.

 # Inventing

1. In your own words, define *inventing*. Then do the following::

(a) Explain to your merit badge counselor the role of inventors and their inventions in the economic development of the United States.

(b) List three inventions and state how they have helped humankind.

2. Do ONE of the following:

(a) Identify and interview with a buddy (and with your parent's permission and merit badge counselor's approval) an individual in your community who has invented a useful item. Report what you learned to your counselor.

(b) Read about three inventors. Select the one you find most interesting and tell your counselor what you learned.

3. Do EACH of the following:

(a) Define the term *intellectual property*. Explain which government agencies oversee the protection of intellectual property, the types of intellectual property that can be protected, how such property is protected, and why protection is necessary.

(b) Explain the components of a patent and the different types of patents available.

(c) Examine your Scouting gear and find a patent number on a camping item you have used. With your parent's permission, use the internet to find out more about that patent. Compare the finished item with the claims and drawings in the patent. Report what you learned to your counselor.

(d) Explain to your counselor the term *patent infringement.*

4. Discuss with your counselor the types of inventions that are appropriate to share with others, and explain why. Tell your counselor about one nonpatented or noncopyrighted invention and its impact on society.

5. Choose a commercially available product that you have used on an overnight camping trip with your troop. Make recommendations for improving the product, and make a sketch that shows your recommendations. Discuss your recommendations with your counselor.

6. Think of an item you would like to invent that would solve a problem for your family, troop, chartered organization, community, or a special-interest group. Then do EACH of the following, while keeping a notebook to record your progress.

(a) Talk to potential users of your invention and determine their needs. Then, based on what you have learned, write a statement describing the invention and how it would help solve a problem. This statement should include a detailed sketch of the invention.

(b) Create a model of the invention using clay, cardboard, or any other readily available material. List the materials necessary to build a prototype of the invention.

(c) Share the idea and the model with your counselor and potential users of your invention. Record their feedback in your notebook.

7. Build a working prototype of the item you invented for requirement 6*. Test and evaluate the invention. Among the aspects to consider in your evaluation are cost, usefulness, marketability, appearance, and function. Describe how your original vision and expectations for your invention are similar or dissimilar to the prototype you built. Have your counselor evaluate and critique your prototype.

8. Do ONE of the following:

(a) Participate with a club or team (robotics team, science club, or engineering club) that builds a useful item. Share your experience with your counselor.

(b) Visit a museum or exhibit dedicated to an inventor or invention, and create a presentation of your visit to share with a group such as your troop or patrol.

9. Discuss with your counselor the diverse skills, education, training, and experience it takes to be an inventor. Discuss how you can prepare yourself to be creative and inventive to solve problems at home, in school, and in your community. Discuss three career fields that might utilize the skills of an inventor.

---

*Before you begin building the prototype, you must have your counselor's approval, based on the design and building plans you have already shared.

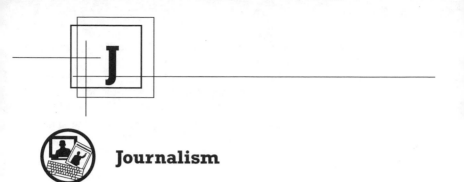

Journalism

1. Explain what freedom of the press is and how the First Amendment guarantees that you can voice your opinion. In your discussion, tell how to distinguish between fact and opinion, and explain the terms *libel, slander, defamation, fair comment and criticism, public figure, privacy,* and *malice.* Discuss how these matters relate to ethics in journalism.

2. Do either A OR B:

   (a) Newspaper, magazine, and online journalism

   (1) All on the same day, read a local newspaper, a national newspaper, a newsmagazine, and (with your parent's permission) an online news source. From each source, clip, read, and compare a story about the same event. Tell your counselor how long each story is and how fair and accurate the stories are in presenting different points of view. Tell how each source handled the story differently, depending on its purpose or audience.

   (2) Visit the office of a newspaper, magazine, or internet news site. Ask for a tour of the various divisions (editorial, business, and printing). During your tour, talk to an executive from the business side about management's relations with reporters, editors, and photographers and what makes a "good" newspaper, magazine, or internet news site.

   (b) Radio and television journalism

   (1) All on the same day, watch a local and national network newscast, listen to a radio newscast, and (with your parent's permission) view a national broadcast news source online. List the different news items and features presented, the different elements used, and the time in minutes and seconds and the online space devoted to each story. Compare the story lists and discuss whether the stories are fair and accurate. Explain why different news outlets treated the stories differently and/or presented a different point of view.

   (2) Visit a radio or television station. Ask for a tour of the various departments, concentrating on those related to news broadcasts. During your tour, talk to the station manager or other station management executive about station operations, particularly how management and the news staff work together, and what makes a "good" station. If possible, go with a reporter to cover a news event.

3. Discuss the differences between a hard news story and a feature story. Explain what is the "five W's and H." Then do ONE of the following:

(a) Choose a current or an unusual event of interest to you, and write either a hard news article OR a feature article about the event. Gear the article for print OR audio OR video journalism. Share your article with your counselor.

(b) With your parent's permission and counselor's approval, interview someone in your community who is influential because of his or her leadership, talent, career, or life experiences. Then present to your counselor either a written or oral report telling what you learned about this person.

(c) With your parent's permission and counselor's approval, read an autobiography written by a journalist you want to learn more about. Write an article that tells what you learned about this person and the contributions this person has made to the field of journalism.

(d) Attend a Scouting event and write a 200-word article (feature or hard news) about the event. Use either the inverted pyramid style or the chronological style. Review the article with your counselor, then submit it to your community newspaper or BSA local council or district newsletter for consideration.

4. Attend a public event and do ONE of the following:

(a) Write two newspaper articles about the event, one using the inverted pyramid style and one using the chronological style.

(b) Using a radio or television broadcasting style, write a news story, a feature story, and a critical review of the event.

(c) Take a series of photographs to help tell the story of the event in pictures. Include news photos and feature photos in your presentation. Write a brief synopsis of the event as well as captions for your photos.

5. Find out about three career opportunities in journalism. Pick one and find out the education, training, and experience required for this profession. Discuss this with your counselor, and explain why this profession might interest you.

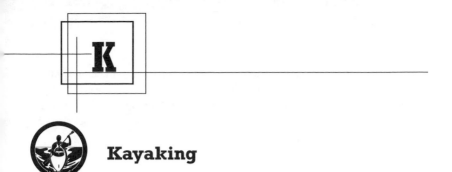

Kayaking

1. Do the following:

   (a) Explain to your counselor the hazards you are most likely to encounter while participating in kayaking activities, including weather and water-related hazards, and what you should do to anticipate, help prevent, mitigate, and respond to these hazards.

   (b) Review prevention, symptoms, and first-aid treatment for the following injuries or illnesses that can occur while kayaking: blisters, cold-water shock and hypothermia, heat-related illnesses, dehydration, sunburn, sprains, and strains.

   (c) Review the BSA Safety Afloat policy. Explain to your counselor how this applies to kayaking.

2. Before doing requirements 3 through 8, successfully complete the BSA swimmer test: Jump feetfirst into water over the head in depth. Level off and swim 75 yards in a strong manner using one or more of the following strokes: sidestroke, breaststroke, trudgen, or crawl; then swim 25 yards using an easy, resting backstroke. The 100 yards must be completed in one swim without stops and must include at least one sharp turn. After completing the swim, rest by floating.

3. Do the following:

   (a) Review the characteristics of life jackets most appropriate for kayaking and understand why one must always be worn while paddling. Then demonstrate how to select and fit a life jacket for kayaking.

   (b) Review the importance of safety equipment such as a signal device, extra paddle, sponge, bilge pump, and throw bag.

4. Do the following:

   (a) Name and point out the major parts of a kayak.

   (b) Review the differences in the design between recreational, whitewater, and sea or touring kayaks. Include how length, width, stability, and rocker are involved in the design of each type.

   (c) Review the advantages and disadvantages of the materials most commonly used to make kayaks. Explain the care, maintenance, and storage of a kayak.

   (d) Using the trucker's hitch and bowline, demonstrate how to secure a kayak to a rack on a vehicle or a trailer, or to a rack on land.

5. Discuss the following:

   (a) How to choose a kayak paddle.

   (b) The different materials from which paddles are made, parts of a paddle, and the care and maintenance of a paddle.

6. Using a properly equipped kayak with an open cockpit, a sit-on-top, or an inflatable kayak, do the following:

   (a) Safely capsize and perform a wet exit.

   (b) Reenter the kayak with assistance from a buddy boat.

   (c) Demonstrate a kayak-over-kayak rescue.

   (d) Demonstrate the HELP position.

   (e) Capsize the kayak, swim it and the paddle to shore, and empty water from the kayak with assistance, if needed.

7. As a solo paddler, use a properly equipped kayak to demonstrate the following:

   (a) Forward stroke

   (b) Backstroke

   (c) Forward sweep

   (d) Reverse sweep

   (e) Draw stroke

   (f) Stern draw

8. As a solo paddler, use a properly equipped kayak to demonstrate the following:

   (a) Paddle a straight line for 25 yards, make a sharp turn, and return 25 yards in a straight line.

   (b) Spin or pivot 360 degrees to the right and 360 degrees to the left.

   (c) Move abeam to the right 10 feet and to the left 10 feet.

   (d) Stop the boat in one boat length.

   (e) Paddle a buoyed course of a length determined by your counselor that includes two right turns and two left turns performed while underway.

Landscape Architecture

1. Go to a completed landscape project that a landscape architect has designed. Before you visit the site, obtain a plan of the design from the landscape architect if one is available.

2. After completing requirement 1, discuss the following with your merit badge counselor:

   (a) Tell whether the design had separate spaces, a defined point of entry, a clear path system, and sun and shade variety.

   (b) Discuss how any structures, the designated seating, eating, or parking areas suited the overall design.

   (c) Explain how the design reflected consideration for the comfort, shelter, and security of the users.

   (d) Discuss how the choice of trees, shrubs, and ground covers used in the project contributed to its appeal and function.

3. Identify five shrubs, five trees, and one ground cover, being sure that you select examples of different shapes, sizes, and textures. With the help of your counselor or a local nursery, choose plants that will grow in your area. Bring pictures of the different planting materials or, if possible, examples of their branches, leaves, or flowers to a group such as your troop or class at school. Be prepared to tell how you might use each in the design of a landscape and the maintenance that would follow.

4. After obtaining permission from the appropriate authority, look at and study a place of worship, school grounds, or a public building and identify where most people arrive by bus or car. Then do the following:

   (a) Using a measuring tape, measure and draw the main site entry and its nearby area. Define the scale of your drawing. Be sure to include the driveway and sidewalk or path that leads to the building's main entry. Indicate any sidewalks, structures, trees and plants, lights, drains, utilities, or other site furnishings within the study area. Make two copies of this plan and save the original, then do 4b and 4c using the copies.

   (b) On one copy of your site plan, use directional arrows to indicate where the water drains across the site, where ditches occur, and where water stands for a longer period of time.

(c) Decide how you can make the place safer and more comfortable for those using it. Redesign the area on another copy of the plan. You may want to include new walks, covered waiting areas, benches, space-defining plantings of trees and shrubs, and drainage structures.

5. Find out about three career opportunities in landscape architecture. Pick one and find out the education, training, and experience required for this profession. Discuss this with your counselor, and explain why this profession might interest you.

 **Law**

1. Define "law." Tell some of its sources. Describe functions it serves.

2. Discuss TWO of the following:

    (a) Justinian's Code, the Code of Hammurabi, and the Magna Carta

    (b) The development of the jury system

    (c) Two famous trials in history

3. Tell what civil law is; tell what criminal law is. Tell the main differences between them. Give examples of each.

4. Ask five people (not more than one from your immediate family) about the role of law enforcement officers in our society. Discuss their answers with them. Go to a law enforcement officer in your neighborhood and ask about his or her responsibilities and duties. Report your findings.

5. Tell about several laws that were passed to protect the consumer and the seller. Tell about several organizations that provide help to consumers and sellers.

6. Do ONE of the following:

    (a) Attend a session of a civil or criminal court. Write 250 words or more on what you saw.

    (b) Plan and conduct a mock trial with your troop or school class. After the trial is over, discuss it with the group.

7. Arrange a visit with a lawyer who works for a business, bank, title company, or government agency. Find out his or her duties and responsibilities. Report what you have learned.

8. Explain the requirements for becoming a lawyer in your state. Describe how judges are selected in your state.

9. Make a list of 15 jobs that deal with some aspects of law or legal processes. Tell which you prefer. Why?

10. Tell where people can go to obtain the help of a lawyer if they are unable to pay for one. Tell what you can do if you can afford a lawyer but do not know of any in your area.

11. Discuss with your counselor the importance in our society of TWO of the following areas of the law:

    (a) Environmental law

    (b) Computers and the internet

    (c) Copyright and the internet

    (d) Immigration

    (e) Patents

    (f) Biotechnology

    (g) Privacy law

    (h) International law

 # Leatherwork

1. Do the following:

    (a) Explain to your counsel the hazards you are most likely to encounter while using leatherwork tools and materials, and what you should do to anticipate, help prevent, mitigate, or lessen these hazards.

    (b) Show that you know first aid for injuries or illnesses that could occur while working with leather, including minor cuts and scratches, puncture wounds, ingested poisoning, and reactions from exposure to chemicals such as dyes, cements, and finishes used in leatherworking.

2. Explain to your counselor

    (a) Where leather comes from

    (b) What kinds of hides are used to make leather

    (c) What are five types of leather

    (d) What are the best uses for each type of leather

3. Make one or more articles of leather that use at least five of the following steps:

    (a) Pattern layout and transfer

    (b) Cutting leather

(c) Punching holes

(d) Carving or stamping surface designs

(e) Applying dye or stain and finish to the project

(f) Assembly by lacing or stitching

(g) Setting snaps and rivets

(h) Dressing edges

4. Braid or plait an article out of leather, vinyl lace, or paracord.

5. Do ONE of the following:

(a) Learn about the commercial tanning process. Report about it to your merit badge counselor.

(b) Tan the skin of a small animal. Describe the safety precautions you will take and the tanning method that you used.

(c) Recondition or show that you can take proper care of your shoes, a baseball glove, a saddle, furniture, or other articles of leather. Discuss with your counselor the advantages or disadvantages of leather vs. synthetic materials.

(d) Visit a leather-related business. This could be a leathercraft supply company, a tannery, a leather goods or shoe factory, or a saddle shop. Report on your visit to your counselor.

 Lifesaving

1. Before doing requirements 2 through 17:

(a) Complete Second Class rank requirements 5a through 5d and First Class rank requirements 6a, 6b, and 6e.

Second Class rank requirements 5a through 5d:

(5a) Tell what precautions must be taken for a safe swim.

(5b) Demonstrate your ability to pass the BSA beginner test: Jump feetfirst into water over your head in depth, level off and swim 25 feet on the surface, stop, turn sharply, resume swimming, then return to your starting place.

(5c) Demonstrate water rescue methods by reaching with your arm or leg, by reaching with a suitable object, and by throwing lines and objects.

(5d) Explain why swimming rescues should not be attempted when a reaching or throwing rescue is possible. Explain why and how a rescue swimmer should avoid contact with the victim.

First Class rank requirements 6a, 6b, and 6e:

(6a) Successfully complete the BSA swimmer test.

(6b) Tell what precautions must be taken for a safe trip afloat.

(6e) With a helper and a practice victim, show a line rescue both as tender and as rescuer. (The practice victim should be approximately 30 feet from shore in deep water.)

For more information about the BSA swimmer test, see the Swimming merit badge requirements found in this publication.

(b) Swim continuously for 400 yards using each of the following strokes in a strong manner, in good form with rhythmic breathing, for at least 50 continuous yards: front crawl, sidestroke, breaststroke, and elementary backstroke.

2. Discuss and review with your counselor the principles of BSA Safe Swim Defense.

3. Explain the following:

(a) Common drowning situations and how to prevent them.

(b) How to identify persons in the water who need assistance.

(c) The order of methods in water rescue.

(d) How rescue techniques vary depending on the setting and the condition of the person needing assistance.

(e) Situations for which in-water rescues should not be undertaken.

4. Demonstrate "reaching" rescues using various items such as arm, leg, towels, shirts, paddles, and poles.

5. Demonstrate "throwing" rescues using various items such as a line, ring buoy, rescue bag, and free-floating support. Successfully place at least one such aid within reach of a practice victim 25 feet from shore.

6. With your counselor's approval, view in-person or on video a rowing rescue performed using a rowboat, canoe, kayak, or stand up paddleboard. Discuss with your counselor how effectively and efficiently the rescue was performed.

7. List various items that can be used as aids in a "go" rescue. Explain why buoyant aids are preferred.

8. Correctly demonstrate rescues of a *conscious* practice subject 30 feet from shore in deep water using two types of buoyant aids provided by your counselor. Use a proper entry and a strong approach stroke. Speak to the subject to determine his or her condition and to provide instructions and encouragement.

(a) Present one aid to a subject, release it, and swim at a safe distance as the subject moves to safety.

(b) In a separate rescue, present the other aid to a subject and use it to tow the subject to safety.

9. Discuss with your counselor when it is appropriate to remove heavy clothing before attempting a swimming rescue. Remove street clothes in 20 seconds or less, enter the water, and approach a *conscious* practice subject 30 feet from shore in deep water. Speak to the subject and use a nonbuoyant aid, such as a shirt or towel, to tow the subject to safety.

10. Discuss with your counselor the importance of avoiding contact with an active subject and demonstrate lead-and-wait techniques.

11. Perform the following *nonequipment* rescues for a *conscious* practice subject 30 feet from shore. Begin in the water from a position near the subject. Speak to the subject to determine his or her condition and to provide instructions and encouragement.

    (a) Perform an armpit tow for a calm, responsive, tired swimmer resting with a back float.

    (b) Perform a cross-chest carry for an exhausted, responsive subject treading water.

12. In deep water, show how to escape from a victim's grasp on your wrist. Repeat for front and rear holds about the head and shoulders.

13. Perform the following rescues for an *unconscious* practice subject at or near the surface 30 feet from shore. Use a proper entry and strong approach stroke. Speak to the subject and splash water on the subject to determine his or her condition before making contact. Quickly remove the victim from the water, with assistance if needed, and position for CPR.

    (a) Perform an equipment assist using a buoyant aid.

    (b) Perform a front approach and wrist tow.

    (c) Perform a rear approach and armpit tow.

14. Discuss with your counselor how to respond if a victim submerges before being reached by a rescuer, and do the following:

    (a) Recover a 10-pound weight in 8 to 10 feet of water using a feetfirst surface dive.

    (b) Repeat using a headfirst surface dive.

15. Demonstrate knowledge of resuscitation procedures:

    (a) Describe how to recognize the need for rescue breathing and CPR.

    (b) Demonstrate CPR knowledge and skills, including rescue breathing, consistent with current guidelines.*

16. Demonstrate management of a spinal injury to your counselor:

    (a) Discuss the causes, signs, and symptoms of a spinal injury.

    (b) Support a faceup subject in calm water of standing depth.

    (c) Turn a subject from a facedown to a faceup position in water of standing depth while maintaining support.

17. With your counselor, discuss causes, prevention, and treatment of other injuries or illnesses that could occur while swimming or boating, including hypothermia, dehydration, heat-related illnesses, muscle cramps, sunburn, stings, and hyperventilation.

---

*Your counselor may accept recent training in CPR by a recognized agency as completion of this requirement only if he or she feels your skills are satisfactory and need no additional reinforcement.

Mammal Study

1. Explain the meaning of "animal," "invertebrate," "vertebrate," and "mammal." Name three characteristics that distinguish mammals from all other animals.

2. Explain how the animal kingdom is classified. Explain where mammals fit in the classification of animals. Classify three mammals from phylum through species.

3. Do ONE of the following:

   (a) Spend three hours in each of two different kinds of natural habitats or at different elevations. List the different mammal species and individual members that you identified by sight or sign. Tell why all mammals do not live in the same kind of habitat.

   (b) Spend three hours on each of five days on at least a 25-acre area (about the size of 3½ football fields). List the mammal species you identified by sight or sign.

   (c) From study and reading, write a simple life history of one nongame mammal that lives in your area. Tell how this mammal lived before its habitat was affected in any way by humans. Tell how it reproduces, what it eats, and its natural habitat. Describe its dependency upon plants and other animals (including humans), and how they depend upon it. Tell how it is helpful or harmful to humankind.

4. Do ONE of the following:

   (a) Under the guidance of a nature center or natural history museum, make two study skins of rats or mice. Tell the uses of study skins and mounted specimens respectively.

   (b) Take good pictures of two kinds of mammals in the wild. Record the date(s), time of day, weather conditions, approximate distance from the animal, habitat conditions, and any other factors you feel may have influenced the animal's activity and behavior.

   (c) Write a life history of a native game mammal that lives in your area, covering the points outlined in requirement 3c. List sources for this information.

   (d) Make and bait a tracking pit. Report what mammals and other animals came to the bait.

(e) Visit a natural history museum. Report on how specimens are prepared and cataloged. Explain the purposes of museums.

(f) Write a report of 500 words on a book about a mammal species.

(g) Trace two possible food chains of carnivorous mammals from soil through four stages to the mammal.

5. Working with your counselor, select and carry out one project that will influence the numbers of one or more mammals.

 # Medicine

1. Discuss with your counselor the influence that EIGHT of the following people had on the history of health care:
   (a) Hippocrates
   (b) William Harvey
   (c) Antonie van Leewenhoek
   (d) Edward Jenner
   (e) Florence Nightingale
   (f) Louis Pasteur
   (g) Gregor Mendel
   (h) Joseph Lister
   (i) Robert Koch
   (j) Daniel Hale Williams
   (k) Wilhelm Conrad Roentgen
   (l) Marie and Pierre Curie
   (m) Walter Reed
   (n) Karl Landsteiner
   (o) Alexander Fleming
   (p) Charles Richard Drew
   (q) Helen Taussig
   (r) James Watson and Francis Crick
   (s) Jonas Salk

2. Explain the Hippocratic Oath to your counselor, and compare the original version to a more modern one. Discuss to whom those subscribing to the original version of the oath owe the greatest allegiance.

3. Discuss the health-care provider–patient relationship with your counselor, and the importance of such a relationship in the delivery of quality care to the patient. Describe the role of confidentiality in this relationship.

4. Do the following:
   (a) Describe the roles the following people play in the delivery of health care:
      (1) Allopathic physician (M.D.) and osteopathic physician (D.O.)

    (2) Chiropractor (D.C.)

    (3) Emergency medical technician

    (4) Licensed practical/vocational nurse

    (5) Medical assistant

    (6) Medical laboratory technologist

    (7) Nurse-midwife

    (8) Nurse practitioner

    (9) Occupational therapist

  (10) Optometrist

  (11) Pharmacist

  (12) Physical therapist

  (13) Physician's assistant

  (14) Podiatrist

  (15) Psychologist

  (16) Radiologic technologist

  (17) Registered nurse

  (18) Respiratory therapist

(b) Describe the educational and licensing requirements to practice health care in your state for FIVE of the professions in requirement 4a. (Not all professions may exist in your state.)

5. (a) Tell what is meant by the term "primary care" with regard to a medical specialty.

(b) Briefly describe the types of work done by physicians in the following specialties:

    (1) Internal medicine*

    (2) Family practice*

    (3) Obstetrics/gynecology*

    (4) Pediatrics*

    (5) Psychiatry

    (6) Surgery

(c) Describe the additional educational requirements for these specialties.

6. (a) Briefly describe the types of work performed by physicians in FIVE of the following specialties or subspecialties:

    (1) Allergy/immunology

    (2) Anesthesiology

    (3) Cardiology

    (4) Colorectal surgery

    (5) Critical care medicine (intensive care medicine)

    (6) Dermatology

    (7) Emergency medicine

    (8) Endocrinology

---

*"Primary care" specialties

(9) Gastroenterology

(10) Geriatric medicine

(11) Hematology/oncology

(12) Hospitalist

(13) Infectious disease

(14) Nephrology

(15) Neurosurgery

(16) Neurology

(17) Nuclear medicine

(18) Ophthalmology

(19) Orthopedic surgery

(20) Otolaryngology/head and neck surgery

(21) Pathology

(22) Physical medicine and rehabilitation

(23) Plastic, reconstructive, and maxillofacial surgery

(24) Preventive medicine

(25) Pulmonology

(26) Radiology

(27) Rheumatology

(28) Thoracic/cardiothoracic surgery

(29) Urology

(30) Vascular surgery

(b) Describe the additional educational requirements for the FIVE specialties or subspecialties you chose in 6a.

7. (a) Visit a physician's office*, preferably one who delivers "primary care." (This may be that of your counselor.) Discuss the components of a medical history and physical examination (an official BSA health form may be used to guide this discussion), and become familiar with the instruments used.

(b) Describe the characteristics of a good diagnostic test to screen for disease (e.g., routine blood pressure measurement). Explain briefly why diagnostic tests are not "perfect."

(c) Show how to take a blood pressure and a pulse reading.

8. Do the following:

(a) Discuss the roles medical societies, employers, the insurance industry, and the government play in influencing the practice of medicine in the United States.

(b) Briefly tell how your state monitors the quality of health care within its borders, and how it provides care to those who do not have health insurance.

9. Compare and discuss with your counselor at least two types of health care delivery systems used throughout the world.

---

*If this cannot be arranged, demonstrate to your counselor that you understand the components of a medical history and physical, and discuss the instruments involved.

10. Serve as a volunteer at a health-related event or facility in your community (e.g., blood drive, "health fair," blood pressure screening, etc.) approved by your counselor.

 # Metalwork

1. Read the safety rules for metalwork. Discuss how to be safe while working with metal. Discuss with your counselor the additional safety rules that apply to the metalwork option you choose for requirement 5.

2. Define the terms native metal, malleable, metallurgy, alloy, nonferrous, and ferrous. Then do the following:

   (a) Name two nonferrous alloys used by pre–Iron Age metalworkers. Name the metals that are combined to form these alloys.

   (b) Name three ferrous alloys used by modern metalworkers.

   (c) Describe how to work-harden a metal.

   (d) Describe how to anneal a nonferrous and a ferrous metal.

3. Do the following:

   (a) Work-harden a piece of 26- or 28-gauge sheet brass or sheet copper. Put a 45-degree bend in the metal, then heavily peen the area along the bend line to work-harden it. Note the amount of effort that is required to overcome the yield point in this unworked piece of metal.

   (b) Soften the work-hardened piece from requirement 3a by annealing it, and then try to remove the 45-degree bend. Note the amount of effort that is required to overcome the yield point.

   (c) Make a temper color index from a flat piece of steel. Using hand tools, make and temper a center punch of medium-carbon or high-carbon steel.

4. Find out about three career opportunities in metalworking. Pick one and find out the education, training, and experience required for this profession. Discuss this with your counselor, and explain why this profession might interest you.

5. After completing the first four requirements, complete at least ONE of the options listed below.

   (a) Option 1—Sheet Metal Mechanic/Tinsmith

   (1) Name and describe the use of the basic sheet metalworking tools.

   (2) Create a sketch of two objects to make from sheet metal. Include each component's dimensions on your sketch, which need not be to scale.

   (3) Make two objects out of 24- or 26-gauge sheet metal. Use patterns either provided by your counselor or made by you and approved by your

counselor. Construct these objects using a metal that is appropriate to the object's ultimate purpose, and using cutting, bending, edging, and either soldering or brazing.

(a) One object also must include at least one riveted component.

(b) If you do not make your objects from zinc-plated sheet steel or tin-plated sheet steel, preserve your work from oxidation.

(b) Option 2—Silversmith

(1) Name and describe the use of a silversmith's basic tools.

(2) Create a sketch of two objects to make from sheet silver. Include each component's dimensions on your sketch, which need not be to scale.

(3) Make two objects out of 18- or 20-gauge sheet copper. Use patterns either provided by your counselor or made by you and approved by your counselor. Both objects must include a soldered joint. If you have prior silversmithing experience, you may substitute sterling silver, nickel silver, or lead-free pewter.

(a) At least one object must include a sawed component you have made yourself.

(b) At least one object must include a sunken part you have made yourself.

(c) Clean and polish your objects.

(c) Option 3—Founder

(1) Name and describe the use of the basic parts of a two-piece mold. Name at least three different types of molds.

(2) Create a sketch of two objects to cast in metal. Include each component's dimensions on your sketch, which need not be to scale.

(3) Make two molds, one using a pattern provided by your counselor and another one you have made yourself that has been approved by your counselor. Position the pouring gate and vents yourself. *Do not use copyrighted materials as patterns.*

(a) Using lead-free pewter, make a casting using a mold provided by your counselor.

(b) Using lead-free pewter, make a casting using the mold that you have made.

(d) Option 4—Blacksmith

(1) Name and describe the use of a blacksmith's basic tools.

(2) Make a sketch of two objects to hot-forge. Include each component's dimensions on your sketch, which need not be to scale.

(3) Using low-carbon steel at least $1/4$ inch thick, perform the following exercises:

(a) Draw out by forging a taper.

(b) Use the horn of the anvil by forging a U-shaped bend.

(c) Form a decorative twist in a piece of square steel.

(d) Use the edge of the anvil to bend metal by forging an L-shaped bend.

(4) Using low-carbon steel at least ¼ inch thick, make the two objects you sketched that require hot-forging. Be sure you have your counselor's approval before you begin.

(a) Include a decorative twist on one object.

(b) Include a hammer-riveted joint in one object.

(c) Preserve your work from oxidation.

Mining in Society

1. Do the following:

(a) Select 10 different minerals. For each one, name a product for which the mineral is used.

(b) Explain the role mining has in producing and processing things that are grown.

(c) From the list of minerals you chose for requirement 1a, determine the countries where those minerals can be found, and discuss what you learned from your counselor.

2. Obtain a map of your state or region showing major cities, highways, rivers, and railroads. Mark the locations of five mining enterprises. Find out what resource is processed at each location, and identify the mine as a surface or underground operation. Discuss with your counselor how the resources mined at these locations are used.

3. Discuss with your counselor the potential hazards a miner may encounter at an active mine and the protective measures used by miners. In your discussion, explain how:

(a) The miner's personal protective equipment is worn and used, including a hard hat, safety glasses, earplugs, dust mask or respirator, self-rescue device, and high-visibility vest.

(b) Miners protect their hands and feet from impact, pinch, vibration, slipping, and tripping/falling hazards.

(c) Monitoring equipment warns miners of imminent danger, and how robots are used in mine rescues.

4. Discuss with your counselor the dangers someone might encounter at an abandoned mine. Include information about the "Stay Out—Stay Alive" program.

5. Do ONE of the following:

(a) With your parent's approval and your counselor's assistance, use the internet to find and take a virtual tour of two types of mines. Determine the similarities and differences between them regarding resource exploration, mine planning, and permitting, types of equipment used, and the minerals produced. Discuss with your counselor what you learned from your internet-based mine tours.

(b) With your parent's permission and counselor's approval, visit a mining or minerals exhibit at a museum. Find out about the history of the museum's exhibit and the type of mining it represents. Give three examples of how mineral resources have influenced history.

(c) With your parent's permission and counselor's approval, visit an active mine.* Find out about the tasks required to explore, plan, permit, mine, and process the resource mined at that site. Take photographs if allowed, and request brochures from your visit. Share photos, brochures, and what you have learned with your counselor.

(d) With your parent's permission and counselor's approval, visit a mining equipment manufacturer or supplier.* Discuss the types of equipment produced or supplied there, and in what part of the mining process this equipment is used. Take photographs if allowed, and request brochures from your visit. Share photos, brochures, and what you have learned with your counselor.

(e) Discuss with your counselor two methods used to reduce rock in size, one of which uses a chemical process to extract a mineral. Explain the difference between smelting and refining.

(f) Learn about the history of a local mine, including what is or was mined there, how the deposit was found, the mining techniques and processes used, and how the mined resource is or was used. Find out from a historian, community leader, or business person how mining has affected your community. Note any social, cultural, or economic consequences of mining in your area. Share what you have learned with your counselor.

6. Do the following:

(a) Choose a modern mining site. Find out what is being done to help control environmental impacts. Share what you have learned about mining and sustainability.

(b) Explain reclamation as it is used in mining and how mine reclamation pertains to Scouting's no-trace principles.

(c) Discuss with your counselor what values society has about returning the land to the benefit of wildlife and people after mining has ended. Discuss the transformation of the BSA Summit Bechtel Family National Scout Reserve from

---

*Visiting a mine site, a mining equipment manufacturer, or an equipment supplier requires advance planning. These sites can be potentially dangerous. You will need permission from your parent and counselor, and the manager of the mine site, or equipment manufacturer or supplier. While there, you will be required to follow closely the site manager's instructions and comply with all safety rules and procedures, including wearing appropriate clothing, footwear, and personal safety equipment.

a mine site to its current role.

7. Do ONE of the following:

(a) Explore the anticipated benefits of interplanetary mining. Learn how NASA and private investors may search for, extract, and process minerals in outer space, and the primary reasons for mining the moon, other planets, or near-Earth asteroids. Find out how exploration and mineral processing in space differ from exploration on Earth. Share what you have learned with your counselor, and discuss the difficulties encountered in exploring, collecting, and analyzing surface or near-surface samples in space.

(b) Identify three minerals found dissolved in seawater or found on the ocean floor, and list three places where the ocean is mined today. Share this information with your counselor, and discuss the chief incentives for mining the oceans for minerals, the reclamation necessary after mining is over, and any special concerns when mining minerals from the ocean. Find out what sustainability problems arise from mining the oceans. Discuss what you learn with your counselor.

(c) Learn what metals and minerals are recycled after their original use has ended. List four metals and two nonmetals, and find out how each can be recycled. Find out how recycling affects the sustainability of natural resources and how this idea is related to mining. Discuss what you learn with your counselor.

(d) With your parent's permission, use the internet and other resources to determine the current price of gold, copper, aluminum, or other commodities like cement or coal, and find out the five-year price trend for two of these. Report your findings to your counselor.

8. Do ONE of the following:

(a) With your parent's and counselor's approval, meet with a worker in the mining industry. Discuss the work, equipment, and technology used in this individual's position, and learn about a current project. Ask to see reports, drawings, and/or maps made for the project. Find out about the educational and professional requirements for this individual's position. Ask how the individual's mining career began. Discuss with your counselor what you have learned.

(b) Find out about three career opportunities in the mining industry. Pick one and find out the education, training, and experience required for this profession. Discuss this with your counselor, and explain why this profession might interest you.

(c) With your parent's permission and counselor's approval, visit a career academy or community college to learn about educational and training requirements for a position in the mining industry that interests you. Find out why this position is critical to the mining industry, and discuss what you learned with your counselor.

Model Design and Building

1. Study and understand the requirements for personal safety when using such modelmaker hand tools as knives, handsaws, vises, files, hammers, screwdrivers, hand drills and drill bits, pliers, and portable power tools, and when to use proper protective equipment such as goggles when grinding or drilling. Know what precautions to take when using flammable or hazardous products such as glue, epoxy, paint, and thinners. Discuss these with your counselor before you begin your modelmaking project and tell why they are important.

2. Explain the uses for each of the following types of models: architectural, structural, process, mechanical, and industrial. Do research into the different types of materials that could be used in making these models.

3. With your counselor's advice, select a subject from requirement 4 for your model project (no kits). Prepare the necessary plans to the proper scale. Make a list of materials and a list of the required tools. This model should be your own original work. Tell why you selected this subject.

4. Do ONE of the following:

    (a) Make an architectural model. Build a model of a house to a scale of ¼" = 1'0" (50:1 metric). Discuss with your counselor the materials you intend to use, the amount of detail required, outside treatment (finish, shrubbery, walks, etc.), and color selections. After completing the model, present it to your counselor for approval.

    (b) Build a structural model. Construct a model showing corner construction of a wood-frame building to a scale of 1 ½" = 1'0" (8:1 metric). All structures shown must be to scale. Cardboard or flat sheet wood stock may be used for sheeting or flooring on the model. Review with your counselor the problems you encountered in gathering the materials and supporting the structure. Be able to name the parts of the floor and wall frames, such as intermediate girder, joist, bridging, subfloor, sill, sole plate, stud, and rafter.

    (c) Make a process model. Build a model showing the plumbing system in your house. Show hot and cold water supply, all waste returns, and venting to a scale of ¾" = 1'0" (15:1 metric). Talk to your counselor about how to begin this model, and present the scale and the materials you will use. After completion, present the model to your counselor, and be prepared to discuss any problems you had building this model.

    (d) Complete a mechanical model. Build a model of a mechanical device that uses at least two of the six simple machines. After completing the model, present it to your counselor. Be prepared to discuss materials used, the machine's function, and any particular difficulty you might have encountered.

(e) Make an industrial model. Build a model of an actual passenger-carrying vehicle to a scale of 1" = 1'0" or ½" = 1'0" (10:1 or 25:1 metric). Take the dimensions of the vehicle and record the important dimensions. Draw the top, front, rear, and sides of the vehicle to scale. From your plans, build a model of the vehicle and finish it in a craftsmanlike manner. Discuss with your counselor the most difficult part of completing the model.

5. Build a special-effects model of a fantasy spacecraft that might appear in a Hollywood science-fiction movie. Determine an appropriate scale for your design—one that makes practical sense. Include a cockpit or control area, living space, storage unit, engineering spaces, and propulsion systems. As you plan and build your model, do the following:

(a) Study aircraft, submarines, and naval ships for design ideas.

(b) Arrange and assemble the parts.

(c) Sketch your completed model.

(d) Write a short essay in which you discuss your design, scale, and materials choices. Describe how you engineered your model and discuss any difficulties you encountered and what you learned.

6. List at least six occupations in which modelmaking is used and discuss with your counselor some career opportunities in this field.

 # Motorboating

1. Do the following:

(a) Explain to your counselor the most likely hazards you may encounter while motorboating, and what you should do to anticipate, help prevent, mitigate, and respond to these hazards.

(b) Explain first aid for injuries or illnesses that could occur while motorboating, including hypothermia, heat reactions, dehydration, motion sickness, bugbites, and blisters.

(c) Identify the conditions that must exist before performing CPR on a person, and explain how such conditions are recognized. Demonstrate proper technique for performing CPR using a training device approved by your counselor.

2. Do the following:

(a) Before doing requirements 3 through 6, successfully complete the BSA swimmer test.*

(b) Name the different types of personal flotation devices (PFDs), and explain when each type should be used. Show how to choose and properly fit a PFD.

3. Do the following:

(a) Explain inboard, outboard, and inboard/outboard motors, and the uses and advantages of each. Discuss the special features of a bass boat and a ski boat.

---

*See the Swimming merit badge requirements later in this pamphlet for details about the BSA swimmer test.

(b) Explain the safety procedures and precautions involving handling fuel and engine servicing, and equipment storage and placement.

(c) Explain how to winterize a boat motor and tell why this procedure is necessary.

(d) Explain the safety procedures and precautions involving swimmers and skiers in the water, passenger positions underway, and boat wakes.

4. Show you know safety laws for motorboating by doing the following:

(a) Have a permit to run a motorboat, if needed.

(b) Explain the rules or laws that apply to recreational boating in your area or state.

(c) Discuss how the hazards of weather and heavy water conditions can affect both safety and performance in motorboating.

(d) Promise that you will follow BSA Safety Afloat guidelines. Explain the meaning of each point.

(e) Discuss with your counselor the nautical rules of the road and describe the national and your state's aids to navigation.

(f) Explain and show the correct use of equipment required by both state and federal regulations to be carried aboard a motorboat.

(g) Explain federal and state rules for a ventilation system, and tell why these rules are required.

(h) Explain the use of lights (sight signals) and sound signals on motorboats.

(i) Discuss the common types of anchors used in motorboating and under what conditions each would be preferred. Explain proper anchoring techniques.

5. With your counselor or other adults on board, demonstrate proper boat-handling procedures and skills by doing the following:

(a) Board and assist others in boarding.

(b) Fuel the boat and complete a safety check.

(c) Get underway from dockside or from a beach launch.

(d) Run a course for at least a mile, showing procedures for overtaking and passing slower craft, yielding right-of-way, passing oncoming traffic, making turns, reversing direction, and using navigation aids.

(e) Stop and secure the boat in position on the open water using anchors. Raise and stow the anchor and get underway.

(f) Land or dock the boat, disembark, and assist others in doing the same.

(g) Moor, dock, or beach the boat and secure all gear.

Moviemaking

1. Discuss and demonstrate the proper elements of a good motion picture. In your discussion, include visual storytelling, rhythm, the 180-axis rule, camera movement, framing and composition of camera shots, and lens selection.

2. Do the following:

   (a) In a three- or four-paragraph treatment, tell the story you plan to produce, making sure that the treatment conveys a visual picture.

   (b) Prepare a storyboard for your motion picture. (This can be done with rough sketches and stick figures.)

   (c) Demonstrate the following motion picture shooting techniques:

     (1) Using a tripod

     (2) Panning a camera

     (3) Framing a shot

     (4) Selecting an angle

     (5) Selecting proper lighting

     (6) Handheld shooting

   (d) Using motion picture shooting techniques, plan ONE of the following programs. Start with a treatment and complete the requirement by presenting this program to a pack or your troop, patrol, or class.

     (1) Film or videotape a court of honor and show it to an audience.

     (2) Create a short feature of your own design, using the techniques you learned.

     (3) Shoot a vignette that could be used to train a new Scout in a Scouting skill.

3. Do ONE of the following:

   (a) With your parent's permission and your counselor's approval, visit a film set or television production studio and watch how production work is done.

   (b) Explain to your counselor the elements of the zoom lens and three important parts.

4. Find out about three career opportunities in moviemaking. Pick one and find out the education, training, and experience required for this profession. Discuss this career with your counselor. Explain why this profession might interest you.

 **Music**

1. Sing or play a simple song or hymn chosen by your counselor, using good technique, phrasing, tone, rhythm, and dynamics. Read all the signs and terms of the score.

2. Name the five general groups of musical instruments. Create an illustration that shows how tones are generated and how instruments produce sound.

3. Do TWO of the following:

   (a) Attend a live performance, or listen to three hours of recordings from any two of the following musical styles: blues, jazz, classical, country, bluegrass, ethnic, gospel, musical theater, opera. Describe the sound of the music and the instruments used. Identify the composers or songwriters, the performers, and the titles of the pieces you heard. If it was a live performance, describe the setting and the reaction of the audience. Discuss your thoughts about the music.

   (b) Interview an adult member of your family about music. Find out what the most popular music was when he or she was your age. Find out what his or her favorite music is now, and listen to three of your relative's favorite tunes with him or her. How do those favorites sound to you? Had you ever heard any of them? Play three of your favorite songs for your relative, and explain why you like these songs. Ask what he or she thinks of your favorite music.

   (c) Serve for six months as a member of a school band, choir, or other organized musical group, or perform as a soloist in public six times.

   (d) List five people who are important in the history of American music and explain to your counselor why they continue to be influential. Include at least one composer, one performer, one innovator, and one person born more than 100 years ago.

4. Do ONE of the following:

   (a) Teach three songs to a group of people. Lead them in singing the songs, using proper hand motions.

   (b) Compose and write the score for a piece of music of 12 measures or more, and play this music on an instrument.

   (c) Make a traditional instrument and learn to play it.

5. Define for your counselor *intellectual property* (IP). Explain how to properly obtain and share recorded music.

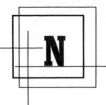

Nature

1. Name three ways in which plants are important to animals. Name a plant that is protected in your state or region, and explain why it is at risk.

2. Name three ways in which animals are important to plants. Name an animal that is protected in your state or region, and explain why it is at risk.

3. Explain the term "food chain." Give an example of a four-step land food chain and a four-step water food chain.

4. Do all of the requirements in FIVE of the following fields:

    (a) Birds

       (1) In the field, identify eight species of birds.

       (2) Make and set out a birdhouse OR a feeding station OR a birdbath. List what birds used it during a period of one month.

    (b) Mammals

       (1) In the field, identify three species of wild mammals.

       (2) Make plaster casts of the tracks of a wild mammal.

    (c) Reptiles and Amphibians

       (1) Show that you can recognize the venomous snakes in your area.

       (2) In the field, identify three species of reptiles or amphibians.

       (3) Recognize one species of toad or frog by voice; OR identify one reptile or amphibian by eggs, den, burrow, or other signs.

    (d) Insects and Spiders

       (1) Collect and identify either in the field or through photographs 10 species of insects or spiders.*

       (2) Hatch an insect from the pupa or cocoon; OR hatch adults from nymphs; OR keep larvae until they form pupae or cocoons; OR keep a colony of ants or bees through one season.

    (e) Fish

       (1) Identify two species of fish native to your area.

       (2) Collect four kinds of animal food eaten by fish in the wild.

---

*Photos may be those taken with your own equipment or gathered from other sources.

(f) Mollusks and Crustaceans

   (1) Identify five species of mollusks and crustaceans.

   (2) Collect, mount, and label six shells.

(g) Plants

   (1) In the field, identify 15 species of wild plants.

   (2) Collect and label the seeds of six plants OR the leaves of 12 plants.

(h) Soils and Rocks

   (1) Collect and identify soils found in different layers of a soil profile.

   (2) Collect and identify five different types of rocks from your area.

NOTE: In most cases all specimens should be returned to the wild at the location of original capture after the requirements have been met. Check with your merit badge counselor for those instances where the return of these specimens would not be appropriate.

Under the Endangered Species Act of 1973, some plants and animals are or may be protected by federal law. The same ones and/or others may be protected by state law. Be sure that you do not collect protected species.

Your state may require that you purchase and carry a license to collect certain species. Check with the wildlife and fish and game officials in your state regarding species regulations before you begin to collect.

 Nuclear Science

1. Do the following:

   (a) Tell what radiation is.

   (b) Describe the hazards of radiation to humans, the environment, and wildlife. Explain the difference between radiation exposure and contamination. In your explanation, discuss the nature and magnitude of radiation risks to humans from nuclear power, medical radiation (e.g., chest or dental X-ray), and background radiation including radon. Explain the ALARA principle and measures required by law to minimize these risks.

(c) Describe the radiation hazard symbol and explain where it should be used. Tell why and how people must use radiation or radioactive materials carefully.

(d) Compare the amount of radiation exposure of a nuclear power plant worker to that of someone receiving a chest and dental X-ray.

2. Do the following:

(a) Tell the meaning of the following: atom, nucleus, proton, neutron, electron, quark, isotope; alpha particle, beta particle, gamma ray, X-ray; ionization, radioactivity, radioisotope, and stability.

(b) Choose an element from the periodic table. Construct 3-D models for the atoms of three isotopes of this element, showing neutrons, protons, and electrons. Use the three models to explain the difference between atomic number and mass number and the difference between the atom and nuclear and quark structures of isotopes.

3. Do ONE of the following; then discuss modern particle physics with your counselor:

(a) Visit an accelerator (research lab) or university where people study the properties of the nucleus or nucleons.

(b) Name three particle accelerators and describe several experiments that each accelerator performs.

4. Do TWO of the following; then discuss with your counselor the different kinds of radiation and how they can be used:

(a) Build an electroscope. Show how it works. Place a radiation source inside and explain the effect it causes.

(b) Make a cloud chamber. Show how it can be used to see the tracks caused by radiation. Explain what is happening.

(c) Obtain a sample of irradiated and non-irradiated foods. Prepare the two foods and compare their taste and texture. Store the leftovers in separate containers and under the same conditions. For a period of 14 days, observe their rate of decomposition or spoilage, and describe the differences you see on days 5, 10, and 14.

(d) Visit a place where radioisotopes are being used. Using a drawing, explain how and why they are used.

5. Do ONE of the following; then discuss with your counselor the principles of radiation safety:

(a) Using a radiation survey meter and a radioactive source, show how the counts per minute change as the source gets closer to or farther from the radiation detector. Place three different materials between the source and the detector, then explain any differences in the measurements per minute. Explain how time, distance, and shielding can reduce an individual's radiation dose.

(b) Describe how radon is detected in homes. Discuss the steps taken for the long-term and short-term test methods, tell how to interpret the results, and explain when each type of test should be used. Explain the health concern related to radon gas and tell what steps can be taken to reduce radon in buildings.

(c) Visit a place where X-rays are used. Draw a floor plan of this room. Show where the unit, the unit operator, and the patient would be when the X-ray unit is operated. Explain the precautions taken and the importance of those precautions.

6. Do ONE of the following; then discuss with your counselor how nuclear energy is used to produce electricity:

(a) Make a drawing showing how nuclear fission happens, labeling all details. Draw another picture showing how a chain reaction could be started and how it could be stopped. Explain what is meant by a "critical mass."

(b) Build a model of a nuclear reactor. Show the fuel, control rods, shielding, moderator, and cooling material. Explain how a reactor could be used to change nuclear energy into electrical energy or make things radioactive.

(c) Find out how many nuclear power plants exist in the United States. Locate the one nearest your home. Find out what percentage of electricity in the United States is generated by nuclear power plants, by coal, and by gas.

7. Give an example of each of the following in relation to how energy from an atom can be used: nuclear medicine, environmental applications, industrial applications, space exploration, and radiation therapy. For each example, explain the application and its significance to nuclear science.

8. Find out about three career opportunities in nuclear science that interest you. Pick one and find out the education, training, and experience required for this profession and discuss this with your counselor. Tell why this profession interests you.

Oceanography

1. Name four branches of oceanography. Describe at least five reasons why it is important for people to learn about the oceans.

2. Define salinity, temperature, and density, and describe how these important properties of seawater are measured by the physical oceanographer. Discuss the circulation and currents of the ocean. Describe the effects of the oceans on weather and climate.

3. Describe the characteristics of ocean waves. Point out the differences among the storm surge, tsunami, tidal wave, and tidal bore. Explain the difference between sea, swell, and surf. Explain how breakers are formed.

4. Draw a cross-section of underwater topography. Show what is meant by:

   (a) Continental shelf

   (b) Continental slope

   (c) Abyssal plain

   Name and put on your drawing the following: seamount, guyot, rift valley, canyon, trench, and oceanic ridge. Compare the depths in the oceans with the heights of mountains on land.

5. List the main salts, gases, and nutrients in seawater. Describe some important properties of water. Tell how the animals and plants of the ocean affect the chemical composition of seawater. Explain how differences in evaporation and precipitation affect the salt content of the oceans.

6. Describe some of the biologically important properties of seawater. Define benthos, nekton, and plankton. Name some of the plants and animals that make up each of these groups. Describe the place and importance of phytoplankton in the oceanic food chain.

7. Do ONE of the following:

   (a) Make a plankton net. Tow the net by a dock, wade with it, hold it in a current, or tow it from a rowboat.* Do this for about 20 minutes. Save the sample. Examine it under a microscope or high-power glass. Identify the three most common types of plankton in the sample.

   (b) Make a series of models (clay or plaster and wood) of a volcanic island. Show the growth of an atoll from a fringing reef through a barrier reef. Describe the Darwinian theory of coral reef formation.

---

*May be done in lakes or streams.

(c) Measure the water temperature at the surface, midwater, and bottom of a body of water four times daily for five consecutive days. You may measure depth with a rock tied to a line. Make a Secchi disk to measure turbidity (how much suspended sedimentation is in the water). Measure the air temperature. Note the cloud cover and roughness of the water. Show your findings (air and water temperature, turbidity) on a graph. Tell how the water temperature changes with air temperature.

(d) Make a model showing the inshore sediment movement by littoral currents, tidal movement, and wave action. Include such formations as high and low waterlines, low-tide terrace, berm, and coastal cliffs. Show how offshore bars are built up and torn down.

(e) Make a wave generator. Show reflection and refraction of waves. Show how groins, jetties, and breakwaters affect these patterns.

(f) Track and monitor satellite images available on the internet for a specific location for three weeks. Describe what you have learned to your counselor.

8. Do ONE of the following:

(a) Write a 500-word report on a book about oceanography approved by your counselor.

(b) Visit one of the following:

(1) Oceanographic research ship

(2) Oceanographic institute, marine laboratory, or marine aquarium

Write a 500-word report about your visit.

(c) Explain to your troop in a five-minute prepared speech "Why Oceanography Is Important" or describe "Career Opportunities in Oceanography." (Before making your speech, show your speech outline to your counselor for approval.)

9. Describe four methods that marine scientists use to investigate the ocean, underlying geology, and organisms living in the water.

 **Orienteering**

1. Show that you know first aid for the types of injuries that could occur while orienteering, including cuts, scratches, blisters, snakebite, insect stings, tick bites, heat and cold reactions (sunburn, heatstroke, heat exhaustion, hypothermia), and dehydration. Explain to your counselor why you should be able to identify poisonous plants and poisonous animals that are found in your area.

2. Explain what orienteering is.

3. Do the following:

(a) Explain how a compass works. Describe the features of an orienteering compass.

(b) In the field, show how to take a compass bearing and follow it.

4. Do the following:

   (a) Explain how a topographic map shows terrain features. Point out and name five terrain features on a map and in the field.

   (b) Point out and name 10 symbols on a topographic map.

   (c) Explain the meaning of *declination.* Tell why you must consider declination when using map and compass together.

   (d) Show a topographic map with magnetic north-south lines.

   (e) Show how to measure distances on a map using an orienteering compass.

   (f) Show how to orient a map using a compass.

5. Set up a 100-meter pace course. Determine your walking and running pace for 100 meters. Tell why it is important to pace-count.

6. Do the following:

   (a) Identify 20 international control description symbols. Tell the meaning of each symbol.

   (b) Show a control description sheet and explain the information provided.

   (c) Explain the following terms and tell when you would use them: attack point, collecting feature, catching feature, aiming off, contouring, reading ahead, handrail, relocation, rough versus fine orienteering.

7. Do the following:

   (a) Take part in three orienteering events. One of these must be a cross-country course.*

   (b) After each event, write a report with (1) a copy of the master map and control description sheet, (2) a copy of the route you took on the course, (3) a discussion of how you could improve your time between control points, and (4) a list of your major weaknesses on this course. Describe what you could do to improve.

8. Do ONE of the following:

   (a) Set up a cross-country course that is at least 2,000 meters long with at least five control markers. Prepare the master map and control description sheet.

   (b) Set up a score orienteering course with at least 12 control points and a time limit of at least 60 minutes. Set point values for each control. Prepare the master map and control description sheet.

9. Act as an official during an orienteering event. This may be during the running of the course you set up for requirement 8.

10. Teach orienteering techniques to your patrol, troop, or crew.

---

*Note to the counselor: While orienteering is primarily an individual sport, BSA Youth Protection procedures call for using the buddy system. Requirement 7a can be completed by pairs or groups of Scouts.

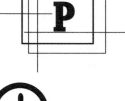

Painting

1. Explain the proper safety procedures to follow when preparing surfaces and applying coatings.

2. Do the following:

   (a) Explain three ways that coatings can improve a surface.

   (b) Explain the differences between oil-based paints, acrylic-based paints, and water-based paints.

   (c) Explain where you would apply enamel paint, flat paint, wood stain, and varnish, and explain the importance of sheen.

   (d) Tell why each is best for these uses.

3. Prepare and paint two different surfaces using patching material, caulking, and the proper primers and topcoats. Suggested projects include an interior or exterior wall, a door, a piece of furniture, a concrete wall or floor, a porch rail, or a fence. Your counselor must preapprove the projects.

4. Prepare and paint an item using harmonizing colors that you have selected using the color wheel in the *Painting* merit badge pamphlet.

5. Show the right way to use, clean, maintain, and store painting equipment.

6. Explain the importance of ladder safety, environmental responsibility, and personal hygiene when painting.

7. Explain some of the environmental and health issues concerning removing paint, applying paint, and discarding old paint.

8. Find out about career opportunities in the paint industry. Discuss the training and experience required, and explain why this profession might interest you.

Personal Fitness

If meeting any of the requirements for this merit badge is against the Scout's religious convictions, the requirement does not have to be done if the Scout's parents and the proper religious advisors state in writing that to do so would be against religious convictions. The Scout's parents must also accept full responsibility for anything that might happen because of this exemption.

1. Do the following:

(a) Before completing requirements 2 through 9, have your health-care practitioner give you a physical examination, using the Scout medical examination form. Explain the following:

(1) Why physical exams are important

(2) Why preventive habits (such as exercising regularly) are important in maintaining good health, and how the use of tobacco products, alcohol, and other harmful substances can negatively affect your personal fitness

(3) Diseases that can be prevented and how

(4) The seven warning signs of cancer

(5) The youth risk factors that affect cardiovascular health in adulthood

(b) Have a dental examination. Get a statement saying that your teeth have been checked and cared for. Tell how to care for your teeth.

2. Explain to your merit badge counselor verbally or in writing what personal fitness means to you, including

(a) Components of personal fitness.

(b) Reasons for being fit in all components.

(c) What it means to be mentally healthy.

(d) What it means to be physically healthy and fit.

(e) What it means to be socially healthy. Discuss your activity in the areas of healthy social fitness.

(f) What you can do to prevent social, emotional, or mental problems.

3. With your counselor, answer and discuss the following questions:

(a) Are you free from all curable diseases? Are you living in such a way that your risk of preventable diseases is minimized?

(b) Are you immunized and vaccinated according to the advice of your health-care provider?

(c) Do you understand the meaning of a nutritious diet and know why it is important for you? Does your diet include foods from all food groups?

(d) Are your body weight and composition what you would like them to be, and do you know how to modify them safely through exercise, diet, and lifestyle?

(e) Do you carry out daily activities without noticeable effort? Do you have extra energy for other activities?

(f) Are you free from habits relating to poor nutrition and the use of alcohol, tobacco, drugs, and other practices that could be harmful to your health?

(g) Do you participate in a regular exercise program or recreational activities?

(h) Do you sleep well at night and wake up feeling ready to start the new day?

(i) Are you actively involved in the religious organization of your choice, and do you participate in their youth activities?

(j) Do you spend quality time with your family and friends in social and recreational activities?

(k) Do you support family activities and efforts to maintain a good home life?

4. Explain the following about physical fitness:

   (a) The components of physical fitness

   (b) Your weakest and strongest component of physical fitness

   (c) The need to have a balance in all five components of physical fitness

   (d) How a program like ScoutStrong can lead to lifelong healthful habits

   (e) How the components of personal fitness relate to the Scout Law and Scout Oath

5. Explain the following about nutrition:

   (a) The importance of good nutrition

   (b) What good nutrition means to you

   (c) How good nutrition is related to the other components of personal fitness

   (d) The three components of a sound weight (fat) control program

6. Before doing requirements 7 and 8, complete the aerobic fitness, flexibility, muscular strength, and body composition tests as described in the *Personal Fitness* merit badge pamphlet. Record your results and identify those areas where you feel you need to improve.

7. Outline a comprehensive 12-week physical fitness program using the results of your fitness tests. Be sure your program incorporates the endurance, intensity, and warm-up guidelines discussed in the *Personal Fitness* merit badge pamphlet. Before beginning your exercises, have the program approved by your counselor and parents.

8. Complete the physical fitness program you outlined in requirement 7. Keep a log of your fitness program activity (how long you exercised; how far you ran, swam, or biked; how many exercise repetitions you completed; your exercise heart rate; etc.). Repeat the aerobic fitness, muscular strength, and flexibility tests every two weeks and record your results. After the 12th week, repeat the three tests, record your results, and show improvement in each one. For the body composition test, compare and analyze your preprogram and postprogram body composition measurements. Discuss the meaning and benefit of your experience, and describe your long-term plans regarding your personal fitness.

9. Find out about three career opportunities in personal fitness. Pick one and find out the education, training, and experience required for this profession. Discuss what you learned with your counselor, and explain why this profession might interest you.

Personal Management

1. Do the following:

   (a) Choose an item that your family might want to purchase that is considered a major expense.

   (b) Write a plan that tells how your family would save money for the purchase identified in requirement 1a.

       (1) Discuss the plan with your merit badge counselor.

       (2) Discuss the plan with your family.

       (3) Discuss how other family needs must be considered in this plan.

   (c) Develop a written shopping strategy for the purchase identified in requirement 1a.

       (1) Determine the quality of the item or service (using consumer publications or ratings systems).

       (2) Comparison shop for the item. Find out where you can buy the item for the best price. (Provide prices from at least two different price sources.) Call around; study ads. Look for a sale or discount coupon. Consider alternatives. Can you buy the item used? Should you wait for a sale?

2. Do the following:

   (a) Prepare a budget reflecting your expected income (allowance, gifts, wages), expenses, and savings for a period of 13 consecutive weeks.

   (b) Compare expected income with expected expenses.

       (1) If expenses exceed budget income, determine steps to balance your budget.

       (2) If income exceeds budget expenses, state how you would use the excess money (new goal, savings).

   (c) Track and record your actual income, expenses, and savings for 13 consecutive weeks (the same 13-week period for which you budgeted). (You may use the forms provided in this pamphlet, devise your own, or use a computer-generated version.) When complete, present the records showing the results to your merit badge counselor.

   (d) Compare your budget with your actual income and expenses to understand when your budget worked and when it did not work. With your merit badge counselor, discuss what you might do differently the next time.

3. Discuss with your merit badge counselor FIVE of the following concepts:

   (a) The emotions you feel when you receive money.

   (b) Your understanding of how the amount of money you have with you affects your spending habits.

(c) Your thoughts when you buy something new and your thoughts about the same item three months later. Explain the concept of buyer's remorse.

(d) How hunger affects you when shopping for food items (snacks, groceries).

(e) Your experience of an item you have purchased after seeing or hearing advertisements for it. Did the item work as well as advertised?

(f) Your understanding of what happens when you put money into a savings account.

(g) Charitable giving. Explain its purpose and your thoughts about it.

(h) What you can do to better manage your money.

4. Explain the following to your merit badge counselor:

(a) The differences between saving and investing, including reasons for using one over the other.

(b) The concepts of return on investment and risk and how they are related.

(c) The concepts of simple interest and compound interest.

(d) The concept of diversification in investing.

(e) Why it is important to save and invest for retirement.

5. Explain to your merit badge counselor what the following investments are and how each works:

(a) Common stocks

(b) Mutual funds

(c) Life insurance

(d) A certificate of deposit (CD)

(e) A savings account

(f) A U.S. savings bond

6. Explain to your counselor why people might purchase the following types of insurance and how they work:

(a) Automobile

(b) Health

(c) Homeowner's/renter's

(d) Whole life and term life

7. Explain to your merit badge counselor the following:

(a) What a loan is, what interest is, and how the annual percentage rate (APR) measures the true cost of a loan.

(b) The different ways to borrow money.

(c) The differences between a charge card, debit card, and credit card. What are the costs and pitfalls of using these financial tools? Explain why it is unwise to make only the minimum payment on your credit card.

---

*Always be sure to have proper permission before using the internet. To learn about appropriate behavior and etiquette while online, consider earning the BSA Cyber Chip. Go to www.scouting.org/training/youth-protection/cyber-chip/ for more information.

(d) Credit reports and how personal responsibility can affect your credit report.

(e) Ways to reduce or eliminate debt.

8. Demonstrate to your merit badge counselor your understanding of time management by doing the following:

(a) Write a "to do" list of tasks or activities, such as homework assignments, chores, and personal projects, that must be done in the coming week. List these in order of importance to you.

(b) Make a seven-day calendar or schedule. Put in your set activities, such as school classes, sports practices or games, jobs or chores, and/or Scout or place of worship or club meetings, then plan when you will do all the tasks from your "to do" list between your set activities.

(c) Follow the one-week schedule you planned. Keep a daily diary or journal during each of the seven days of this week's activities, writing down when you completed each of the tasks on your "to do" list compared to when you scheduled them.

(d) With your merit badge counselor, review your "to do" list, one-week schedule, and diary/journal to understand when your schedule worked and when it did not work. Discuss what you might do differently the next time.

9. Prepare a written project plan demonstrating the steps below, including the desired outcome. This is a project on paper, not a real-life project. Examples could include planning a camping trip, developing a community service project or a school or religious event, or creating an annual patrol plan with additional activities not already included in the troop annual plan. Discuss your completed project plan with your merit badge counselor.

(a) Define the project. What is your goal?

(b) Develop a timeline for your project that shows the steps you must take from beginning to completion.

(c) Describe your project.

(d) Develop a list of resources. Identify how these resources will help you achieve your goal.

(e) Develop a budget for your project.

10. Do the following:

(a) Choose a career you might want to enter after high school or college graduation. Discuss with your counselor the needed qualifications, education, skills, and experience.

(b) Explain to your counselor what the associated costs might be to pursue this career, such as tuition, school or training supplies, and room and board. Explain how you could prepare for these costs and how you might make up for any shortfall.

 **Pets**

1. Present evidence that you have cared for a pet for four months. Get approval before you start.*

2. Write in 200 words or more about the care, feeding, and housing of your pet. Tell some interesting facts about it. Tell why you have this kind of pet. Give local laws, if any, relating to the pet you keep.

3. Show that you have read a book or pamphlet, approved by your counselor, about your kind of pet. Discuss with your counselor what you have learned from what you read.

4. Do any ONE of the following:

   (a) Show your pet in a pet show.

   (b) Start a friend raising a pet like yours. Help your friend get a good start.

   (c) Train a pet in three or more tricks or special abilities.

*Work done for other merit badges cannot be used for this requirement.

 **Photography**

1. Safety. Do the following:

   (a) Explain to your counselor the most likely hazards you may encounter while working with photography and what you should do to anticipate, mitigate, prevent, and respond to these hazards. Explain how you would prepare for exposure to environmental situations such as weather, sun, and water.

   (b) Show your counselor your current, up-to-date Cyber Chip.

2. Explain how the following elements and terms can affect the quality of a picture:

   (a) Light—natural light (ambient/existing), low light (such as at night), and artificial light (such as from a flash)

   (b) Exposure—aperture (f-stops), shutter speed, ISO

   (c) Depth of field

   (d) Composition—rule of thirds, leading lines, framing, depth

   (e) Angle of view

   (f) Stop action and blur motion

   (g) Decisive moment (action or expression captured by the photographer)

3. Explain the basic parts and operation of a camera. Explain how an exposure is made when you take a picture.

4. Do TWO of the following, then share your work with your counselor.

   (a) Photograph one subject from two different angles or perspectives.

   (b) Photograph one subject from two different light sources—artificial and natural.

   (c) Photograph one subject with two different depth of fields.

   (d) Photograph one subject with two different compositional techniques.

5. Photograph THREE of the following, then share your work your counselor.

   (a) Close-up of a person

   (b) Two to three people interacting

   (c) Action shot

   (d) Animal shot

   (e) Nature shot

   (f) Picture of a person—candid, posed, or camera aware

6. Describe how software allows you to enhance your photograph after it is taken. Select a photo you have taken, then do ONE of the following, and share what you have done with your counselor.

   (a) Crop your photograph.

   (b) Adjust the exposure or make a color correction.

   (c) Show another way you could improve your picture for impact.

7. Using images other than those created for requirements 4, 5, or 6, produce a visual story to document an event to photograph OR choose a topic that interests you to photograph. Do the following:

   (a) Plan the images you need to photograph for your photo story.

   (b) Share your plan with your counselor, and get your counselor's input and approval before you proceed.

   (c) Select eight to 12 images that best tell your story. Arrange your images in order and mount the prints on a poster board, OR create an electronic presentation. Share your visual story with your counselor.

8. Identify three career opportunities in photography. Pick one and explain to your counselor how to prepare for such a career. Discuss what education and training are required, and why this profession might interest you.

Pioneering

1. Do the following:

   (a) Explain to your counselor the most likely hazards you might encounter while participating in pioneering activities and what you should do to anticipate, help prevent, mitigate, and respond to these hazards.

(b) Discuss the prevention of, and first-aid treatment for, injuries and conditions that could occur while working on pioneering projects, including rope splinters, rope burns, cuts, scratches, insect bites and stings, hypothermia, dehydration, heat exhaustion, heatstroke, sunburn, and falls.

2. Do the following:

   (a) Demonstrate the basic and West Country methods of whipping a rope. Fuse the ends of a rope.

   (b) Demonstrate how to tie the following knots: clove hitch, butterfly knot, roundturn with two half hitches, rolling hitch, water knot, carrick bend, sheepshank, and sheet bend.

   (c) Demonstrate and explain when to use the following lashings: square, diagonal, round, shear, tripod, and floor lashing.

3. Explain why it is useful to be able to throw a rope, then demonstrate how to coil and throw a 40-foot length of ¼- or ⅜-inch rope. Explain how to improve your throwing distance by adding weight to the end of your rope.

4. Explain the differences between synthetic ropes and natural fiber ropes. Discuss which types of rope are suitable for pioneering work and why. Include the following in your discussion: breaking strength, safe working loads, and the care and storage of rope.

5. Explain the uses for the back splice, eye splice, and short splice. Using ¼- or ⅜-inch three-stranded rope, demonstrate how to form each splice.

6. Using a rope-making device or machine, make a rope at least 6 feet long consisting of three strands, each having three yarns. Whip the ends.

7. Explain the importance of effectively anchoring a pioneering project. Describe to your counselor the 1-1-1 anchoring system and the log-and-stake anchoring methods.

8. With the approval of your counselor, demonstrate and use a rope tackle. Be sure the rope tackle is secured properly. Explain the advantages and limitations of using a rope tackle. Describe the potential damage that friction can do to a rope.

All pioneering projects constructed for this merit badge must comply with height standards as outlined in the *Guide to Safe Scouting.*

9. By yourself, build a trestle using square and diagonal lashings. Explain why trestles are used when constructing pioneering projects.

10. With the approval of your counselor and using appropriate lashings and pioneering techniques, build and use one full-size pioneering project from either group A or group B. Your project must comply with the requirements of the *Guide to Safe Scouting.* (Requirement 10 may be done at summer camp, at district or council events, or on a troop camp outing.)

   Group A: Tower **OR** bridge

   Anchor your project as appropriate and necessary. Explain how your anchoring system works. Group A projects may be worked on in a group and with others.

Group B: Camp chair **OR** camp table

Group B projects must be worked on individually.

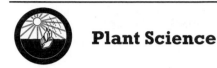 **Plant Science**

1. Make a drawing and identify five or more parts of a flowering plant. Tell what each part does.

2. Explain photosynthesis and tell why this process is important. Tell at least five ways that humans depend on plants.

3. Explain how honeybees and other pollinating insects are important to plant life.

4. Explain how water, light, air, temperature, and pests affect plants. Describe the nature and function of soil and explain its importance. Tell about the texture, structure, and composition of fertile soil. Tell how soil may be improved.

5. Tell how to propagate plants by seeds, roots, cuttings, tubers, and grafting. Grow a plant by ONE of these methods.

6. List by common name at least 10 native plants and 10 cultivated plants that grow near your home. List five invasive nonnative plants in your area and tell how they may be harmful. Tell how the spread of invasive plants may be avoided or controlled in ways that are not damaging to humans, wildlife, and the environment.

7. Name and tell about careers in agronomy, horticulture, and botany. Write a paragraph about a career in one of these fields that interests you.

8. Choose ONE of the following options and complete each requirement:

Option 1: Agronomy

A. Describe how to prepare a seedbed.

B. Make and use a seed germination tester to test 50 seeds of four of the following plants: corn, cotton, alfalfa, soybeans, clover, wheat, rice, rye, barley. Determine the percentage of live seeds.

C. Tell about one important insect pest and one important disease that damage each of the following: corn, small grains, cotton. Collect and name five weeds that compete with crops in your locality. Tell how to control these weeds without harming people, wildlife, or useful insects.

D. On a map of the United States, identify the chief regions where corn, cotton, forage crops, small grain crops, and oil crops grow. Tell how climate and location of these regions make them leaders in the production of these crops.

E. Complete ONE of the following alternatives:

(1) Corn

>(a) Grow a plot of corn and have your plot inspected by your counselor. Record seed variety or experimental code number.
>
>(b) Tell about modern methods of commercial corn farming and the contributions that corn makes to today's food and fuel supply.
>
>(c) Tell about an insect that can damage corn, and explain how it affects corn production and how it is controlled.

(2) Cotton

>(a) Grow a plot of cotton and have your plot inspected by your counselor.
>
>(b) Tell about modern methods of commercial cotton farming, and about the uses of cotton fiber and seed and the economic value of this crop.
>
>(c) Tell about an insect that can damage cotton, and explain how it affects cotton production and how it is controlled.

(3) Forage Crops

>(a) Collect, count, and label samples of each for display: perennial grasses, annual grasses, legumes, and broadleaf weeds. Indicate how each grass and legume is used. Keep a log of the site where you found each sample and share it with your counselor.
>
>(b) Explain how legumes can be used to enrich the soil and how they may deplete it under certain conditions. Explain how livestock may enrich or deplete the soil.
>
>(c) Name five poisonous plants that are dangerous to livestock, and tell the different ways of using forage crops as feed for livestock.

(4) Small Grains

>(a) Give production figures for small grain crops listed in the U.S. Statistical Report or Agricultural Statistics Handbook for the latest year available.
>
>(b) Help in harvesting a crop of grain. Tell how to reduce harvesting losses and about modern methods of growing one small grain crop.
>
>(c) Visit a grain elevator, flour mill, cereal plant, feed or seed company. Talk with the operator. Take notes, and describe the processes used and tell your patrol, troop, or class about your visit.

(5) Oil Crops

>(a) Grow a plot of soybeans and have your plot inspected by your counselor.
>
>(b) Tell about modern methods of growing soybeans on a commercial scale, and discuss the contributions soybeans make to our food supply.
>
>(c) Explain why a killing frost just after emergence is critical for soybeans.

Option 2: Horticulture

A. Visit one of the following places and tell what you learned about horticulture there: public garden, arboretum, retail nursery, wholesale nursery, production greenhouse, or conservatory greenhouse.

B. Explain the following terms: hardiness zone, shade tolerance, pH, moisture requirement, native habitat, texture, cultivar, ultimate size, disease resistance, habit, evergreen, deciduous, annual, perennial. Find out what hardiness zone you live in and list 10 landscape plants you like that are suitable for your climate, giving the common name and scientific name for each.

C. Do ONE of the following:

(1) Explain the difference between vegetative and sexual propagation methods, and tell some horticultural advantages of each. Grow a plant from a stem or root cutting or graft.

(2) Transplant 12 seedlings or rooted cuttings to larger containers and grow them for at least one month.

(3) Demonstrate good pruning techniques and tell why pruning is important.

(4) After obtaining permission, plant a tree or shrub properly in an appropriate site.

D. Do EACH of the following:

(1) Explain the importance of good landscape design and selection of plants that are suitable for particular sites and conditions.

(2) Tell why it is important to know how big a plant will grow.

(3) Tell why slower-growing landscape plants are sometimes a better choice than faster-growing varieties.

E. Choose ONE of the following alternatives and complete EACH of the requirements:

(1) Bedding Plants

(a) Grow bedding plants appropriate for your area in pots or flats from seed or cuttings in a manufactured soil mix. Explain why you chose the mix and tell what is in it.

(b) Transplant plants to a bed in the landscape and maintain the bed until the end of the growing season. Record your activities, observations, materials used, and costs.

(c) Demonstrate mulching, fertilizing, watering, weeding, and deadheading, and tell how each practice helps your plants.

(d) Tell some differences between gardening with annuals and perennials.

(2) Fruit, Berry, and Nut Crops

(a) Plant five fruit or nut trees, grapevines, or berry plants that are suited to your area. Take full care of fruit or nut trees, grapevines, or berry plants through one season.

(b) Prune a tree, vine, or shrub properly. Explain why pruning is necessary.

(c) Demonstrate one type of graft and tell why this method is useful.

(d) Describe how one fruit, nut, or berry crop is processed for use.

(3) Woody Ornamentals

(a) Plant five or more trees or shrubs in a landscape setting. Take full care of the trees or shrubs you have planted for one growing season.

(b) Prune a tree or shrub properly. Explain why pruning is necessary.

(c) List 10 trees (in addition to those listed in general requirement 5 above) and tell your counselor how each is used in the landscape. Give the common and scientific names.

(d) Describe the size, texture, color, flowers, leaves, fruit, hardiness, cultural requirements, and any special characteristics that make each type of tree or shrub attractive or interesting.

(e) Tell five ways trees help improve the quality of our environment.

(4) Home Gardening

(a) Design and plant a garden or landscape that is at least 10 by 10 feet.

(b) Plant 10 or more different types of plants in your garden. Tell why you selected particular varieties of vegetables and flowers. Take care of the plants in your garden for one season.

(c) Demonstrate soil preparation, staking, watering, weeding, mulching, composting, fertilizing, pest management, and pruning. Tell why each technique is used.

(d) Tell four types of things you could provide to make your home landscape or park a better place for birds and wildlife. List the common and scientific names of 10 kinds of native plants that are beneficial to birds and wildlife in your area.

Option 3: Field Botany

A. Visit a park, forest, Scout camp, or other natural area near your home. While you are there:

(1) Determine which species of plants are the largest and which are the most abundant. Note whether they cast shade on other plants.

(2) Record environmental factors that may influence the presence of plants on your site, including latitude, climate, air and soil temperature, soil type and pH, geology, hydrology, and topography.

(3) Record any differences in the types of plants you see at the edge of a forest, near water, in burned areas, or near a road or railroad.

B. Select a study site that is at least 100 by 100 feet. Make a list of the plants in the study site by groups of plants: canopy trees, small trees, shrubs, herbaceous wildflowers and grasses, vines, ferns, mosses, algae, fungi, lichens. Find out which of these are native plants and which are exotic (or nonnative).

C. Tell how an identification key works and use a simple key to identify 10 kinds of plants (in addition to those in general requirement 5 above). Tell the difference between common and scientific names and tell why scientific names are important.

D. After gaining permission, collect, identify, press, mount, and label 10 different plants that are common in your area. Tell why voucher specimens are important for documentation of a field botanist's discoveries.

E. Obtain a list of rare plants of your state. Tell what is being done to protect rare plants and natural areas in your state. Write a paragraph about one of the rare plants in your state.

F. Choose ONE of the following alternatives and complete EACH of its requirements:

(1) Tree Inventory

(a) Identify the trees of your neighborhood, a park, a section of your town, or a Scout camp.

(b) Collect, press, and label leaves, flowers, or fruits to document your inventory.

(c) List the types of trees by scientific name and give common names. Note the number and size (diameter at 4 feet above ground) of trees observed and determine the largest of each species in your study area.

(d) Lead a walk to teach others about trees and their value, OR write and distribute materials that will help others learn about trees.

(2) Transect Study

(a) Visit two sites, at least one of which is different from the one you visited for Field Botany requirement 1.

(b) Use the transect method to study the two different kinds of plant communities. The transects should be at least 500 feet long.

(c) At each site, record observations about the soil and other influencing factors AND do the following. Then make a graph or chart to show the results of your studies.

(1) Identify each tree within 10 feet of the transect line.

(2) Measure the diameter of each tree at 4 feet above the ground, and map and list each tree.

(3) Nested Plot

(a) Visit two sites, at least one of which is different from the one you visited for Field Botany requirement 1.

(b) Mark off nested plots and inventory two different kinds of plant communities.

(c) At each site, record observations about the soil and other influencing factors AND do the following. Then make a graph or chart to show the results of your studies.

(1) Identify, measure, and map each tree in a 100-by-100-foot plot. (Measure the diameter of each tree at 4 feet above the ground.)

(2) Identify and map all trees and shrubs in a 10-by-10-foot plot within each of the larger areas.

(3) Identify and map all plants (wildflowers, ferns, grasses, mosses, etc.) of a 4-by-4-foot plot within the 10-by-10-foot plot.

(4) Herbarium Visit

(a) Write ahead and arrange to visit an herbarium at a university, park, or botanical garden; OR, visit an herbarium website (with your parent's permission).

(b) Tell how the specimens are arranged and how they are used by researchers. If possible, observe voucher specimens of a plant that is rare in your state.

(c) Tell how a voucher specimen is mounted and prepared for permanent storage. Tell how specimens should be handled so that they will not be damaged.

(d) Tell about the tools and references used by botanists in an herbarium.

(5) Plant Conservation Organization Visit

(a) Write ahead and arrange to visit a private conservation organization or government agency that is concerned with protecting rare plants and natural areas.

(b) Tell about the activities of the organization in studying and protecting rare plants and natural areas.

(c) If possible, visit a nature preserve managed by the organization. Tell about land management activities such as controlled burning, or measures to eradicate invasive (nonnative) plants or other threats to the plants that are native to the area.

 # Plumbing

1. Do the following:

(a) Describe how a properly working plumbing system protects your family's health and safety.

(b) List five important local health regulations related to plumbing and tell how they protect health and safety.

(c) Describe the safety precautions you must take when making home plumbing repairs.

2. Do the following:

(a) Make a drawing and explain how a home hot- and cold-water supply system works. Tell how you would make it safe from freezing.

(b) Make a drawing and explain the drainage system of the plumbing in a house. Show and explain the use of drains and vents.

3. Show how to use five important plumber's tools.

4. Identify and describe the use of each of the following: washer, retaining nut, plunger (rubber force cup), solder, flux, elbow, tee, nipple, coupling, plug, union, trap, drainpipe, and water meter.

5. Name the kinds of pipe that are used most often in a plumbing system. Explain why these pipes are used.

6. Cut, thread, and connect two pieces of metal pipe.

7. Under the supervision of a knowledgeable adult, solder three copper tube connections using a gas torch. Include one tee, two straight pieces, and one coupling.

8. Do the following:

   (a) Replace a washer in a faucet.

   (b) Clean out a sink or lavatory trap.

 # Pottery

1. Explain to your counselor the precautions that must be followed for the safe use and operation of a potter's tools, equipment, and other materials.

2. Do the following:

   (a) Explain the properties and ingredients of a good clay body for the following:

      (1) Making sculpture

      (2) Throwing on the wheel

   (b) Tell how three different kinds of potter's wheels work.

3. Make two drawings of pottery forms, each on an 8½-by-11-inch sheet of paper. One must be a historical pottery style. The other must be of your own design.

4. Explain the meaning of the following pottery terms: bat, wedging, throwing, leather hard, bone dry, greenware, bisque, terra-cotta, grog, slip, score, earthenware, stoneware, porcelain, pyrometric cone, and glaze.

5. Do the following. Each piece is to be painted, glazed, or otherwise decorated by you:

   (a) Make a slab pot, a coil pot, and a pinch pot.

   (b) Make a human or animal figurine or decorative sculpture.

   (c) Throw a functional form on a potter's wheel.

   (d) Help to fire a kiln.

6. Explain the scope of the ceramic industry in the United States. Tell some things made other than craft pottery.

7. With your parent's permission and your counselor's approval, do ONE of the following:

   (a) Visit the kiln yard at a local college or other craft school. Learn how the different kinds of kilns work, including low fire electric, gas or propane high fire, wood or salt/soda, and raku.

(b) Visit a museum, art exhibit, art gallery, artists' co-op, or artist's studio that features pottery. After your visit, share with your counselor what you have learned.

(c) Using resources from the library, magazines, the internet (with your parent's permission), and other outlets, learn about the historical and cultural importance of pottery. Share what you discover with your counselor.

8. Find out about career opportunities in pottery. Pick one and find out the education, training, and experience required for this profession. Discuss this with your counselor, and explain why this profession might interest you.

 Programming

1. **Safety.** Do the following:

(a) Show your counselor your current, up-to-date Cyber Chip.

(b) Discuss first aid and prevention for potential injuries, such as eyestrain and repetitive stress injuries, that could occur during programming activities.

Earn the Cyber Chip

Earning the Cyber Chip can help you learn how to stay safe while you are online and using social networks or the latest electronic gadgets. Topics include cell phone use, texting, blogging, gaming, cyberbullying, and identity theft. Find out more about the Cyber Chip at www.scouting.org/cyberchip.

2. **History.** Do the following:

(a) Give a brief history of programming, including at least three milestones related to the advancement or development of programming.

(b) Discuss with your counselor the history of programming and the evolution of programming languages.

3. **General knowledge.** Do the following:

(a) Create a list of 10 popular programming languages in use today and describe which industry or industries they are primarily used in and why.

(b) Describe three different programmed devices you rely on every day.

4. **Intellectual property.** Do the following:

(a) Explain the four types of intellectual property used to protect computer programs.

(b) Describe the difference between licensing and owning software.

(c) Describe the differences between freeware, open source, and commercial software, and why it is important to respect the terms of use of each.

5. **Projects.** Do the following:

(a) With your counselor's approval, choose a sample program. Modify the code or add a function or subroutine to it. Debug and demonstrate the modified program to your counselor.

The Programming merit badge website, www.boyslife.org/programming, has a number of sample programs that you could use for requirement 5a. However, you have the option of finding a program on your own. It's a good idea to seek your merit badge counselor's guidance.

(b) With your counselor's approval, choose a second programming language and development environment, different from those used for requirement 5a and in a different industry from 5a. Then write, debug, and demonstrate a functioning program to your counselor, using that language and environment.

(c) With your counselor's approval, choose a third programming language and development environment, different from those used for requirements 5a and 5b and in a different industry from 5a or 5b. Then write, debug, and demonstrate a functioning program to your counselor, using that language and environment.

(d) Explain how the programs you wrote for requirements 5a, 5b, and 5c process inputs, how they make decisions based on those inputs, and how they provide outputs based on the decision making.

6. **Careers.** Find out about three career opportunities that require knowledge in programming. Pick one and find out the education, training, and experience required. Discuss this with your counselor and explain why this career might be of interest to you.

Public Health

1. Do the following:

   (a) Explain what public health is. Explain how *Escherichia coli (E. coli)*, tetanus, HIV/AIDS, malaria, salmonellosis, and Lyme disease are contracted.

   (b) Choose any FOUR of the following diseases or conditions, and explain how each one is contracted and possibly prevented: gonorrhea, West Nile virus, Zika, botulism, influenza, syphilis, hepatitis, emphysema, meningitis, herpes, lead poisoning.

   (c) For each disease or condition in requirement 1b, explain:

   (i) The type or form of the malady (viral, bacterial, environmental, toxin)

   (ii) Any possible vectors for transmission

   (iii) Ways to help prevent exposure or the spread of infection

   (iv) Available treatments

2. Do the following:

   (a) Explain the meaning of *immunization.*

   (b) Name eight diseases against which a young child should be immunized, two diseases against which everyone should be reimmunized periodically, and one immunization everyone should receive annually.

   (c) Using the list of diseases and conditions in requirement 1b, discuss with your counselor those which currently have no immunization available.

3. Discuss the importance of safe drinking water in terms of the spread of disease. Then, demonstrate two ways for making water safe to drink that can be used while at camp. In your demonstration, explain how dishes and utensils should be washed, dried, and kept sanitary at home and in camp.

4. Explain what a vector is and how insects and rodents can be controlled in your home, in your community, and at camp. Tell why this is important. In your discussion, explain which vectors can be easily controlled by individuals and which ones require long-term, collective action.

5. With your parent's and counselor's approval, do ONE of the following:

   (a) Visit a municipal wastewater treatment facility OR a solid-waste management operation in your community.

   (i) Describe how the facility safely treats and disposes of sewage or solid waste.

   (ii) Discuss your visit and what you learned with your counselor.

   (iii) Describe how sewage and solid waste should be disposed of under wilderness camping conditions.

(b) Visit a food service facility, such as a restaurant or school cafeteria.

(i) Observe food preparation, handling, and storage. Learn how the facility keeps food from becoming contaminated.

(ii) Find out what conditions allow micro-organisms to multiply in food, what can be done to help prevent them from growing and spreading, and how to kill them.

(iii) Discuss the importance of using a thermometer to check food temperatures.

(iv) Discuss your visit and what you learned with your counselor.

6. Do the following:

(a) Describe the health dangers from air, water, and noise pollution.

(b) Describe health dangers from tobacco use and alcohol and drug abuse.

(c) Describe the health dangers from abusing illegal and prescription drugs.

7. With your parent's and counselor's approval, do ONE of the following:

(a) Visit your city, county, or state public health agency.

(b) Familiarize yourself with your city, county, or state health agency's website.

After completing either 7a or 7b, do the following:

(i) Compare the four leading causes of mortality (death) in your community for any of the past five years with the four leading causes of disease in your community. Explain how the public health agency you visited is trying to reduce the mortality and morbidity rates of these leading causes of illness and death.

(ii) Explain the role of your health agency as it relates to the outbreak of diseases.

(iii) Discuss the kinds of public assistance the agency is able to provide in case of disasters such as floods, storms, tornadoes, earthquakes, and other acts of destruction. Your discussion can include the cleanup necessary after the disaster.

8. Pick a profession in the public health sector that interests you. Find out the education, training, and experience required to work in this profession. Discuss what you learn with your counselor.

Public Speaking

1. Give a three- to five-minute introduction of yourself to an audience such as your troop, class at school, or some other group.

2. Prepare a three- to five-minute talk on a topic of your choice that incorporates body language and visual aids.

3. Give an impromptu talk of at least two minutes either as part of a group discussion or before your counselor. Use a subject selected by your counselor that is interesting to you but that is not known to you in advance and for which you do not have time to prepare.

4. Select a topic of interest to your audience. Collect and organize information about the topic and prepare an outline. Write an eight- to 10-minute speech, practice it, then deliver it in a conversational way.

5. Show you know parliamentary procedure by leading a discussion or meeting according to accepted rules of order, or by answering questions on the rules of order.

 # Pulp and Paper

1. Tell the history of papermaking. Describe the part paper products play in our society and economy.

2. Learn about the pulp and paper industry.

   (a) Describe the ways the industry plants, grows, and harvests trees.

   (b) Explain how the industry manages its forests so that the supply of trees keeps pace with the demand.

   (c) Tell how the industry has incorporated the concepts of sustainable forest management (SFM).

   (d) Describe two ways the papermaking industry has addressed pollution.

3. Name at least four types of trees that are major sources of papermaking fibers. Then do the following:

   (a) Discuss what other uses are made of the trees and the forestland owned by the pulp and paper industry.

   (b) Describe two ways of getting fibers from wood, and explain the major differences between them.

   (c) Tell why some pulps are bleached, and describe the process.

4. Describe how paper is made. Discuss how paper is recycled. Make a sheet of paper by hand.

5. Explain what coated paper is and why it is coated. Describe the major uses for different kinds of coated papers. Describe one other way that paper is changed by chemical or mechanical means to make new uses possible.

6. Make a list of 15 pulp or paper products found in your home. Share examples of 10 such products with your counselor.

7. With your parent's and counselor's approval, do ONE of the following:

   (a) Visit a pulp mill. Describe how the mill converts wood to cellulose fibers.

   (b) Visit a paper mill and get a sample of the paper made there. Describe the processes used for making this paper. Tell how it will be used.

(c) Visit a container plant or box plant. Describe how the plant's products are made.

(d) Visit a recycled paper collection or sorting facility. Describe the operations there.

(e) Using books, magazines, your local library, the internet (with your parent's permission), and any other suitable research tool, find out how paper products are developed. Find out what role research and development play in the papermaking industry. Share what you learn with your counselor.

8. Find out about three career opportunities in the papermaking industry that interest you. Pick one and find out the education, training, and experience required for this profession. Discuss this with your counselor, and explain why this profession might interest you.

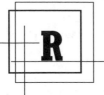

Radio

1. Explain what radio is. Then discuss the following:

   (a) The differences between broadcast radio and hobby radio

   (b) The differences between broadcasting and two-way communications

   (c) Radio station call signs and how they are used in broadcast radio and amateur radio

   (d) The phonetic alphabet and how it is used to communicate clearly

2. Do the following:

   (a) Sketch a diagram showing how radio waves travel locally and around the world.

   (b) Explain how the radio stations WWV and WWVH can be used to help determine what you can expect to hear when you listen to a shortwave radio.

   (c) Explain the difference between a distant (DX) and a local station.

   (d) Discuss what the Federal Communications Commission (FCC) does and how it is different from the International Telecommunication Union.

3. Do the following:

   (a) Draw a chart of the electromagnetic spectrum covering 300 kilohertz (kHz) to 3,000 megahertz (MHz).

   (b) Label the MF, HF, VHF, UHF, and microwave portions of the spectrum on your diagram.

   (c) Locate on your chart at least eight radio services, such as AM and FM commercial broadcast, citizens band (CB), television, amateur radio (at least four amateur radio bands), and public service (police and fire).

4. Explain how radio waves carry information. Include in your explanation: transceiver, transmitter, receiver, amplifier, and antenna.

5. Do the following:

   (a) Explain the differences between a block diagram and a schematic diagram.

   (b) Draw a block diagram for a radio station that includes a transceiver, amplifier, microphone, antenna, and feed line.

   (c) Discuss how information is sent when using amplitude modulation (AM), frequency modulation (FM), continuous wave (CW) Morse Code transmission, single sideband (SSB) transmission, and digital transmission.

(d) Explain how NOAA Weather Radio (NWR) can alert you to danger.

(e) Explain how cellular telephones work. Identify their benefits and limitations in an emergency.

6. Explain the safety precautions for working with radio gear, including the concept of grounding for direct current circuits, power outlets, and antenna systems.

7. Visit a radio installation (an amateur radio station, broadcast station, or public service communications center, for example) approved in advance by your counselor. Discuss what types of equipment you saw in use, how it was used, what types of licenses are required to operate and maintain the equipment, and the purpose of the station.

8. Find out about three career opportunities in radio. Pick one and find out the education, training, and experience required for this profession. Discuss this with your counselor, and explain why this profession might interest you.

9. Do ONE of the following (a OR b OR c OR d):

(a) **Amateur Radio**

(1) Tell why the FCC has an amateur radio service. Describe activities that amateur radio operators can do on the air, once they have earned an amateur radio license.

(2) Explain differences between the Technician, General, and Extra Class license requirements and privileges. Explain who administers amateur radio exams.

(3) Explain at least five Q signals or amateur radio terms.

(4) Explain how you would make an emergency call on voice or Morse code.

(5) Explain the differences between handheld transceivers and home "base" transceivers. Explain the uses of mobile amateur radio transceivers and amateur radio repeaters.

(6) Using proper call signs, Q signals, and abbreviations, carry on a 10-minute real or simulated amateur radio contact using voice, Morse code, or digital mode. (Licensed amateur radio operators may substitute five QSL cards as evidence of contacts with five amateur radio operators.) Properly log the real or simulated ham radio contact, and record the signal report.

(b) **Radio Broadcasting**

(1) Discuss with your counselor FCC broadcast regulations. Include power levels, frequencies, and the regulations for low-power stations.

(2) Prepare a program schedule for radio station "KBSA" of exactly one-half hour, including music, news, commercials, and proper station identification. Record your program on audiotape or in a digital audio format, using proper techniques.

(3) Listen to and properly log 15 broadcast stations. Determine the program format and target audience for five of these stations.

(4) Explain to your counselor at least eight terms used in commercial broadcasting, such as segue, cut, fade, continuity, remote, Emergency Alert System, network, cue, dead air, PSA, and playlist.

(5) Discuss with your counselor alternative radio platforms such as internet streaming, satellite radio, and podcasts.

(c) **Shortwave and Medium-Wave Listening**

(1) Listen across several shortwave bands for four one-hour periods—at least one period during daylight hours and at least one period at night. Log the stations properly and locate them geographically on a map, globe, or web-based mapping service.

(2) Listen to several medium-wave stations for two one-hour periods, one period during daylight hours and one period at night. Log the stations properly and locate them on a map, globe, or web-based mapping service.

(3) Compare your daytime and nighttime shortwave logs; note the frequencies on which your selected stations were loudest during each session. Explain differences in the signal strength from one period to the next.

(4) Compare your medium-wave broadcast station logs and explain why some distant stations are heard at your location only during the night.

(5) Demonstrate listening to a radio broadcast using a smartphone/cell phone. Include international broadcasts in your demonstration.

(d) **Amateur Radio Direction Finding**

(1) Describe amateur radio direction finding and explain why direction finding is important as both an activity and in competition.

(2) Describe what frequencies and equipment are used for ARDF or fox hunting.

(3) Build a simple directional antenna for either of the two frequencies used in ARDF.

(4) Participate in a simple fox hunt using your antenna along with a provided receiver.

(5) Show, on a map, how you located the "fox" using your receiver.

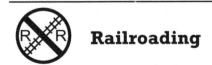 # Railroading

1. Do THREE of the following:

(a) Name three types of modern freight trains. Explain why unit trains are more efficient than mixed freight trains.

(b) Name one Class I or regional railroad. Explain what major cities it serves, the locations of major terminals, service facilities and crew change points, and the major commodities it carries.

(c) Using models or pictures, identify 10 types of railroad freight or passenger cars. Explain the purpose of each type of car.

(d) Explain how a modern diesel or electric locomotive develops power. Explain the terms dynamic braking and radial steering trucks.

2. Do the following:

(a) Explain the purpose and formation of Amtrak. Explain, by the use of a timetable, a plan for making a trip by rail between two cities at least 500 miles apart. List the times of departure and arrival at your destination, the train number and name, and the type of service you want.

(b) List and explain the various forms of public/mass transit using rail.

3. Do ONE of the following:

(a) Name four departments of a railroad company. Describe what each department does.

(b) Tell about the opportunities in railroading that interest you most and why.

(c) Name four rail support industries. Describe the function of each one.

(d) With your parent's and counselor's approval, interview someone employed in the rail industry. Learn what that person does and how this person became interested in railroading. Find out what type of schooling and training are required for this position.

4. Explain the purpose of Operation Lifesaver and its mission.

5. Do THREE of the following:

(a) List five safety precautions that help make trains safer for workers and passengers.

(b) Explain to your merit badge counselor why safety around rights-of-way is important.

(c) List 10 safety tips to remember when you are near a railroad track (either on the ground or on a station platform) or aboard a train.

(d) Tell your counselor about the guidelines for conduct that should be followed when you are near or on railroad property. Explain the dangers of trespassing on railroad property.

(e) Tell what an automobile driver can do to safely operate a car at grade crossings, and list three things an automobile driver should never do at a grade crossing.

(f) Tell how to report a malfunction of grade crossing warning devices.

(g) List safety precautions a pedestrian should follow at a public crossing.

6. Explain the appearance and meaning of the following warning signs and devices: advance warning sign, pavement markings, crossbucks, flashing red lights, crossing gates.

7. Do EACH of the following:

(a) Explain how railroad signals operate and show two basic signal types using color or configuration.

(b) Explain the meaning of three horn signals.

(c) Describe a way to signal a train for an emergency stop.

(d) Explain the use and function of the EOTD (end-of-train device), or FRED (flashing rear end device), used on the last car of most freight trains.

8. Select ONE of the following special-interest areas and complete the requirements.

(a) **Model Railroading**

With your parent's and counselor's approval, do TWO of the following:

(1) Draw a layout of your own model railroad or one that could be built in your home. Design a point-to-point track or loop with different routings. Include one of the following: turnaround or terminal or yard or siding.

(2) Build one model railroad car kit or one locomotive kit.

(3) Name the scale of four popular model railroad gauges. Identify the scale of four model cars or locomotives.

(4) Locate the website of four model railroad–related manufacturers or magazine publishers. Print information on their products and services and discuss the information with your counselor.

(5) Build one railroad structure (from scratch or using a kit), paint and weather the structure, mount it on your layout or diorama, and make the surrounding area on the diorama scenic.

(6) Alone or with others, build a model railroad or modular layout including ballast and scenery. Make electrical connections and operate a train. Describe what you enjoyed most.

(7) Participate in a switching contest on a timesaver layout and record your time.

(8) Explain the difference between powering and controlling a model railroad by using direct current, and powering and controlling a model railroad using digital command control.

(b) **Railfanning**

With your parent's and counselor's approval, do TWO of the following:

(1) Visit a railroad museum, historical display, or a prototype railroad-sponsored public event. With permission, photograph, videotape, or sketch items of interest. Explain what you saw and describe your photos, sketches, or videotape.

(2) Purchase tickets and ride a scenic or historic railroad. Under supervision, photograph the equipment and discuss with your counselor the historic significance of the operation.

(3) Locate the website of four rail historical groups, then find information on the history of the rail preservation operations and purpose of each group. Talk with a member of one of the groups and find out how you might help.

(4) Plan a trip by rail between two points. Obtain a schedule and explain when the train should arrive at two intermediate points. Purchase the tickets and make the trip. Explain to your counselor what you saw.

Reading

1. Do EACH of the following:

   (a) Learn how to search your library's card catalog or computerized catalog by author, title, and subject.

   (b) With the assistance of your merit badge counselor or a librarian, select six books of four different types (such as poetry, drama/plays, fiction, nonfiction, biographies, etc.). Ask your librarian or counselor about award-winning books that are recommended for readers your age and include at least one of those titles.

   (c) Find the books in the library catalog. With your counselor's or a librarian's assistance, locate the books on the shelves.

   (d) Read each book. Keep a log of your reading that includes the title of the book, the pages or chapters read, the date you completed them, and your thoughts about what you have read so far. Discuss your reading with your counselor. Using your log as a reference, explain why you chose each book and tell whether you enjoyed it and what it meant to you.

2. Read about the world around you from any two sources—books, magazines, newspapers, the internet (with your parent's permission), field manuals, etc. Topics may include sports, environmental problems, politics, social issues, current events, nature, religion, etc. Discuss what you have learned with your counselor.

3. Do ONE of the following:

   (a) From a catalog of your choice, fill out an order form for merchandise as if you intended to place an order. Share the completed form with your counselor and discuss it.

   (b) With your parent's permission, locate at least five websites that are helpful for your Scouting or other activities. Write the internet addresses of these sites in your log. Talk with your counselor or a librarian about safety rules for using the internet.

4. With your counselor's and your parent's permission, choose ONE of the following activities and devote at least four hours of service to that activity. Discuss your participation with your counselor.

   (a) Read to a sick, blind, or homebound person in a hospital or in an extended-care facility.

   (b) Perform volunteer work at your school library or a public library.

   (c) Read stories to younger children, in a group or individually.

Reptile and Amphibian Study

1. Describe the identifying characteristics of six species of reptiles and four species of amphibians found in the United States. For any four of these, make sketches from your own observations or take photographs. Show markings, color patterns, or other characteristics that are important in the identification of each of the four species. Discuss the habits and habitats of all 10 species.

2. Discuss with your merit badge counselor the approximate number of species and general geographic distribution of reptiles and amphibians in the United States. Prepare a list of the most common species found in your local area or state.

3. Describe the main differences between

   (a) Amphibians and reptiles

   (b) Alligators and crocodiles

   (c) Toads and frogs

   (d) Salamanders and lizards

   (e) Snakes and lizards

4. Explain how reptiles and amphibians are an important component of the natural environment. List four species that are officially protected by the federal government or by the state you live in, and tell why each is protected. List three species of reptiles and three species of amphibians found in your local area that are not protected. Discuss the food habits of all 10 species.

5. Describe how reptiles and amphibians reproduce.

6. From observation, describe how snakes move forward. Describe the functions of the muscles, ribs, and belly plates.

7. Describe in detail six venomous snakes and the one venomous lizard found in the United States. Describe their habits and geographic range. Tell what you should do in case of a bite by a venomous species.

8. Do ONE of the following:

   (a) Maintain one or more reptiles or amphibians for at least a month. Record food accepted, eating methods, changes in coloration, shedding of skins, and general habits; or keep the eggs of a reptile from the time of laying until hatching; or keep the eggs of an amphibian from the time of laying until their transformation into tadpoles (frogs) or larvae (salamanders). Whichever you chose, keep records of and report to your counselor how you cared for your animal/eggs/larvae to include lighting, habitat, temperature and humidity maintenance, and any veterinary care requirements.

   (b) Choose a reptile or amphibian that you can observe at a local zoo, aquarium, nature center, or other such exhibit (such as your classroom or school). Study the specimen weekly for a period of three months. At each visit, sketch the specimen in its captive habitat and note any changes in its coloration, shedding of skins, and general habits and behavior. Discuss with your counselor how the animal you observed was cared for to include its housing and habitat, how the lighting, temperature, and humidity were maintained, and any veterinary care requirements.

Find out, either from information you locate on your own or by talking to the caretaker, what this species eats and what are its native habitat and home range, preferred climate, average life expectancy, and natural predators. Also identify any human-caused threats to its population and any laws that protect the species and its habitat. After the observation period, share what you have learned with your counselor.

9. Do TWO of the following:

(a) Identify at night three kinds of toads or frogs by their voices. Imitate the song of each for your counselor. Stalk each with a flashlight and discover how each sings and from where.

(b) Identify by sight eight species of reptiles or amphibians.

(c) Using visual aids, give a brief talk to a small group on three different reptiles and amphibians.

10. Tell five superstitions or false beliefs about reptiles and amphibians and give a correct explanation for each. Give seven examples of unusual behavior or other true facts about reptiles and amphibians.

NOTE: Scouts must not use venomous reptiles in fulfilling requirement 8a. Species listed by federal or state law as endangered, protected, or threatened must not be used as live specimens in completing requirement 8a. When you decide keeping your specimen is no longer possible or desired, be sure to find another appropriate home for it or return it to the wild at the location of capture. Check with your merit badge counselor for those instances where the return of these specimens would not be appropriate.

Under the Endangered Species Act of 1973, some plants and animals are, or may be, protected by federal law. The same ones and/or others may be protected by state law. Be sure that you do not collect protected species.

Your state may require that you purchase and carry a license to collect certain species. Check with the wildlife and fish and game officials in your state regarding species regulations before you begin to collect.

 # Rifle Shooting

1. Do the following:

(a) Explain why BB and pellet air guns must always be treated with the same respect as firearms.

(b) Describe how you would react if a friend visiting your home asked to see your or your family's firearm(s).

(c) Explain the need for, and use and types of, eye and hearing protection. Demonstrate their proper use.

(d) Give the main points of the laws for owning and using guns in your community and state.

(e) Explain how hunting is related to the wise use of renewable wildlife resources.

(f) Successfully complete a state hunter education course or obtain a copy of the hunting laws for your state, then do the following:

   (1) Explain the main points of hunting laws in your state and give any special laws on the use of guns and ammunition.

   (2) List the kinds of wildlife that can be legally hunted in your state.

(g) Identify and explain how you can join or be a part of shooting sports activities.

(h) Explain to your counselor the proper hygienic guidelines used in shooting.

(i) Give your counselor a list of sources that you could contact for information on firearms and their uses.

2. Do ONE of the following options:

Option A—Rifle Shooting (Modern cartridge type)

(a) Identify the three main parts of a rifle, and tell how they function.

(b) Identify and demonstrate the three fundamental rules for safe gun handling.

(c) Identify the two types of cartridges, their parts, and how they function.

(d) Explain to your counselor what a misfire, hangfire, and squib fire are, and explain the procedures to follow in response to each.

(e) Identify and demonstrate the five fundamentals of shooting a rifle safely.

(f) Explain to your counselor the fundamental rules for safe gun handling. Explain each rule for using and storing a gun. Identify and explain each rule for safe shooting.

(g) Explain the range commands and range procedures.

(h) Demonstrate the knowledge, skills, and attitude necessary to safely shoot a rifle from the benchrest position or supported prone position while using the five fundamentals of rifle shooting.

(i) Identify the basic safety rules for cleaning a rifle, and identify the materials needed.

(j) Demonstrate how to clean a rifle properly and safely.

(k) Discuss what points you would consider in selecting a rifle.

(l) Using a .22 caliber rimfire rifle and shooting from a benchrest or supported prone position at 50 feet, fire five groups (three shots per group) that can be covered by a quarter. Using these targets, explain how to adjust sights to zero a rifle.

(m) Adjust sights to center the group on the target* and fire five groups (five shots per group). According to the target used, each shot in the group must meet the following minimum score: (1) A-32 targets—9; (2) A-17 or TQ-1 targets—7; (3) A-36 targets—5.

---

*NOTE: It is not always practical to adjust the sights (i.e., when using a borrowed fixed-sight rifle). For requirement 2(l), you may demonstrate your ability to use the shooting fundamentals by shooting five shot groups (five shots per group) in which all shots can be covered by or touch a quarter and then explain how to adjust the sights to zero the rifle used.

Option B—Air Rifle Shooting (BB or pellet)

(a) Identify the three main parts of an air rifle, and tell how they function.

(b) Identify and demonstrate the three fundamental rules for safe gun handling.

(c) Explain the range commands and range procedures.

(d) Identify the two most common types of air rifle ammunition.

(e) Identify and demonstrate the five fundamentals of shooting a rifle safely.

(f) Identify and explain each rule for shooting an air rifle safely.

(g) Demonstrate the knowledge, skills, and attitude necessary to safely shoot a target from the benchrest position or supported prone position while using the five fundamentals of rifle shooting.

(h) Identify the basic safety rules for cleaning an air rifle, and identify the materials needed.

(i) Demonstrate how to clean an air rifle safely.

(j) Discuss what points you would consider in selecting an air rifle.

(k) Using a BB gun or pellet air rifle and shooting from a benchrest or supported prone position at 15 feet for BB guns or 33 feet for air rifles, fire five groups (three shots per group) that can be covered by a quarter.

(l) Adjust sights to center the group on the target and fire five groups (five shots per group). According to the target used, each shot in the group must meet the following minimum score: (1) BB rifle at 15 feet or 5 meters using TQ-5 targets—8; (2) pellet air rifle at 25 feet using TQ-5 targets—8, at 33 feet or 10 meters using AR-1 targets—6.

Option C—Muzzleloading Rifle Shooting

(a) Give a brief history of the development of muzzleloading rifles.

(b) Identify principal parts of percussion rifles and discuss how they function.

(c) Demonstrate and discuss the safe handling of muzzleloading rifles.

(d) Identify the various grades of black powder and black powder substitutes and explain their proper use.

(e) Discuss proper safety procedures pertaining to black powder use and storage.

(f) Discuss proper components of a load.

(g) Identify proper procedures and accessories used for loading a muzzleloading rifle.

(h) Demonstrate the knowledge, skills, and attitude necessary to safely shoot a muzzleloading rifle on a range, including range procedures. Explain what a misfire, hangfire, and squib fire are, and explain the procedures to follow in response to each.

(i) Shoot a target with a muzzleloading rifle using the five fundamentals of firing a shot.

(j) Identify the materials needed to clean a muzzleloading rifle safely. Using these materials, demonstrate how to clean a muzzleloading rifle safely.

(k) Identify the causes of a muzzleloading rifle's failure to fire and explain or demonstrate proper correction procedures.

(l) Discuss what points you would consider in selecting a muzzleloading rifle.

(m) Using a muzzleloading rifle of .45 or .50 caliber and shooting from a benchrest or supported prone position, fire three groups (three shots per group) at 50 feet that can be covered by the base of a standard-size soft drink can.

(n) Center the group on the target and fire three groups (five shots per group). According to the target used, each shot in the group must meet the following minimum score: (1) at 25 yards using NRA A-23 or NMLRA 50-yard targets—7; (2) at 50 yards using NRA A-25 or NMLRA 100-yard targets—7.

Robotics

1. **Safety.** Do each of the following:

   (a) Explain to your counselor the most likely hazards you may encounter while working with robots and what you should do to anticipate, mitigate and prevent, and respond to these hazards. Describe the appropriate safety gear and clothing that should be used when working with robotics.

   (b) Discuss first aid and prevention for the types of injuries that could occur while participating in robotics activities and competitions, including cuts, eye injuries, and burns (chemical or heat).

2. **Robotics industry.** Discuss the following with your counselor:

   (a) The kinds of things robots can do and how robots are best used today.

   (b) The similarities and differences between remote-control vehicles, telerobots, and autonomous robots.

   (c) Three different methods robots can use to move themselves other than wheels or tracks. Describe when it would be appropriate to use each method.

3. **General knowledge.** Discuss with your counselor three of the five major fields of robotics (human-robot interface, mobility, manipulation, programming, sensors) and their importance to robotics development. Discuss either the three fields as they relate to a single robot system OR talk about each field in general. Find pictures or at least one video to aid your discussion.

4. **Design, build, program, test.** Do each of the following:

   (a) With your counselor's approval, choose a task for the robot or robotic subsystem that you plan to build. Include sensor feedback and programming in the task. Document this information in your robot engineering notebook.

(b) Design your robot. The robot design should use sensors and programming and have at least 2 degrees of freedom. Document the design in your robot engineering notebook using drawings and a written description.

(c) Build a robot or robotic subsystem of your original design to accomplish the task you chose for requirement 4a.

(d) Discuss with your counselor the programming options available for your robot. Then do either option 1 OR option 2.

(1) Option 1. Program your robot to perform the task you chose for your robot in 4a. Include a sample of your program's source code in your robot engineering notebook.

(2) Option 2. Prepare a flowchart of the desired steps to program your robot for accomplishing the task in 4a. Include procedures that show activities based on sensor inputs. Place this in your robot engineering notebook.

(e) Test your robot and record the results in your robot engineering notebook. Include suggestions on how you could improve your robot, as well as pictures or sketches of your finished robot.

5. **Demonstrate.** Do the following:

(a) Demonstrate for your counselor the robot you built in requirement 4.

(b) Share your robot engineering notebook with your counselor. Talk about how well your robot accomplished the task, the improvements you would make in your next design, and what you learned about the design process.

6. **Competitions.** Do ONE of the following.

(a) Attend a robotics competition and report to your counselor what you saw and learned about the competition and how teams are organized and managed.

(b) Learn about three youth robotics competitions. Tell your counselor about these, including the type of competition, time commitment, age of the participants, and how many teams are involved.

7. **Careers.** Name three career opportunities in robotics. Pick one and find out the education, training, and experience required for this profession. Discuss this with your counselor, and explain why this profession might interest you.

 **Rowing**

1. Do the following:

(a) Explain to your counselor the most likely hazards you may encounter while participating in rowing activities, including weather- and water-related hazards, and what you should do to anticipate, help prevent, mitigate, and respond to these hazards.

(b) Review prevention, symptoms, and first-aid treatment for the following injuries or illnesses that can occur while rowing: blisters, hypothermia, heat-related illnesses, dehydration, sunburn, sprains, and strains.

(c) Review the BSA Safety Afloat policy. Explain to your counselor how this applies to rowing activities.

2. Before doing the following requirements, successfully complete the BSA swimmer test.

3. Review the characteristics of life jackets most appropriate for rowing and why one must always be worn while rowing. Then demonstrate how to select and fit a life jacket.

4. Do ONE of the following:

(a) Alone or with a passenger, do the following in either a fixed-seat or sliding-seat rowboat:

(1) Launch.

(2) Row in a straight line for 100 yards. Stop, pivot, and return to the starting point.

(3) Backwater in a straight line for 25 yards. Make a turn underway and return to the starting point.

(4) Land and moor or rack your craft.

(5) Tie the following mooring knots—clove hitch, roundturn with two half-hitches, bowline, Wellman's knot, and mooring hitch.

(b) Participate as a rowing team member in a competitive rowing meet. The team may be sponsored by a school, club, or Scout unit. The meet must include competition between two or more teams with different sponsors. Complete at least 10 hours of team practice prior to the meet.

5. Do ONE of the following:

(a) In a fixed-seat rowboat, come alongside a pier and help a passenger into the boat. Pull away from the pier, change positions with your passenger, and demonstrate sculling over the stern or side. Resume your rowing position, return alongside the pier, and help your passenger out of the boat.

(b) In a sliding-seat rowboat, come alongside a pier and, with your buddy assisting you, get out onto the pier. Help your buddy into the boat. Reverse roles with your buddy and repeat the procedure.

6. Participate in a swamped boat drill including righting and stabilizing the craft, reboarding in deep water, and making headway. Tell why you should stay with a swamped boat.

7. Alone in a rowboat, push off from the shore or a pier. Row 20 yards to a swimmer. While giving instructions to the swimmer, pivot the boat so that the swimmer can hold on to the stern. Tow the swimmer to shore.

8. Describe the following:

    (a) Types of craft used in commercial, competitive, and recreational rowing.

    (b) Four common boatbuilding materials. Give some positive and negative points of each.

    (c) Types of oarlocks used in competitive and recreational rowing.

9. Discuss the following:

    (a) The advantage of feathering oars while rowing

    (b) Precautions regarding strong winds and heavy waves, and boat-handling procedures in rough water and windstorms

    (c) How to properly fit out and maintain a boat in season, and how to prepare and store a boat for winter

    (d) How to determine the proper length of oars

    (e) The differences between fixed-seat and sliding-seat rowing

    (f) The different meanings of the term sculling in fixed- and sliding-seat rowing

    (g) The health benefits from rowing for exercise

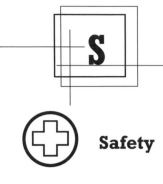

Safety

1. Explain what safety is and what it means to be safe. Then prepare a notebook to include:

   (a) Newspaper and other stories, facts, and statistics showing common types and causes of injuries in the home and in the workplace, and how these injuries could be prevented

   (b) Newspaper and other stories, facts, and statistics showing common types of crimes and ways to avoid being a crime victim

   (c) Facts you have obtained concerning the frequency of accidents and of crimes in your local area

   (d) A paragraph or more, written by you, explaining how a serious fire, accident, or crime could change your family life

   (e) A list of safe practices and safety devices currently used by your family, such as safety practices used while driving or working and safety devices that prevent injuries or help in an emergency

2. Do the following:

   (a) Using a safety checklist approved by your counselor, make an inspection of your home. Identify any hazards found and explain how these can be corrected.

   (b) Review or develop your family's plan of escape in case of fire in your home. As you develop the escape plan with family members, share with them facts about the common causes of fire in the home, such as smoking, cooking, electrical appliances, and candles.

3. Do the following:

   (a) Discuss with your counselor how you contribute to the safety of yourself, your family, and your community.

   (b) Show your family members how to protect themselves and your home from accidents, fire, burglary, robbery, and assault.

   (c) Discuss with your counselor the tips for online safety. Explain the steps individuals can take to help prevent identity theft.

   (d) Discuss with your counselor the three R's of Youth Protection and how to recognize child abuse.

4. Show your family the exits you would use from different public buildings (such as a theater, municipal building, library, supermarket, shopping center, or your place of worship) in the event of an emergency. Teach your family what to do in the event that they need to take shelter in or evacuate a public place.

5. Make an accident prevention plan for five family activities outside the home (at your place of worship, at a theater, on a picnic, at the beach, and while traveling, for example). Each plan should include an analysis of possible hazards, proposed action to correct hazards, and reasons for the correction you propose in each plan.

6. Plan and complete a safety project approved by your counselor for your home, school, place of worship, place of employment, or community.

7. Explain what the National Terrorism Advisory System is and how you would respond to each type of alert.

8. Learn about three career opportunities in the field of safety. Pick one career and find out the education, training, and experience required for this profession. Discuss this choice with your counselor, and explain why this profession might interest you.

 # Salesmanship

1. Do the following:

   (a) Explain the responsibilities of a salesperson and how a salesperson serves customers and helps stimulate the economy.

   (b) Explain the differences between a business-to-business salesperson and a consumer salesperson.

2. Explain why it is important for a salesperson to do the following:

   (a) Research the market to be sure the product or service meets the needs of customers.

   (b) Learn all about the product or service to be sold.

   (c) If possible, visit the location where the product is built and learn how it is constructed. If a service is being sold, learn about the benefits of the service to the customer.

   (d) Follow up with customers after their purchase to confirm their satisfaction and discuss their concerns about the product or service.

3. Write and present a sales plan for a product or service and a sales territory assigned by your counselor.

4. Make a sales presentation of a product or service assigned by your counselor.

5. Do ONE of the following and keep a record (cost sheet). Use the sales techniques you have learned, and share your experience with your counselor:

   (a) Help your unit raise funds through sales of merchandise or of tickets to a Scout event.

   (b) Sell your services such as lawn raking or mowing, pet watching, dog walking, snow shoveling, and car washing to your neighbors. Follow up after the service has been completed and determine the customer's satisfaction.

   (c) Earn money through retail selling.

6. Do ONE of the following:

   (a) Interview a salesperson and learn the following:

      (1) What made the person choose sales as a profession?

      (2) What are the most important things to remember when talking to customers?

      (3) How is the product or service sold?

      (4) Include your own questions.

   (b) Interview a retail store owner and learn the following:

      (1) How often is the owner approached by a sales representative?

      (2) What good traits should a sales representative have? What habits should the sales representative avoid?

      (3) What does the owner consider when deciding whether to establish an account with a sales representative?

      (4) Include at least two of your own questions.

7. Investigate and report on career opportunities in sales, then do the following:

   (a) Prepare a written statement of your qualifications and experience. Include relevant classes you have taken in school and merit badges you have earned.

   (b) Discuss with your counselor what education, experience, or training you should obtain so you are prepared to serve in a sales position.

 **Scholarship**

1. Do ONE of the following:

   (a) Show that your school grades have been an average of B or higher (80 percent or higher) for one term or semester.

   (b) Show that for one term or semester you have improved your school grades over the previous period.

2. Do TWO of the following:

   (a) Make a list of educational places located where you live (other than schools). Visit one, and report on how you used the place for self-education.

   (b) With your counselor's and your parent's approval, interview two professionals (other than teachers or other professionals at your school) with established careers. Find out where they were educated, what training they received, and how their education and training have helped prepare them for the career they have chosen. Find out how they continue to educate themselves. Discuss what you find out with your counselor.

   (c) Using a daily planner, show your counselor how you keep track of assignments and activities, and discuss how you manage your time.

(d) Discuss the advantages and disadvantages of the different methods of research available to you for school assignments, such as the library, books and periodicals, and the internet.

3. Get a note from the principal* of your school (or another school official named by the principal) that states that during the past year your behavior, leadership, and service have been satisfactory.

4. Do ONE of the following:

(a) Show that you have taken part in an extracurricular school activity, and discuss with your counselor the benefits of participation and what you learned about the importance of teamwork.

(b) Discuss your participation in a school project during the past semester where you were a part of a team. Tell about the positive contributions you made to the team and the project.

5. Do ONE of the following:

(a) Write a report of 250 to 300 words about how the education you receive in school will be of value to you in the future and how you will continue to educate yourself in the future.

(b) Write a report of 250 to 300 words about two careers that interest you and how specific classes and good scholarship in general will help you achieve your career goals.

---

*If you are home-schooled or your school environment does not include a principal, you may obtain a note from a counterpart such as your parent.

 # Scouting Heritage

1. Discuss with your counselor the life and times of Lord Baden-Powell of Gilwell. Explain why he felt a program like Scouting would be good for the young men of his day. Include in your discussion how Scouting was introduced in the United States, and the origins of Boy Scouting and Cub Scouting under Baden-Powell.

2. Do the following:

(a) Give a short biographical summary of any TWO of the following, and tell of their roles in how Scouting developed and grew in the United States.

(1) Daniel Carter Beard	(4) Ernest Thompson Seton
(2) William D. Boyce	(5) James E. West
(3) Waite Phillips	(6) "Green Bar Bill" Hillcourt

(b) Discuss the significance to Scouting of any TWO of the following:

    (1) Brownsea Island

    (2) The First World Scout Jamboree

    (3) Boy Scout Handbook

    (4) Boys' Life magazine

3. Discuss with your counselor how Scouting's programs have developed over time and been adapted to fit different age groups and interests (Cub Scouting, Boy Scouting, Exploring, Venturing).

4. Do ONE of the following:

(a) Attend either a BSA national jamboree, OR world Scout jamboree, OR a national BSA high-adventure base. While there, keep a journal documenting your day-to-day experiences. Upon your return, report to your counselor what you did, saw, and learned. You may include photos, brochures, and other documents in your report.

(b) Write or visit the National Scouting Museum. Obtain information about this facility. Give a short report on what you think the role of this museum is in the Scouting program.

(c) Visit an exhibit of Scouting memorabilia or a local museum with a Scouting history gallery, or (with your parent's permission and counselor's approval) visit with someone in your council who is recognized as a dedicated Scouting historian or memorabilia collector. Learn what you can about the history of Boy Scouting. Give a short report to your counselor on what you saw and learned.

5. Learn about the history of your unit or Scouting in your area. Interview at least two people (one from the past and one from the present) associated with your troop. These individuals could be adult unit leaders, Scouts, troop committee members, or representatives of your troop's chartered organization. Find out when your unit was originally chartered. Create a report of your findings on the history of your troop, and present it to your patrol or troop or at a court of honor, and then add it to the troop's library. This presentation could be in the form of an oral/written report, an exhibit, a scrapbook, or a computer presentation such as a slide show.

6. Make a collection of some of your personal patches and other Scouting memorabilia. With their permission, you may include items borrowed from family members or friends who have been in Scouting in the past, or you may include photographs of these items. Show this collection to your counselor, and share what you have learned about items in the collection. (There is no requirement regarding how large or small this collection must be.)

7. Reproduce the equipment for an old-time Scouting game such as those played at Brownsea Island. You may find one on your own (with your counselor's approval), or pick one from the Scouting Heritage merit badge pamphlet. Teach and play the game with other Scouts.

8. Interview at least three people (different from those you interviewed for requirement 5) over the age of 40 who were Scouts. Find out about their Scouting experiences. Ask about the impact that Scouting has had on their lives. Share what you learned with your counselor.

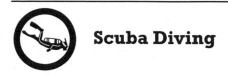

Scuba Diving

1. Do the following:

   (a)   Show that you know first aid for injuries or illnesses that could occur while scuba diving, including hypothermia, hyperventilation, squeezes, decompression illness, nitrogen narcosis, motion sickness, fatigue, overexertion, heat reactions, dehydration, injuries by aquatic life, and cuts and scrapes.

   (b)   Identify the conditions that must exist before performing CPR on a person, and explain how to recognize such conditions. Demonstrate the proper technique for performing CPR using a training device approved by your counselor.

2. Before completing requirements 3 through 6, earn the Swimming merit badge.

3. Discuss the Scuba Diver's Code with your merit badge counselor, and explain the importance of each guideline to a scuba diver's safety.

4. Earn an Open Water Diver Certification from a scuba organization recognized by the Boy Scouts of America scuba policy.

5. Explain what an ecosystem is, and describe four aquatic ecosystems a diver might experience.

6. Find out about three career opportunities in the scuba industry. Pick one and find out the education, training, and experience required for this profession. Discuss this with your counselor, and explain why this profession might interest you.

Sculpture

1. Explain to your counselor the precautions that must be followed for the safe use and operation of a sculptor's tools, equipment, and other materials.

2. Do TWO of the following:

    (a) Model in clay a life-size human head. Then sculpt in modeling clay, carve in wood or plaster, or use 3D modeling software to make a small-scale model of an animal or person. Explain to your counselor the method and tools you used to sculpt the figure.

    (b) Make a plaster mold of a fruit or vegetable. In this mold, make a copy of the fruit or vegetable. Explain to your counselor the method and tools you used to make the copy.

    (c) With your parent's permission and your counselor's approval, visit a museum, art exhibit, art gallery, artists' co-op, or artist's studio. After your visit, share with your counselor what you have learned. Discuss the importance of visual arts and how it strengthens social tolerance and helps stimulate cultural, intellectual, and personal development.

3. Find out about career opportunities in sculpture. Pick one and find out the education, training, and experience required for this profession. Discuss this with your counselor, and explain why this profession might interest you.

Search and Rescue

1. Do the following:

    (a) Explain to your counselor the hazards you are most likely to encounter while participating in search and rescue (SAR) activities, and what you should do to anticipate, help prevent, mitigate, and respond to these hazards.

    (b) Discuss first aid and prevention for the types of injuries or illnesses that could occur while participating in SAR activities, including: snakebites, dehydration, shock, environmental emergencies such as hypothermia or heatstroke, blisters, and ankle and knee sprains.

2. Demonstrate knowledge to stay found and prevent yourself from becoming the subject of a SAR mission.

    (a) How does the buddy system help in staying found and safe?

    (b) How can knowledge of the area and its seasonal weather changes affect your plans?

    (c) Explain how the Ten Essentials are similar to a "ready pack."

3. Discuss the following with your counselor:

    (a) The difference between *search* and *rescue*

(b) The difference between *PLS (place last seen)* and *LKP (last known point)*

(c) The meaning of these terms:

    (1) AFRCC (Air Force Rescue Coordination Center)

    (2) IAP (Incident Action Plan)

    (3) ICS (Incident Command System)

    (4) Evaluating search urgency

    (5) Establishing confinement

    (6) Scent item

    (7) Area air scent dog

    (8) Briefing and debriefing

4. Find out who in your area has authority for search and rescue and what their responsibilities are. Discuss this with your counselor, and explain the official duties of a search and rescue team.

5. Working with your counselor, become familiar with the Incident Command System. You may use any combination of resource materials, such as printed or online. Discuss with your counselor how features of the ICS compare with Scouting's patrol method.*

6. Identify four types of search and rescue teams and discuss their use or role with your counselor. Then do the following:

(a) Interview a member of one of the teams you have identified above, and learn how this team contributes to a search and rescue operation. Discuss what you learned with your counselor.

(b) Describe the process and safety methods of working around at least two of the specialized SAR teams you identified above.

(c) Explain the differences between wilderness, urban, and water SARs.

A Note About Unauthorized and Restricted Activities

The BSA's *Guide to Safe Scouting* states under "Unauthorized and Restricted Activities" that flying in aircraft as part of a search and rescue mission is an unauthorized activity for youth members. For complete information, see www.scouting.org/health-and-safety.

7. Discuss the Universal Transverse Mercator (UTM) system, latitude, and longitude. Then do the following:

(a) Using a 1:24,000 scale USGS topographic map, show that you can identify a location of your choice using UTM coordinates.

(b) Using a 1:24,000 scale map, ask your counselor to give you a UTM coordinate on the map, then identify that location.

(c) Show that you can identify your current location using the UTM coordinates on a Global Positioning System (GPS) unit and verify it on a 1:24,000 scale map.

(d) Determine a hypothetical place last seen, and point out an area on your map that could be used for containment using natural or human-made boundaries.

---

*Scouts who have already completed the original requirement 5 as published in the current *Search and Rescue* merit badge pamphlet need not redo this updated requirement in order to earn the badge.

8. Choose a hypothetical scenario, either one presented in this merit badge pamphlet or one created by your counselor. Then do the following:

(a) Complete an incident objectives form for this scenario.

(b) Complete an Incident Action Plan (IAP) to address this scenario.

(c) Discuss with your counselor the behavior of a lost person and how that would impact your incident action plan (for example, the differences between searching for a young child versus a teen).

(d) After completing 8a–8c, discuss the hypothetical scenario with your counselor.

9. Discuss with your counselor the terms *hasty team* and *hasty search*. Then do the following:

(a) Plan and carry out a practice hasty search—either urban or wilderness— for your patrol or troop. Include the following elements in the search: clue awareness, evidence preservation, tracking the subject, and locating the subject using attraction or trail sweep.

(b) When it's over, hold a team debriefing to discuss the hasty search. Discuss problems encountered, successful and unsuccessful tactics, and ideas for improvement.

10. Find out about three career or volunteer opportunities in search and rescue. Pick one and find out the education, training, and experience required for this professional or volunteer position. Discuss this with your counselor, and explain why this position might interest you.

 Shotgun Shooting

1. Do the following:

(a) Explain why BB and pellet air guns must always be treated with the same respect as firearms.

(b) Describe how you would react if a friend visiting your home asked to see your or your family's firearm(s).

(c) Explain the need for and use and types of eye and hearing protection.

(d) Explain the main points of the laws for owning and using guns in your community and state.

(e) Explain how hunting is related to the wise use of renewable wildlife resources.

(f) Successfully complete a state hunter education course, or obtain a copy of the hunting laws for your state, then do the following.

(1) Explain the main points of hunting laws in your state and give any special laws on the use of guns and ammunition, and

(2) List the kinds of wildlife that can be legally hunted in your state.

(g) Explain to your counselor the proper hygienic guidelines used in shooting.

(h) Identify and explain three shotgun sports. Identify places in your community where you could shoot these sports and explain how you can join or be a part of shooting sports activities.

(i) Give your counselor a list of sources that you could contact for information on firearms and their use.

2. Do ONE of the following options:

Shotgun Shooting (Modern Shotshell Type) Option A

(a) Identify the principal parts of a shotgun, action types, and how they function.

(b) Identify and demonstrate the rules for safely handling a shotgun.

(c) Identify the parts of a shotgun shell and their functions.

(d) Identify the various gauges of shotguns. Explain which one you would pick for use and why.

(e) Identify and explain the fundamentals of safely shooting a shotgun. Explain what a misfire, hangfire, and squib fire are, and explain the procedures to follow in response to each.

(f) Identify and explain each rule for safely shooting a shotgun.

(g) Demonstrate the knowledge, skills, and attitude necessary to safely shoot moving targets, using the fundamentals of shotgun shooting.

(h) Identify the materials needed to clean a shotgun.

(i) Demonstrate how to clean a shotgun safely.

(j) Discuss what points you would consider in selecting a shotgun.

(k) Shooting score required—Hit at least 12 (48 percent) out of 25 targets in two 25-target groups. The two groups need not be shot in consecutive order. A minimum of 50 shots must be fired.

Shooting skill rules:

• Targets may be thrown by a hand trap, manual mechanical trap, or on any trap or skeet field. Note: If using a hand trap or manual mechanical trap, the trap operator should be at least five feet to the right and three feet to the rear of the shooter. If throwing left-handed with a hand trap, the trap operator should be at least 5 feet to the left and 3 feet to the rear of the shooter.

• All targets should be thrown at a reasonable speed and in the same direction.

• Targets should be generally thrown so as to climb in the air after leaving the trap.

• Scores may be fired at any time, either in formal competition or in practice.

• Any gauge shotgun not exceeding 12 gauge may be used.

• Only commercially manufactured ammunition may be used. Reloads may not be used in BSA shooting sports programs.

• Shooters must shoot in rounds of 25. Rounds need not be shot continuously or on the same day (the term "round" refers to a single series of 25 shots).

- If using a trap field, shoot station 3 with traps set to throw straightaway targets.
- If using a skeet field, shoot station 7 low house.

Muzzleloading Shotgun Shooting Option B

(a) Discuss a brief history of the development of the muzzleloading shotgun.

(b) Identify principal parts of percussion and flintlock shotguns and discuss how they function.

(c) Demonstrate and explain the rules of safely handling a muzzleloading shotgun.

(d) Identify the various grades of black powder and their proper and safe use.

(e) Discuss proper safety procedures pertaining to black powder use and storage.

(f) Discuss proper components of a load.

(g) Identify proper procedures and accessories used for safety loading a muzzleloading shotgun.

(h) Demonstrate the knowledge, skills, and attitude necessary to safely shoot a muzzleloading shotgun on a range, including range procedures. Explain what a misfire, hangfire, and squib fire are, and explain the procedures to follow in response to each.

(i) Shoot a moving target with a muzzleloading shotgun using the five fundamentals of firing the shot.

(j) Identify the materials needed to clean a muzzleloading shotgun properly and safely.

(k) Demonstrate how to clean to clear a muzzleloading shotgun's failure to fire and explain or demonstrate proper correction procedures.

(l) Identify the causes of a muzzleloading shotgun's failure to fire and explain or demonstrate proper preventive procedures.

(m) Discuss what points you would consider if selecting a muzzleloading shotgun.

(n) Shooting score required—Hit at least five out of 15 targets in each of two 15-target groups. The two groups need not be shot in consecutive order. A minimum of 30 shots must be fired. Shooting skill rules:

- Targets may be thrown by a hand trap, manual mechanical trap, or on any trap or skeet field. Note: If using a hand trap or manual mechanical trap, the trap operator should be at least five feet to the right and three feet to the rear of the shooter. If throwing left-handed with a hand trap, the trap operator should be at least 5 feet to the left and 3 feet to the rear of the shooter.
- All targets should be thrown at a reasonable speed and in the same direction.
- Targets should be generally thrown so as to climb in the air after leaving the trap.
- Scores may be fired at any time, either in formal competition or in practice.

- Any gauge shotgun not exceeding 10 gauge may be used.
- Standard clay targets customarily used for trap and skeet are to be used.
- On a standard trap field, the shooter should be positioned 8 yards behind the trap house. The trap should be set to throw only straightaway targets.
- On a skeet field, use station 7 low house.

Signs, Signals, and Codes

1. Discuss with your counselor the importance of signs, signals, and codes, and why people need these different methods of communication. Briefly discuss the history and development of signs, signals, and codes.

2. Explain the importance of signaling in emergency communications. Discuss with your counselor the types of emergency or distress signals one might use to attract airborne search-and-rescue personnel if lost in the outdoors or trying to summon assistance during a disaster. Illustrate these signaling examples by the use of photos or drawings.

3. Do the following:

   (a) Describe what Morse code is and the various means by which it can be sent. Spell your first name using Morse code. Send or receive a message of six to 10 words using Morse code.

   (b) Describe what American Sign Language (ASL) is and how it is used today. Spell your first name using American Sign Language. Send or receive a message of six to 10 words using ASL.

4. Give your counselor a brief explanation about semaphore, why it is used, how it is used, and where it is used. Explain the difference between semaphore flags and nautical flags. Then do the following:

   (a) Spell your first name using semaphore. Send or receive a message of six to 10 words using semaphore.

   (b) Using illustrations or photographs, identify 10 examples of nautical flags and discuss their importance.

5. Explain the braille reading technique and how it helps individuals with sight impairment to communicate. Then do the following:

   (a) Either by sight or by touch, identify the letters of the braille alphabet that spell your name. By sight or touch, decode a braille message at least six words long.

   (b) Create a message in braille at least six words long, and share this with your counselor.

6. Do the following:

    (a) Describe to your counselor six sound-only signals that are in use today. Discuss the pros and cons of using sound signals versus other types of signals.

    (b) Demonstrate to your counselor six different silent Scout signals. Use these Scout signals to direct the movements and actions of your patrol or troop.

7. On a Scout outing, lay out a trail for your patrol or troop to follow. Cover at least one mile in distance and use at least six different trail signs and markers. After the Scouts have completed the trail, follow no-trace principles by replacing or returning trail markers to their original locations.

8. For THREE of the following activities, demonstrate five signals each. Tell what the signals mean and why they are used:

    (a) Sports official's hand signs/signals

    (b) Heavy-equipment operator's hand signals

    (c) Aircraft carrier catapult crew signals

    (d) Cyclist's hand signals

    (e) An activity selected by you and your counselor

9. Share with your counselor 10 examples of symbols used in everyday life. Design your own symbol. Share it with your counselor and explain what it means. Then do the following:

    (a) Show examples of 10 traffic signs and explain their meaning.

    (b) Using a topographical map, explain what a map legend is and discuss its importance. Point out 10 map symbols and explain the meaning of each.

    (c) Discuss text-message symbols and why they are commonly used. Give examples of your favorite 10 text symbols or emoticons. Then see if your counselor or parent can identify the meaning or usage of each symbol.

10. Briefly discuss the history of secret code writing (cryptography). Make up your own secret code and write a message of up to 25 words using this code. Share the message with a friend or fellow Scout. Then share the message and code key with your counselor and discuss the effectiveness of your code.

Skating

1. Do the following:

   (a) Explain to your counselor the most likely hazards associated with skating and what you should do to anticipate, help prevent, mitigate, and respond to these hazards.

   (b) Show that you know first aid for injuries or illnesses that could occur while skating, including hypothermia, frostbite, lacerations, abrasions, fractures, sprains and strains, blisters, heat-related reactions, and shock.

2. Complete ALL of the requirements for ONE of the following options.

Ice Skating Option

   (a) Do the following:

   (1) Give general safety and courtesy rules for ice skating. Discuss preparations that must be taken when skating outdoors on natural ice. Explain how to make an ice rescue.

   (2) Discuss the parts and functions of the different types of ice skates.

   (3) Describe the proper way to carry ice skates.

   (4) Describe how to store ice skates for long periods of time, such as seasonal storage.

   (b) Do the following:

   (1) Skate forward at least 40 feet and come to a complete stop. Use either a two-footed snowplow stop or a one-footed snowplow stop.

   (2) After skating forward, glide forward on two feet, then on one foot, first right and then left.

   (3) Starting from a T position, stroke forward around the test area, avoiding the use of toe points if wearing figure skates.

   (c) Do the following:

   (1) Glide backward on two feet for at least two times the skater's height.

   (2) Skate backward for at least 20 feet on two skates.

   (3) After gaining forward speed, glide forward on two feet, making a turn of 180 degrees around a cone, first to the right and then to the left.

   (d) Do the following:

   (1) Perform forward crossovers in a figure-eight pattern.

   (2) Explain to your counselor the safety considerations for running or participating in an ice skating race.

   (3) Perform a hockey stop.

Roller Skating Option

(a) Do the following:

(1) Give general safety and etiquette rules for roller skating.

(2) Discuss the parts and functions of the roller skate.

(3) Describe five essential steps to good skate care.

(b) Do the following:

(1) Skate forward with smooth, linked strokes on two feet for at least 100 feet in both directions around the rink and demonstrate proper techniques for stopping.

(2) Skate forward and glide at least 15 feet on one skate, then on the other skate.

(c) Do the following:

(1) Perform the crosscut.

(2) Skate backward for at least 40 feet on two skates, then for at least 15 feet on one skate.

(3) Skate forward in a slalom pattern for at least 40 feet on two skates, then for at least 20 feet on one skate.

(4) Skate backward in a slalom pattern for at least 15 feet on two skates.

(d) Do the following:

(1) Shuttle skate once around the rink, bending twice along the way without stopping.

(2) Perform a widespread eagle.

(3) Perform a mohawk.

(4) Perform a series of two consecutive spins on skates, OR hop, skip, and jump on skates for at least 10 feet.

(e) Do the following:

(1) Race on a speed track, demonstrating proper technique in starting, cornering, passing, and pacing.

(2) Perform the limbo under a pole placed at least chest-high, OR shoot-the-duck under a waist-high pole and rise while still on one foot.

(3) Perform the stepover.

(4) While skating, dribble a basketball the length of the floor, then return to your starting position, OR push a hockey ball with a stick around the entire rink in both directions.

In-Line Skating Option

(a) Do the following:

(1) Give general and in-line skating safety rules and etiquette.

(2) Describe the parts and functions of the in-line skate.

(3) Describe the required and recommended safety equipment.

(4) Describe four essential steps to good skate care.

(b) Do the following:

(1) Skate forward with smooth, linked strokes on two feet for at least 100 feet.

(2) Skate forward and glide at least 15 feet on one skate, then on the other skate.

(3) Stop on command on flat pavement using the heel brake.

(c) Do the following:

(1) Perform the forward crossover.

(2) Perform a series of forward, linked swizzles for at least 40 feet.

(3) Skate backward for at least 40 feet in a series of linked, backward swizzles.

(4) From a strong pace, perform a lunge turn around an object predetermined by your counselor.

(5) Perform a mohawk.

(d) Do the following:

(1) Perform a series of at least four one-footed downhill slaloms on pavement with a gentle slope.

(2) Describe how to pass a pedestrian or another skater from behind.

(3) Describe at least three ways to avoid an unforeseen obstacle while skating.

(4) Describe two ways to get on and off a curb, and demonstrate at least one of these methods.

 # Small-Boat Sailing

1. Do the following:

(a) Explain to your counselor the most likely hazards you may encounter while participating in small-boat activities, and what you should do to anticipate, help prevent, mitigate, and respond to these hazards.

(b) Review prevention, symptoms, and first-aid treatment for the following injuries or illnesses that can occur while canoeing: blisters, cold-water shock and hypothermia, dehydration, heat-related illnesses, sunburn, sprains, and strains.

(c) Discuss the BSA Safety Afloat policy. Tell how it applies to small-boat activities.

2. Before doing requirements 3 through 9, successfully complete the BSA swimmer test:

Jump feetfirst into water over the head in depth. Level off and swim 75 yards in a strong manner using one or more of the following strokes: sidestroke, breaststroke, trudgen, or crawl; then swim 25 yards using an easy resting backstroke. The 100 yards must be completed in one swim without stops and must include at least one sharp turn. After completing the swim, rest by floating.

3. Describe the boat you will be using for the sailing requirement, naming all of the major parts and the function of those parts.*

4. Before going afloat, do the following:

   (a) Discuss the nine points of the BSA Safety Afloat plan.

   (b) Explain the rules of the road in general and any specific rules or laws that apply to your area or state.

   (c) Explain how water conditions, the hazards of weather, and heavy winds can affect both safety and performance in sailing.

   (d) Discuss the warning signs of inclement weather and what to do should heavy winds develop or a storm approach.

   (e) Prepare a typical float plan.

   (f) Discuss the proper clothing, footwear, and personal gear required for small-boat sailing in warm weather and in cool weather. Explain how choosing the proper clothing, footwear, and personal gear will help keep you comfortable and safe while sailing.

5. Discuss with your counselor how to identify the wind direction and wind indicators. Explain the importance of this task before setting sail.

6. Following the BSA Safety Afloat plan, show that you and a buddy can sail a boat properly. Do the following:

   (a) Prepare a boat for sailing, including a safety inspection.

   (b) Get underway from a dock, mooring, or beach.

   (c) Properly set sails for a round-trip course approved by your counselor that will include running, beating, and reaching—the basic points of sail. While sailing, demonstrate good helmsmanship skills.

   (d) Change direction by tacking; change direction by jibing.

   (e) Demonstrate getting out of irons.

   (f) Demonstrate the safety position.

   (g) Demonstrate capsize procedures and the rescue of a person overboard.†

   (h) Demonstrate the procedure to take after running aground.

   (i) Upon returning to the dock, mooring, or beach, properly secure all equipment, furl or stow sails, and prepare the craft for unattended docking or beaching overnight or longer.

7. Demonstrate a working knowledge of marlinespike seamanship. Do the following:

   (a) Show how to tie a square (reef) knot, clove hitch, two half hitches, bowline, cleat hitch, and figure-eight knot. Demonstrate the use of each.

---

*The skills may be demonstrated on any boat available to the Scout; sailboards are not acceptable. While no specific sail plan is recommended, it is suggested that the craft be smaller than 20 feet. The boat must be capsizable and have the capability of sailing to windward.

†Capsize procedures should be conducted under the close supervision of the counselor. A rescue boat should be standing by to assist, if necessary, and to tow the capsized craft to shore. Self-bailing boats are acceptable for this requirement. Extreme care should be taken to avoid personal injury and damage to the boat or equipment.

(b) Show how to heave a line, coil a line, and fake down a line.

(c) Discuss the kinds of lines used on sailboats and the types of fibers used in their manufacture. Explain the advantages and disadvantages of each.

8. Describe how you would care for and maintain a sailboat and its gear throughout the year.

9. With your counselor, review sailing terminology and the points of sail. Discuss various types of sailboats in use today and explain their differences.

 **Snow Sports**

1. Do the following:

(a) Explain to your counselor the hazards you are most likely to encounter while participating in snow sport activities, and what you should do to anticipate, help prevent, mitigate, and respond to these hazards.

(b) Discuss first aid and prevention for the types of injuries or illnesses that could occur while participating in snow sports, including hypothermia, frostbite, shock, dehydration, sunburn, fractures, bruises, sprains, and strains. Tell how to apply splints.

2. Do the following:

(a) Explain why every snow sport participant should be prepared to render first aid in the event of an accident.

(b) Explain the procedure used to report an accident to the local ski patrol for the area where you usually ski, ride, or snowshoe.

3. Explain the international trail-marking system.

4. Discuss the importance of strength, endurance, and flexibility in snow sports. Demonstrate exercises and activities you can do to get fit for the option you choose in requirement 7.

5. Present yourself properly clothed and equipped for the option you choose in requirement 7. Discuss how the clothing you have chosen will help keep you warm and protected.

6. Do EACH of the following:

(a) Tell the meaning of the Your Responsibility Code for skiers, snowboarders, and snowshoers. Explain why each rider must follow this code.

(b) Explain the Smart Style safety program. Tell why it is important and how it applies to participants at snow sport venues like terrain parks and pipes.

(c) Explain the precautions pertaining to avalanche safety, including the responsibility of individuals regarding avalanche safety.

(d) Tell the meaning of the Wilderness Use Policy. Explain why each skier and snowboarder must adopt this policy.

7. Complete ALL of the requirements for ONE of the following options: downhill (Alpine) skiing OR cross-country (Nordic) OR snowboarding OR snowshoeing.

Downhill (Alpine) Skiing Option

(a) Show how to use and maintain your own release bindings and explain the use of two others. Explain the international DIN standard and what it means to skiers.

(b) Explain the American Teaching System and a basic snow-skiing progression.

(c) Discuss the five types of Alpine skis. Demonstrate two ways to carry skis and poles safely and easily.

(d) Demonstrate how to ride one kind of lift and explain how to ride two others.

(e) On a gentle slope, demonstrate some of the beginning maneuvers learned in skiing. Include the straight run, gliding wedge, wedge stop, sidestep, and herringbone maneuvers.

(f) On slightly steeper terrain, show linked wedge turns.

(g) On a moderate slope, demonstrate five to 10 christies.

(h) Make a controlled run down an intermediate slope and demonstrate the following:

(1) Short-, medium-, and long-radius parallel turns

(2) A sideslip and safety (hockey) stop to each side

(3) Traverse across a slope

(i) Demonstrate the ability to ski in varied conditions, including changes in pitch, snow conditions, and moguls. Maintain your balance and ability to turn.

(j) Name the major ski organizations in the United States and explain their functions.

Cross-Country (Nordic) Skiing Option

(a) Show your ability to select, use, and repair, if necessary, the correct equipment for ski touring in safety and comfort.

(b) Discuss classical and telemark skis. Demonstrate two ways to carry skis and poles safely and easily.

(c) Discuss the basic principles of waxing for cross-country ski touring.

(d) Discuss the differences between cross-country skiing, ski touring, ski mountaineering, and downhill skiing.

(e) List the items you would take on a one-day ski tour.

(f) Demonstrate the proper use of a topographic map and compass.

(g) On a gentle, packed slope, show some basic ways to control speed and direction. Include the straight run, traverse, side slip, step turn, wedge stop, and wedge turn maneuvers.

(h) On a cross-country trial, demonstrate effective propulsion by showing proper weight transfer from ski to ski, pole timing, rhythm, flow, and glide.

(i) Demonstrate your ability, on a tour, to cope with an average variety of snow conditions.

(j) Demonstrate several methods of dealing with steep hills or difficult conditions. Include traverses and kick turns going uphill and downhill, sidesteps, pole drag, and ski-pole "glissade."

Snowboarding Option

(a) Discuss forward-fall injuries.

(b) Show your ability to select the correct equipment for snowboarding and to use it for safety and comfort.

(c) Show how to use and maintain your own bindings, and explain the use of the different binding methods. Explain the need for leashes.

(d) Discuss the four types of snowboards. Demonstrate how to carry a snowboard easily and safely.

(e) Demonstrate how to ride one kind of lift and explain how to ride two others.

(f) Demonstrate the basic principles of waxing a snowboard.

(g) Do the following:

   (1) On a gentle slope, demonstrate beginning snowboarding maneuvers. Show basic ways to control speed and direction. Include the side-slipping maneuver.

   (2) On slightly steeper terrain, show traversing.

(h) On a moderate slope, demonstrate an ollie, a nose-end grab, and a wheelie.

(i) Make a controlled run down an intermediate slope and demonstrate the following:

   (1) Skidded, carved, and jump turns

   (2) Stops

   (3) Riding fakie

(j) Demonstrate your ability to ride in varied conditions, including changes in pitch, snow conditions, and moguls. Maintain your balance and ability to turn.

(k) Name the major snowboarding organizations in the United States and explain their functions.

   (1) Skidded, carved, and jump turns

   (2) Stops

   (3) Riding fakie

(l) Demonstrate your ability to ride in varied conditions, including changes in pitch, snow conditions, and moguls. Maintain your balance and ability to turn.

(m) Name the major snowboarding organizations in the United States and explain their functions.

Snowshoeing Option

(a) Name the parts of a snowshoe.

(b) Explain how to choose the correct size of snowshoe.

(c) Describe the different types of snowshoes and their specialized uses. Discuss factors to consider when choosing a snowshoe.

(d) Explain how to properly care for and maintain snowshoes.

(e) Describe how to make an emergency snowshoe.

(f) Describe areas that are best for snowshoeing. Discuss some advantages and dangers of backcountry snowshoeing.

(g) Discuss the benefits of snowshoeing.

(h) Demonstrate the most efficient ways to break trail, climb uphill, travel downhill, and traverse a slope.

(i) Take a two-mile snowshoe hike with a buddy or your troop.

(j) Demonstrate your ability, on a hike, to cope with an average variety of snow conditions.

Soil and Water Conservation

1. Do the following:

   (a) Tell what soil is. Tell how it is formed.

   (b) Describe three kinds of soil. Tell how they are different.

   (c) Name the three main plant nutrients in fertile soil. Tell how they can be put back when used up.

2. Do the following:

   (a) Define soil erosion.

   (b) Tell why it is important. Tell how it affects you.

   (c) Name three kinds of soil erosion. Describe each.

   (d) Take pictures or draw two kinds of soil erosion.

3. Do the following:

   (a) Tell what is meant by conservation practices.

   (b) Describe the effect of three kinds of erosion-control practices.

   (c) Take pictures or draw three kinds of erosion-control practices.

4. Do the following:

   (a) Explain what a watershed is.

   (b) Outline the smallest watershed that you can find on a contour map.

   (c) Then outline on your map, as far as possible, the next larger watershed which also has the smallest in it.

   (d) Explain what a river basin is. Tell why all people living in a river basin should be concerned about land and water use in it.

   (e) Explain what an aquifer is and why it can be important to communities.

5. Do the following:

(a) Make a drawing to show the hydrologic cycle.

(b) Show by demonstration at least two of the following actions of water in relation to soil: percolation, capillary action, precipitation, evaporation, transpiration.

(c) Explain how removal of vegetation will affect the way water runs off a watershed.

(d) Tell how uses of forest, range, and farm land affect usable water supply.

(e) Explain how industrial use affects water supply.

6. Do the following:

(a) Tell what is meant by "water pollution."

(b) Describe common sources of water pollution and explain the effects of each.

(c) Tell what is meant by "primary water treatment," "secondary waste treatment," and "biochemical oxygen demand."

(d) Make a drawing showing the principles of complete waste treatment.

7. Do TWO of the following:

(a) Make a trip to TWO of the following places. Write a report of more than 500 words about the soil and water and energy conservation practices you saw.

   (1) An agricultural experiment

   (2) A managed forest or woodlot, range, or pasture

   (3) A wildlife refuge or a fish or game management area

   (4) A conservation-managed farm or ranch

   (5) A managed watershed

   (6) A waste-treatment plant

   (7) A public drinking water treatment plant

   (8) An industry water use installation

   (9) A desalinization plant

(b) Plant 100 trees, bushes, and/or vines for a good purpose.

(c) Seed an area of at least ⅕ acre for some worthwhile conservation purpose, using suitable grasses or legumes alone or in a mixture.

(d) Study a soil survey report. Describe the things in it. On tracing paper over any of the soil maps, outline an area with three or more different kinds of soil. List each kind of soil by full name and map symbol.

(e) Make a list of places in your neighborhood, camps, school ground, or park that have erosion, sedimentation, or pollution problems. Describe how these could be corrected through individual or group action.

(f) Carry out any other soil and water conservation project approved by your merit badge counselor.

Space Exploration

1. Tell the purpose of space exploration and include the following:

   (a) Historical reasons

   (b) Immediate goals in terms of specific knowledge

   (c) Benefits related to Earth resources, technology, and new products

   (d) International relations and cooperation

2. Design a collector's card, with a picture on the front and information on the back, about your favorite space pioneer. Share your card and discuss four other space pioneers with your counselor.

3. Build, launch, and recover a model rocket.* Make a second launch to accomplish a specific objective. (Rocket must be built to meet the safety code of the National Association of Rocketry. See the "Model Rocketry" chapter of the *Space Exploration* merit badge pamphlet.) Identify and explain the following rocket parts.

   (a) Body tube

   (b) Engine mount

   (c) Fins

   (d) Igniter

   (e) Launch lug

   (f) Nose cone

   (g) Payload

   (h) Recovery system

   (i) Rocket engine

4. Discuss and demonstrate each of the following:

   (a) The law of action-reaction

   (b) How rocket engines work

   (c) How satellites stay in orbit

   (d) How satellite pictures of Earth and pictures of other planets are made and transmitted

5. Do TWO of the following:

   (a) Discuss with your counselor a robotic space exploration mission and a historic crewed mission. Tell about each mission's major discoveries, its importance, and what was learned from it about the planets, moons, or regions of space explored.

---

*If local laws prohibit launching model rockets, do the following activity: Make a model of a NASA rocket. Explain the functions of the parts. Give the history of the rocket.

(b) Using magazine photographs, news clippings, and electronic articles (such as from the internet), make a scrapbook about a current planetary mission.

(c) Design a robotic mission to another planet or moon that will return samples of its surface to Earth. Name the planet or moon your spacecraft will visit. Show how your design will cope with the conditions of the planet's or moon's environment.

6. Describe the purpose, operation, and components of ONE of the following:

(a) Space shuttle or any other crewed orbital vehicle, whether government-owned (U.S. or foreign) or commercial

(b) International Space Station

7. Design an inhabited base located within our solar system, such as Titan, asteroids, or other locations that humans might want to explore in person. Make drawings or a model of your base. In your design, consider and plan for the following:

(a) Source of energy

(b) How it will be constructed

(c) Life-support system

(d) Purpose and function

8. Discuss with your counselor two possible careers in space exploration that interest you. Find out the qualifications, education, and preparation required and discuss the major responsibilities of those positions.

 **Sports**

Note: The activities used to fulfill the requirements for the Sports merit badge may not be used to help fulfill requirements for other merit badges

1. Do the following:

(a) Explain to your counselor the most likely hazards you may encounter while playing sports, and what you should do to anticipate, help prevent, mitigate, and respond to these hazards.

(b) Show that you know first aid for injuries or illnesses that could occur while participating in sports, including sprains, strains, contusions, abrasions, fractures, blisters, muscle cramps, injured teeth, dehydration, heat and cold reactions, and concussions or other suspected injuries to the head, neck, and back.

2. Explain the importance of the following:

   (a) The importance of the physical exam

   (b) The importance of maintaining good health habits for life (such as exercising regularly), and how the use of tobacco products, alcohol, and other harmful substances can negatively affect your health and your performance in sports activities

   (c) The importance of maintaining a healthy diet

3. Discuss the following:

   (a) The importance of warming up and cooling down

   (b) The importance of weight training

   (c) What an amateur athlete is and the differences between an amateur and a professional athlete

   (d) The attributes (qualities) of a good sport, the importance of sportsmanship, and the traits of a good team leader and player who exhibits Scout spirit on and off the playing field

4. With guidance from your counselor, establish a personal training program suited to the activities you choose for requirement 5. Then do the following:

   (a) Create a chart and use it to track your training, practice, and development in these sports for one season (or four months).

   (b) Demonstrate proper technique for your two chosen sports.

   (c) At the end of the season, share your completed chart with your counselor and discuss how your participation in the sports you chose has affected you mentally and physically.

5. Take part for one season (or four months) as a competitive individual or as a member of an organized team in TWO of the following sports: baseball, basketball, bowling, cross-country, field hockey, football, golf, gymnastics, ice hockey, lacrosse, soccer, softball, swimming, table tennis, tennis, track and field, volleyball, water polo, wrestling. Your counselor may approve in advance other recognized sports, but not any sport that is restricted and not authorized by the Boy Scouts of America. Then with your chosen sports do the following:

   (a) Give the rules and etiquette for the two sports you picked.

   (b) List the equipment needed for the two sports you chose. Describe the protective equipment and appropriate clothing (if any) and explain why it is needed.

   (c) Draw diagrams of the playing areas for your two sports.

Stamp Collecting

1. Do the following:

   (a) Discuss how you can better understand people, places, institutions, history, and geography as a result of collecting stamps.

   (b) Briefly describe some aspects of the history, growth, and development of the United States postal system. Tell how it is different from postal systems in other countries.

2. Define topical stamp collecting. Name and describe three other types of stamp collections.

3. Show at least ONE example of each of the following:

   (a) Perforated and imperforate stamps

   (b) Mint and used stamps

   (c) Sheet, booklet, and coil stamps

   (d) Numbers on plate block, booklet, or coil, or marginal markings

   (e) Overprint and surcharge

   (f) Metered mail

   (g) Definitive, commemorative, semipostal, and airmail stamps

   (h) Cancellation and postmark

   (i) First day cover

   (j) Postal stationery (aerogramme, stamped envelope, and postal card)

4. Do the following:

   (a) Demonstrate the use of ONE standard catalog for several different stamp issues. Explain why catalog value can vary from the corresponding purchase price.

   (b) Explain the meaning of the term *condition* as used to describe a stamp. Show examples that illustrate the different factors that affect a stamp's value.

5. Demonstrate the use of at least THREE of the following stamp collector's tools:

   (a) Stamp tongs

   (b) Water and tray

   (c) Magnifiers

   (d) Hinges and stamp mounts

   (e) Perforation gauge

   (f) Glassine envelopes and cover sleeves

   (g) Watermark fluid

6. Do the following:

   (a) Show a stamp album and how to mount stamps with or without hinges. Show at least ONE page that displays several stamps.

   (b) Discuss at least THREE ways you can help to preserve stamps, covers, and albums in first-class condition.

7. Do at least TWO of the following:

   (a) Design a stamp, cancellation, or cachet.

   (b) Visit a post office, stamp club, or stamp show with an experienced collector. Explain what you saw and learned.

   (c) Write a review of an interesting article from a stamp newspaper, magazine, book, or website (with your parent's permission).

   (d) Research and report on a famous stamp-related personality or the history behind a particular stamp.

   (e) Describe the steps taken to produce a stamp. Include the methods of printing, types of paper, perforation styles, and how they are gummed.

   (f) Prepare a two- to three-page display involving stamps. Using ingenuity, as well as clippings, drawings, etc., tell a story about the stamps and how they relate to history, geography, or a favorite topic of yours.

8. Mount and show, in a purchased or homemade album, ONE of the following:

   (a) A collection of 250 or more different stamps from at least 15 countries.

   (b) A collection of a stamp from each of 50 different countries, mounted on maps to show the location of each.

   (c) A collection of 100 or more different stamps from either one country or a group of closely related countries.

   (d) A collection of 75 or more different stamps on a single topic. (Some interesting topics are: Scouting, birds, insects, the Olympics, sports, flowers, animals, ships, holidays, trains, famous people, space, and medicine.) Stamps may be from different countries.

   (e) A collection of postal items discovered in your mail by monitoring it over a period of 30 days. Include at least five different types listed in requirement 3.

Surveying

1. Show that you know first aid for the types of injuries that could occur while surveying, including cuts, scratches, snakebite, insect stings, tick bites, heat and cold reactions, and dehydration. Explain to your counselor why a surveyor should be able to identify the poisonous plants and poisonous animals that are found in your area.

2. Find and mark the corners of a five-sided lot that has been laid out by your counselor to fit the land available. Set an instrument over each of the corners and record the angle turned between each line and the distance measured between each corner. With the assistance of the counselor, compute the error of closure from the recorded notes. The error of closure must not be more than 5 feet. From the corners, take compass readings or turn angles to trees, shrubs, and rocks, and measure to them. All measurements should be made using instruments, methods, and accuracies consistent with current technology.

3. From the field notes gathered for requirement 2, draw to scale a map of your survey. Submit a neatly drawn copy.

4. Write a metes and bounds description for the five-sided lot in requirement 2.

5. Use one of the corner markers from requirement 2 as a benchmark with an assumed elevation of 100 feet. Using a level and rod, determine the elevation of the other four corner markers.

6. Get a copy of the deed to your property, or a piece of property assigned by your counselor, from the local courthouse or title agency.

7. Tell what GPS is; discuss with your counselor the importance of GPS and how it is changing the field of surveying.

8. Discuss the importance of surveying with a licensed surveyor. Also discuss the various types of surveying and mapping, and applications of surveying technology to other fields. Discuss career opportunities in surveying and related fields. Discuss the qualifications and preparation for such a career.

 # Sustainability

1. Before starting work on any other requirements for this merit badge, write in your own words the meaning of *sustainability*. Explain how you think conservation and stewardship of our natural resources relate to sustainability. Have a family meeting, and ask family members to write down what they think sustainability means. Be sure to take notes. You will need this information again for requirement 5.

2. Do the following:

Water. Do A AND either B *OR* C

(a) Develop and implement a plan that attempts to reduce your family's water usage. As a family, discuss water usage. To aid in your discussion, if past water bills are available, you may choose to examine a few. As a family, choose three ways to help reduce water consumption. Implement those ideas for one month. Share what you learn with your counselor, and tell how you think your plan affected your family's water usage.

(b) Using a diagram you have created, explain to your counselor how your household gets its clean water from a natural source and what happens with the water after you use it. Include water that goes down the kitchen, bathroom, and laundry drains, and any runoff from watering the yard or washing the car. Tell two ways to preserve your family's access to clean water in the future.

(c) Discuss with your counselor two areas in the world that have been affected by drought over the last three years. For each area, identify a water conservation practice (successful or unsuccessful) that has been used. Tell whether the practice was effective and why. Discuss what water conservation practice you would have tried and why.

Food. Do A AND either B *OR* C.

(a) Develop and implement a plan that attempts to reduce your household food waste. Establish a baseline and then track and record your results for two weeks. Report your results to your family and counselor.

(b) Discuss with your counselor the ways individuals, families, and communities can create their own food sources (potted plants, family garden, rooftop garden, neighborhood or community garden). Tell how this plan might contribute to a more sustainable way of life if practiced globally.

(c) Discuss with your counselor factors that limit the availability of food and food production in different regions of the world. Tell three ways these factors influence the sustainability of worldwide food supplies.

Community. Do A AND either B *OR* C.

(a) Draw a rough sketch depicting how you would design a sustainable community. Share your sketch with your counselor, and explain how the housing, work locations, shops, schools, and transportation systems affect energy, pollution, natural resources, and the economy of the community.

(b) With your parent's permission and your counselor's approval, interview a local architect, engineer, contractor, or building materials supplier. Find out the factors that are considered when using sustainable materials in renovating or building a home. Share what you learn with your counselor.

(c) Review a current housing needs assessment for your town, city, county, or state. Discuss with your counselor how birth and death rates affect sufficient housing, and how a lack of housing—or too much housing—can influence the sustainability of a local or global area.

Energy. Do A AND either B *OR* C.

(a) Learn about the sustainability of different energy sources, including fossil fuels, solar, wind, nuclear, hydropower, and geothermal. Find out how the production and consumption of each of these energy sources affects the environment and what the term "carbon footprint" means. Discuss what you learn with your counselor, and explain how you think your family can reduce its carbon footprint.

(b) Develop and implement a plan that attempts to reduce consumption for one of your family's household utilities. Examine your family's bills for that utility reflecting usage for three months (past or current). As a family, choose three ways to help reduce consumption and be a better steward of this resource. Implement those ideas for one month. Share what you learn with your counselor, and tell how your plan affected your family's usage.

(c) Evaluate your family's fuel and transportation usage. Review your family's transportation-related bills (gasoline, diesel, electric, public transportation, etc.) reflecting usage for three months (past or current). As a family, choose three ways to help reduce consumption and be a better steward of this resource. Implement those ideas for one month. Share what you learn with your counselor, and tell how your plan affected your family's transportation habits.

Stuff. Do A AND either B *OR* C.

(a) Keep a log of the "stuff" your family purchases (excluding food items) for two weeks. In your log, categorize each purchase as an essential *need* (such as soap) or a desirable *want* (such as a DVD). Share what you learn with your counselor.

(b) Plan a project that involves the participation of your family to identify the "stuff" your family no longer needs. Complete your project by donating, repurposing, or recycling these items.

(c) Discuss with your counselor how having too much "stuff" affects you, your family, and your community. Include the following: the financial impact, time spent, maintenance, health, storage, and waste. Include in your discussion the practices that can be used to avoid accumulating too much "stuff."

3. Do the following:

(a) Explain to your counselor how the planetary life-support systems (soil, climate, freshwater, atmospheric, nutrient, oceanic, ecosystems, and species) support life on Earth and interact with one another.

(b) Tell how the harvesting or production of raw materials (by extraction or recycling), along with distribution of the resulting products, consumption, and disposal/repurposing, influences current and future sustainability thinking and planning.

4. Explore TWO of the following categories. Have a discussion with your family about the two you select. In your discussion, include your observations, and best and worst practices. Share what you learn with your counselor.

(a) **Plastic waste.** Discuss the impact plastic waste has on the environment (land, water, air). Learn about the number system for plastic recyclables, and determine which plastics are more commonly recycled. Find out what the trash vortex is and how it was formed.

(b) **Electronic waste.** Choose three electronic devices in your household. Find out the average lifespan of each, what happens to these devices once they pass their useful life, and whether they can be recycled in whole or part. Discuss the impact of electronic waste on the environment.

(c) **Food waste.** Learn about the value of composting and how to start a compost pile. Start a compost pile appropriate for your living situation. Tell what can be done with the compost when it is ready for use.

(d) **Species decline.** Explain the term species (plant or animal) decline. Discuss the human activities that contribute to species decline, what can be done to help reverse the decline, and its impact on a sustainable environment.

(e) **World population.** Learn how the world's population affects the sustainability of Earth. Discuss three human activities that may contribute to putting Earth at risk, now and in the future.

(f) **Climate change.** Find a world map that shows the pattern of temperature change for a period of at least 100 years. Share this map with your counselor, and discuss three factors that scientists believe affect the global weather and temperature.

5. Do the following:

(a) After completing requirements 1 through 4, have a family meeting. Discuss what your family has learned about what it means to be a sustainable citizen. Talk about the behavioral changes and life choices your family can make to live more sustainably. Share what you learn with your counselor.

(b) Discuss with your counselor how living by the Scout Oath and Scout Law in your daily life helps promote sustainability and good stewardship.

6. Learn about career opportunities in the sustainability field. Pick one and find out the education, training, and experience required. Discuss what you have learned with your counselor and explain why this career might interest you.

For more information about sustainability and its connection to people, prosperity, and the planet, go to www.scouting.org/sustainability.

 Swimming

1. Do the following:

(a) Explain to your counselor how Scouting's Safe Swim Defense plan anticipates, helps prevent and mitigate, and provides responses to likely hazards you may encounter during swimming activities.

(b) Discuss the prevention and treatment of health concerns that could occur while swimming, including hypothermia, dehydration, sunburn, heat exhaustion, heatstroke, muscle cramps, hyperventilation, spinal injury, stings and bites, and cuts and scrapes.

2. Before doing the following requirements, successfully complete the BSA swimmer test: Jump feetfirst into water over the head in depth. Level off and swim 75 yards in a strong manner using one or more of the following strokes: sidestroke, breaststroke, trudgen, or crawl; then swim 25 yards using an easy, resting backstroke. The 100 yards must be completed in one swim without stops and must include at least one sharp turn. After completing the swim, rest by floating.

3. Swim continuously for 150 yards using the following strokes in good form and in a strong manner: front crawl or trudgen for 25 yards, back crawl for 25 yards, sidestroke for 25 yards, breaststroke for 25 yards, and elementary backstroke for 50 yards.

4. Do the following:

   (a) Demonstrate water rescue methods by reaching with your arm or leg, by reaching with a suitable object, and by throwing lines and objects. Explain why swimming rescues should not be attempted when a reaching or throwing rescue is possible, and explain why and how a rescue swimmer should avoid contact with the victim.

   (b) With a helper and a practice victim, show a line rescue both as tender and as rescuer. The practice victim should be approximately 30 feet from shore in deep water.

5. Do the following:

   (a) Float faceup in a resting position for at least one minute.

   (b) Demonstrate survival floating for at least five minutes.

   (c) While wearing a properly fitted U.S. Coast Guard–approved life jacket, demonstrate the HELP and huddle positions. Explain their purposes.

   (d) Explain why swimming or survival floating will hasten the onset of hypothermia in cold water.

6. In water over your head, but not to exceed 10 feet, do each of the following:

   (a) Use the feetfirst method of surface diving and bring an object up from the bottom.

   (b) Do a headfirst surface dive (pike or tuck), and bring the object up again.

   (c) Do a headfirst surface dive to a depth of at least 5 feet and swim underwater for three strokes. Come to the surface, take a breath, and repeat the sequence twice.

7. Following the guidelines set in the BSA Safe Swim Defense, in water at least 7 feet deep*, show a standing headfirst dive from a dock or pool deck. Show a long shallow dive, also from the dock or pool deck.

8. Explain the health benefits of regular aerobic exercise, and discuss why swimming is favored as both fitness and therapeutic exercise.

---

*If your state, city, or local community requires a water depth greater than 7 feet, it is important to abide by that mandate.

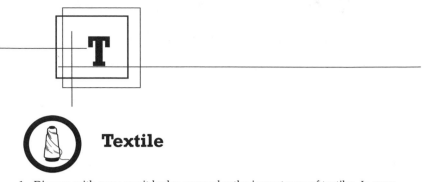

Textile

1. Discuss with your merit badge counselor the importance of textiles. In your discussion, define the terms *fiber, fabric,* and *textile.* Give examples of textiles you use every day.

2. Do the following:

    (a) Get swatches of two natural-fiber fabrics (100 percent cotton, linen, wool, or silk; no blends). Get swatches of two synthetic-fiber fabrics (nylon, polyester, acrylic, olefin, or spandex). Get a sample of one cellulosic fabric (rayon, acetate, or lyocell).

    (b) Give the origin, major characteristics, and general content of each type of fiber obtained for 2a. Explain the difference between a cellulosic manufactured fiber and a synthetic manufactured fiber.

    (c) Describe the main steps in making raw fiber into yarn, and yarn into fabric.

    (d) Assume you will soon buy a new garment or other textile item. Tell your counselor what fiber or blend of fibers you want the item to be, and give reasons for your choice.

3. Do TWO of the following:

    (a) Visit a textile plant, textile products manufacturer, or textile school or college. Report on what you saw and learned.

    (b) Weave a belt, headband, place mat, or wall hanging. Use a simple loom that you have made yourself.

    (c) With a magnifying glass, examine a woven fabric, a nonwoven fabric, and a knitted fabric. Sketch what you see. Explain how the three constructions are different.

    (d) Make a piece of felt.

    (e) Make two natural dyes and use them to dye a garment or a piece of fabric.

    (f) Waterproof a fabric.

    (g) Demonstrate how to identify fibers, using microscope identification or the breaking test.

4. Explain the meaning of 10 of the following terms: warp, harness, heddle, shed, aramid, spandex, sliver, yarn, spindle, distaff, loom, cellulose, sericulture, extrusion, carbon fibers, spinneret, staple, worsted, nonwoven, greige goods.

5. List the advantages and disadvantages of natural plant fibers, natural animal fibers, cellulosic manufactured fibers, and synthetic manufactured fibers. Identify and discuss at least four ecological concerns regarding the production and care of textiles.

6. Explain to your merit badge counselor, either verbally or in a written report, five career possibilities in the textile industry. Tell about two positions that interest you the most and the education, cost of training, and specific duties those positions require.

 **Theater**

1. See or read three full-length plays.* Write a review of each. Discuss with your counselor the plot or story. If you chose to watch the plays, comment on the acting and the staging.

2. Write a one-act play that will take at least eight minutes to perform. The play must have a main character, conflict, and a climax.

3. Discuss with your counselor the safety precautions that should be practiced when working in a theater to protect the cast and crew. Then do THREE of the following:

   (a) Act a major part in a full-length play; or, act a part in three one-act plays.

   (b) Direct a play. Cast, rehearse, and stage it. The play must be at least 10 minutes long.

   (c) Design the set for a play or a theatrical production. Make a model of it.

   (d) Design the costumes for five characters in a theatrical production set in a historical time.

   (e) Show skill in hair and makeup design. Make up yourself or a friend as a historical figure, a clown, an extraterrestrial, or a monster as directed.

   (f) With your counselor's approval, help with the building and painting of the scenery for a theatrical production.

   (g) With your counselor's approval, design the lighting for a play; or help install, focus, color, program, and operate the lighting for a theatrical production.

   (h) With your counselor's approval, help install, focus, equalize, program, and operate the sound for a theatrical production.

   (i) Serve as the stage manager for a theatrical production. Document all cues and stage setups in your calling script.

---

*Watching plays on television, video, or as a movie is not permitted.

4. Mime or pantomime any ONE of the following, chosen by your counselor.

   (a) You have come into a large room. It is full of pictures, furniture, and other things of interest.

   (b) As you are getting on a bus, your books fall into a puddle. By the time you pick them up, the bus has driven off.

   (c) You have failed a school test. You are talking with your teacher, who does not buy your story.

   (d) You are at camp with a new Scout. You try to help them pass a cooking test. The Scout learns very slowly.

   (e) You are at a banquet. The meat is good. You don't like the vegetable. The dessert is ice cream.

   (f) You are a circus performer such as a juggler, high-wire artist, or lion tamer doing a routine.

5. Explain the following: proscenium arch, central or arena staging, center stage, stage right, stage left, downstage, upstage, stage crew, flies, portal, cyclorama, stage brace, spotlight, floodlight, lighting control board, sound mixing desk.

 Traffic Safety

1. Do the following:

   (a) Describe the top 10 mistakes new drivers frequently make. Name the two items you are required by law to carry with you whenever you operate a motor vehicle.

   (b) Describe how alcohol and other drugs affect the human body and why a person should never drink and drive, or drive while under the influence of any mind-altering substances including prescription drugs, cold medications, and illicit drugs. For the state where you live, find out what is the legal blood alcohol concentration and the consequences for driving while intoxicated or driving under the influence. Find out what the open-container law is in your state.

   (c) Describe at least four factors to be considered in the design of a road or highway. Explain how roadside hazards and road conditions contribute to the occurrence and seriousness of traffic crashes.

   (d) Explain why a driver who is fatigued or distracted should not operate a motor vehicle. List five common distractions, explain how driver distractions contribute to traffic accidents, and tell how drivers can minimize distractions. Describe how volunteer drivers can plan to be alert when transporting Scouting participants.

2. Do the following:

   (a) Demonstrate how to properly wear a lap or shoulder belt. Explain why it is important for drivers and passengers to wear safety belts at all times.

(b) List five safety features found in motor vehicles besides occupant restraint systems. Describe each safety feature, how each works, and how each contributes to safety.

3. Do the following:

(a) Using your family car or another vehicle, demonstrate that all lights and lighting systems in the vehicle are working. Describe the function and explain why each type of light is important to safe driving.

(b) Using your family car or another vehicle, demonstrate how to check tire pressure and identify the correct tire pressure for the vehicle. Explain why proper tire pressure is important to safe driving.

(c) Demonstrate a method to check for adequate tire tread. Explain why proper tire tread is important to safe driving.

(d) Demonstrate with a smear-and-clear test if the windshield wiper blades will clear the windshield completely or need to be replaced. Describe instances in good and bad weather when windshield washers are important to safe driving.

4. Do the following:

(a) In a location away from traffic hazards, measure with a tape measure—not in a car—and mark off with stakes the distance that a car will travel during the time needed for decision and reaction, and the braking distances necessary to stop a car traveling 30, 50, and 70 miles per hour on dry, level pavement. Discuss how environmental factors such as bad weather and road conditions will affect the distance.

(b) Describe the difference in nighttime visibility between a properly lit bicycle and rider (or a pedestrian) wearing reflective material and a bicycle and rider with no lights (or a pedestrian) dressed in dark clothing, without reflective material.

(c) Explain how color and shape are used to help road users recognize and understand the information presented on traffic and roadway signs. Explain the purpose of different types of signs, signals, and pavement markings.

(d) Describe at least three examples of traffic laws that apply to drivers of motor vehicles and that bicyclists must also obey.

5. Do ONE of the following:

(a) Interview a traffic law enforcement officer in your community to identify what three traffic safety problems the officer is most concerned about. Discuss with your merit badge counselor possible ways to solve one of those problems.

(b) Using the internet (with your parent's permission), visit five websites that cover safe driving for teenagers. As a group, discuss what you learn with your counselor and at least three other teenagers.

(c) Initiate and organize an activity or event to demonstrate the importance of traffic safety.

(d) Accompanied by an adult and a buddy, pick a safe place to observe traffic at a controlled intersection (traffic signal or stop sign) on three separate days and at three different times of the day, for 30 minutes on each visit. At this intersection, survey (1) such violations as running a red light or stop sign; or (2) seat belt usage. Count the number of violations or number of drivers not wearing a seat belt. Record in general terms if the driver was young or old, male or female. Keep track of the total number of vehicles observed so that you can determine the percentage of compliance vs. violations. Discuss your findings with your merit badge counselor.

 Truck Transportation

1. List the major truck lines serving your town.

2. Do the following:

   (a) Describe the role of truck transportation within commerce (the movement of goods, funds, and information).

   (b) Describe how trucks fit into a company's supply chain. This could be a manufacturer, importer, wholesaler, or retailer.

   (c) On paper, map out how goods that are manufactured overseas are transported to a retailer in this country.

3. Describe the difference between the gasoline engine and the diesel engine that power trucks. List the advantages of each.

4. Visit a truck terminal and complete items 4a through 4e. After your visit, share what you have learned with your counselor.

   (a) Find out what kind of maintenance program the company follows to help keep its fleet, drivers, and the roadway safe.

   (b) Find out how dispatchers maintain communication with drivers on the road.

   (c) Talk with a professional truck driver about safety. Learn about the truck driver's rules of the road for safe driving. List five safe-driving rules every professional truck driver must follow.

   (d) Review the driver's log and find out what kind of information the log contains.

   (e) Learn about important federal regulations that help ensure public safety.

5. Do the following:

   (a) Outline the general organization of a trucking company. Describe what each department does.

   (b) List five positions with trucking companies and describe each one.

6. Name five government agencies that work closely with the trucking industry. Describe their role.

7. List five different kinds of trucks. Tell the service each provides.

8. Assume that you are going to ship by truck 500 pounds of goods (freight class 65) from your town to another town 500 miles away. Your shipment must arrive within three days. Explain in writing:

   (a) How to prepare the shipment

   (b) How to compare at least three carriers for time in transit and rates

   (c) How to choose which carrier to use

   (d) How to insure the shipment for damages

9. Define the following terms: bill of lading, ETA, logbook, intermodal, containers, tariff, shippers, carrier, consignee, drayage, cartage.

10. Learn about opportunities in the field of truck transportation. Choose one career in which you are interested and discuss with your counselor the major responsibilities of that position and the qualifications, education, and training such a position requires.

Veterinary Medicine

1. Discuss with your counselor the roles a veterinarian plays in the following:

    (a) Companion or small animal medicine, and equine medicine

    (b) Food animal or large animal medicine

    (c) Exotic animal medicine

    (d) Marine animal medicine (mammal and fish)

    (e) Poultry medicine

    (f) Wildlife medicine and aquaculture medicine

2. Discuss with your counselor the roles a veterinarian plays in the following:

    (a) Public health medicine and zoonotic disease surveillance and control

    (b) The military

    (c) Food safety and inspection

    (d) Laboratory animal medicine and research

    (e) Teaching and government

3. Describe the training required to become a veterinarian. Where is the veterinary medical college nearest you? Describe the prerequisites for applying to veterinary school.

4. Tell your counselor what a registered veterinary technician (R.V.T.) or animal health technician (A.H.T.) is. Describe the training required to become an R.V.T. or A.H.T. Where is the school or facility for R.V.T. or A.H.T. training nearest you? Describe the role an R.V.T. or A.H.T. would play in assisting a veterinarian working in three of the practice types listed in requirement 1.

5. Discuss with your merit badge counselor the role a veterinarian plays in the human-animal bond.

6. Do ONE of the following:

(a) Visit a veterinary clinic, hospital, or veterinary referral teaching hospital that does work in one of the practices listed in requirement 1. Spend as much time as you can observing the veterinarians and their staff. Write a report on what you observed and learned at the facility. Share your report with your counselor.

(b) Spend as much time as possible with a veterinarian who works in one of the fields listed in requirement 2. Learn what special training beyond veterinary medical school may have been required for that position. Learn about any special or unusual activities required of this position. Write a report on what you have learned about this field of veterinary medicine. Include in your report how this field serves the needs of the general public. Share your report with your counselor.

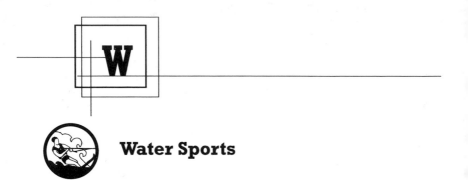

Water Sports

1. Do the following:

   (a) Explain to your counselor the most likely hazards you may encounter while participating in water sports activities and what you should do to anticipate, help prevent, mitigate, and respond to these hazards.

   (b) Review prevention, symptoms, and first-aid treatment for the following injuries or illnesses that could occur while participating in water sports: blisters, cold-water shock and hypothermia, dehydration, heat-related illnesses, sunburn, sprains, strains, minor cuts and bruises, spinal injury, and concussions and head trauma.

   (c) Review the BSA Safety Afloat policy. Tell how it applies to water sports.

2. Do the following:

   (a) Discuss with your counselor the characteristics of life jackets most appropriate for water sports, and tell why one must always be worn while waterskiing or wakeboarding. Then demonstrate how to select and fit a life jacket for water sports activities.

   (b) Review and discuss the Water Sports Safety Code with your counselor. Promise that you will live up to it and follow it in all water work for this merit badge. Review the safety precautions that must be used by the boat operator in pulling waterskiers and wakeboarders.

3. Before doing requirements 4 through 6, successfully complete the BSA swimmer test: Jump feetfirst into water over the head in depth. Level off and swim 75 yards in a strong manner using one or more of the following strokes: sidestroke, breaststroke, trudgen, or crawl; then swim 25 yards using an easy, resting backstroke. The 100 yards must be completed in one swim without stops and must include at least one sharp turn. After completing the swim, rest by floating.

4. Show the following skier signals to the safety observer in the boat: skier safe, faster, slower, turns, back to dock, cut motor, skier in water.

5. Showing reasonable control while using two skis, one ski, or a wakeboard, do EACH of the following:

   (a) Show how to enter the water from a boat and make a deepwater start without help.

   (b) Starting from outside the wakes, show you can cross both wakes four times and return to the center of the wake each time without falling.

(c) Show you can fall properly to avoid an obstacle. Also show that you can drop handle and coast to a stop without losing your balance.

6. While on shore, show that you know how to properly adjust the bindings of your ski(s) or wakeboard to fit yourself. Then, in deep water, show you can adjust bindings to fit. Recover and put on your ski(s) or wakeboard that has come off during a fall.

Weather

1. Define meteorology. Explain what weather is and what climate is. Discuss how the weather affects farmers, sailors, aviators, and the outdoor construction industry. Tell why weather forecasts are important to each of these groups.

2. Name five dangerous weather-related conditions. Give the safety rules for each when outdoors and explain the difference between a severe weather watch and a warning. Discuss the safety rules with your family.

3. Explain the difference between high- and low-pressure systems in the atmosphere. Tell which is related to good and to poor weather. Draw cross sections of a cold front and a warm front, showing the location and movements of the cold and warm air, the frontal slope, the location and types of clouds associated with each type of front, and the location of precipitation.

4. Tell what causes wind, why it rains, and how lightning and hail are formed.

5. Identify and describe clouds in the low, middle, and upper levels of the atmosphere. Relate these to specific types of weather.

6. Draw a diagram of the water cycle and label its major processes. Explain the water cycle to your counselor.

7. Identify some human activities that can alter the environment, and describe how they affect the climate and people.

8. Describe how the tilt of Earth's axis helps determine the climate of a region near the equator, near the poles, and across the area in between.

9. Do ONE of the following:

    (a) Make one of the following instruments: wind vane, anemometer, rain gauge, hygrometer. Keep a daily weather log for one week using information from this instrument as well as from other sources such as local radio and television stations, NOAA Weather Radio All Hazards, and internet sources (with your parent's permission). Record the following information at the same time every day: wind direction and speed, temperature, precipitation, and types of clouds. Be sure to make a note of any morning dew or frost. In the log, also list the weather forecasts from radio or television at the same time each day and show how the weather really turned out.

(b) Visit a National Weather Service office or talk with a local radio or television weathercaster, private meteorologist, local agricultural extension service officer, or university meteorology instructor. Find out what type of weather is most dangerous or damaging to your community. Determine how severe weather and flood warnings reach the homes in your community.

10. Give a talk of at least five minutes to a group (such as your unit or a Cub Scout pack) explaining the outdoor safety rules in the event of lightning, flash floods, and tornadoes. Before your talk, share your outline with your counselor for approval.

11. Find out about a weather-related career opportunity that interests you. Discuss with and explain to your counselor what training and education are required for such a position, and the responsibilities required of such a position.

 **Welding**

1. Do the following:

(a) Explain to your counselor the hazards you are most likely to encounter while welding, and what you should do to anticipate, help prevent, mitigate, or lessen these hazards.

(b) Show that you know first aid for, and the prevention of, injuries or illnesses that could occur while welding, including electrical shock, eye injuries, burns, fume inhalation, dizziness, skin irritation, and exposure to hazardous chemicals, including filler metals and welding gases.

2. Do the following:

(a) With your counselor, discuss general safety precautions and Safety Data Sheets related to welding. Explain the importance of the SDS.

(b) Describe the appropriate safety gear and clothing that must be worn when welding. Then, present yourself properly dressed for welding—in protective equipment, clothing, and footwear.

(c) Explain and demonstrate the proper care and storage of welding equipment, tools, and protective clothing and footwear.

3. Explain the terms welding, electrode, slag, and oxidation. Describe the welding process, how heat is generated, what kind of filler metal is added (if any), and what protects the molten metal from the atmosphere.

4. Name the different mechanical and thermal cutting methods. Choose one method and describe how to use the process. Discuss one advantage and one limitation of this process.

5. Do the following:

(a) Select two welding processes, and make a list of the different components of the equipment required for each process. Discuss one advantage and one limitation for each process.

(b) Choose one welding process. Set up the process you have chosen, including gas regulators, work clamps, cables, filler materials, and equipment settings. Have your counselor inspect and approve the area for the welding process you have chosen.

6. After successfully completing requirements 1 through 5, use the equipment you prepared for the welding process in 5b to do the following:

(a) Using a metal scribe or soapstone, sketch your initial onto a metal plate, and weld a bead on the plate following the pattern of your initial.

(b) Cover a small plate (approximately 3" x 3" x ¼") with weld beads side by side.

(c) Tack two plates together in a square groove butt joint.

(d) Weld the two plates together from 6c on both sides.

(e) Tack two plates together in a T joint, have your counselor inspect it, then weld a T joint with fillet weld on both sides.

(f) Tack two plates together in a lap joint, have your counselor inspect it, then weld a lap joint with fillet weld on both sides.

7. Do the following:

(a) Find out about three career opportunities in the welding industry. Pick one and find out the education, training, and experience required for this profession. Discuss this with your counselor, and explain why the profession might interest you.

(b) Discuss the role of the American Welding Society in the welding profession.

 # Whitewater

1. Do the following:

(a) Explain to your counselor the most likely hazards you may encounter while participating in whitewater activities and what you should do to anticipate, help prevent, mitigate, and respond to these hazards.

(b) Review with your counselor the prevention, symptoms, and first-aid treatment for the following injuries or illnesses that could occur while participating in whitewater activities including cold-water shock; hypothermia; head, neck, and back injuries; heat-related illnesses; sunburn; dehydration; blisters; bruises; cuts; sprains and strains; shoulder dislocation; and submersion injuries.

(c) Discuss with your counselor the BSA Safety Afloat policy and the American Whitewater safety guidelines.

2. Do the following:

   (a) Explain the following river features: upstream V, downstream V, riffle, eddy, eddy line, pillow, ledge, bend, shallows, current, drop, horizon line, wave, standing wave, wave train.

   (b) Explain when, why, and how you should scout a river while ashore and while on the river.

3. Before doing requirements 4 through 12, earn the Canoeing merit badge if you will be using a canoe to earn this merit badge. If you will be using a kayak, earn the Kayaking merit badge. Then do the following:

   (a) If you will be using a canoe to earn this merit badge, demonstrate strokes and maneuvers from the Canoeing merit badge to the satisfaction of your merit badge counselor.

   OR

   (b) If you will be using a kayak to earn this merit badge, demonstrate strokes and maneuvers from the Kayaking merit badge to the satisfaction of your merit badge counselor.

4. Do ONE of the following:

   (a) If you are completing these requirements as a tandem canoeist, perform the following on calm water:

      (1) Demonstrate the following strokes in the bow: cross forward, bow draw, cross bow draw, bow pry, Duffek, sculling draw, and sculling pushaway (reverse scull).

      (2) Demonstrate the following strokes in the stern: stern draw, stern pry, sculling draw, sculling pushaway (reverse scull), and forward with stern pry.

      (3) Demonstrate a high brace, low brace, and a righting pry.

   OR

   (b) If you are completing these requirements as a solo canoeist, perform the following on calm water:

      (1) Demonstrate the following strokes: cross forward, bow draw, cross bow draw, stern draw, pry, stern pry, Duffek, sculling draw, sculling pushaway (reverse scull), and forward with stern pry.

      (2) Demonstrate a high brace, low brace, and righting pry.

   OR

   (c) If you are completing these requirements as a solo kayaker, perform the following on calm water:

      (1) Demonstrate the following strokes: Duffek, bow draw, rudder, and sculling draw.

      (2) Demonstrate a high brace and low brace.

5. Do the following:

   (a) Explain the International Scale of River Difficulty and apply the scale to the stretch of river approved by your counselor.

(b) Identify the specific characteristics of the river that are factors in your classification according to the International Scale.

(c) Discuss how the level of flow changes a river from one class to another and what effects different flow rates have on the features of a river and its hazards.

6. Explain the importance of communication during every whitewater outing. Demonstrate knowledge and ability to use the following American Whitewater Universal River Signals, both visual and auditory: "Stop," "Are you OK?," "Help/emergency," "Run river right," "Run river left," and "All clear—come ahead."

7. Do ONE of the following:

(a) If completing this merit badge in a canoe, describe the various types of canoes used on moving water and how they differ in design, materials, and purpose.

OR

(b) If completing this merit badge in a kayak, describe the various types of kayaks used on moving water and explain how they differ in design, materials, and purpose.

8. Discuss the personal and group equipment necessary for a safe whitewater outing and how and why it is used. Explain how to pack and protect these items.

9. Do the following:

(a) Demonstrate your ability to read a Class II section of river approved by your counselor. Describe the most desirable paths or lines of travel as well as alternative routes and options. Point out how to use the existing water features to your advantage, and explain how to best avoid the hazards present.

(b) Wearing a proper life jacket and being appropriately dressed for the weather and water conditions, perform the following skills in moving water in a properly equipped whitewater craft of your choice (tandem canoe, solo canoe, or solo kayak). If a tandem canoe is used, the skills must be demonstrated from both the bow and stern positions.

    (1) Launch and land.

    (2) Paddle forward in a straight line.

    (3) Backpaddle.

    (4) Ferry upstream.

    (5) Ferry downstream.

    (6) Eddy turn.

    (7) Peel out.

10. Explain and demonstrate the following to your counselor:

(a) Self-rescue and procedures when capsized in moving water, including a wet exit if necessary

(b) Proper use of a throw rope to rescue a swimmer in whitewater

(c) Proper technique for receiving a throw rope as a swimmer

(d) Portaging—where portaging would be appropriate, and when and how to do it

(e) The whitewater buddy system using at least three persons and three craft

11. Discuss the use of inflatable rafts on moving water. In your discussion, explain the special safety precautions that should be taken when using an inflatable raft and the risks of "tubing" on moving water.

12. Participate in a whitewater trip using either a canoe or kayak on a Class I or Class II river. Help to prepare a written plan, specifying the route, schedule, equipment, safety precautions, and emergency procedures. Determine local rules and obtain permission from landowners and land managers in advance. Explain what steps you have taken to comply with BSA Safety Afloat and the American Whitewater safety guidelines. Execute the plan with others.

 # Wilderness Survival

1. Do the following:

   (a) Explain to your counselor the hazards you are most likely to encounter while participating in wilderness survival activities, and what you should do to anticipate, help prevent, mitigate, or lessen these hazards.

   (b) Show that you know first aid for and how to prevent injuries or illnesses that could occur in backcountry settings, including hypothermia, heat reactions, frostbite, dehydration, blisters, insect stings, tick bites, and snakebites.

2. From memory, list the seven priorities for survival in a backcountry or wilderness location. Explain the importance of each one with your counselor.

3. Discuss ways to avoid panic and maintain a high level of morale when lost, and explain why this is important.

4. Describe the steps you would take to survive in the following exposure conditions:

   (a) Cold and snowy

   (b) Wet

   (c) Hot and dry

   (d) Windy

   (e) At or on the water

5. Put together a personal survival kit and explain how each item in it could be useful.

6. Using three different methods (other than matches), build and light three fires.

7. Do the following:

   (a) Show five different ways to attract attention when lost.

(b) Demonstrate how to use a signal mirror.

(c) Describe from memory five ground-to-air signals and tell what they mean.

8. Improvise a natural shelter. For the purpose of this demonstration, use techniques that have little negative impact on the environment. Spend a night in your shelter.

9. Explain how to protect yourself from insects, reptiles, bears, and other animals of the local region.

10. Demonstrate three ways to treat water found in the outdoors to prepare it for drinking.

11. Show that you know the proper clothing to wear while in the outdoors during extremely hot and cold weather and during wet conditions.

12. Explain why it usually is not wise to eat edible wild plants or wildlife in a wilderness survival situation.

 # Wood Carving

1. Do the following:

(a) Explain to your counselor the hazards you are most likely to encounter while wood carving, and what you should do to anticipate, help prevent, mitigate, or lessen these hazards.

(b) Show that you know first aid for injuries that could occur while wood carving, including minor cuts and scratches and splinters.

2. Do the following:

(a) Earn the Totin' Chip recognition.

(b) Discuss with your merit badge counselor your understanding of the Safety Checklist for Carving.

3. Do the following:

(a) Explain to your counselor, orally or in writing, the care and use of five types of tools that you may use in a carving project.

(b) Tell your counselor how to care for and use several types of sharpening devices, then demonstrate that you know how to use these devices.

4. Using a piece of scrap wood or a project on which you are working, show your merit badge counselor that you know how to do the following:

(a) Paring cut

(b) Push cut and levering cut

(c) "V" cut

(d) Stop cut or score line

5. Tell why different woods are used for different projects. Explain why you chose the type of wood you did for your projects in requirements 6 and 7.

6. Plan your own or select a project from this merit badge pamphlet and complete a simple carving in the round.

7. Complete a simple low-relief OR a chip carving project.

 # Woodwork

1. Do the following:

   (a) Explain to your counselor the most likely hazards you may encounter while participating in woodwork activities, and what you should do to anticipate, help prevent, mitigate, and respond to these hazards. Explain what precautions you should take to safely use your tools.

   (b) Show that you know first aid for injuries that could occur while woodworking, including splinters, scratches, cuts, severe bleeding, and shock. Tell what precautions must be taken to help prevent loss of eyesight or hearing, and explain why and when it is necessary to use a dust mask.

   (c) Earn the Totin' Chip recognition.

2. Do the following:

   (a) Describe how timber is grown, harvested, and milled. Tell how lumber is cured, seasoned, graded, and sized.

   (b) Collect and label blocks of six kinds of wood useful in woodworking. Describe the chief qualities of each. Give the best uses of each.

3. Do the following:

   (a) Show the proper care, use, and storage of all working tools and equipment that you own or use at home or school.

   (b) Sharpen correctly the cutting edges of two different tools.

4. Using a saw, plane, hammer, brace, and bit, make something useful of wood. Cut parts from lumber that you have squared and measured from working drawings.

5. Create your own woodworking project. Begin by making working drawings, list the materials you will need to complete your project, and then build your project. Keep track of the time you spend and the cost of the materials.

6. Do any TWO of the following:

   (a) Make working drawings of a project needing beveled or rounded edges and build it.

   (b) Make working drawings of a project needing curved or incised cuttings and build it.

   (c) Make working drawings of a project needing miter, dowel, or mortise and tenon joints and build it.

(d) Make a cabinet, box, or something else with a door or lid fastened with inset hinges.

(e) Help make and repair wooden toys for underprivileged children OR help carry out a woodworking service project approved by your counselor for a charitable organization.

7. Talk with a cabinetmaker or carpenter. Find out about the training, apprenticeship, career opportunities, work conditions, work hours, pay rates, and union organization that woodworking experts have in your area.

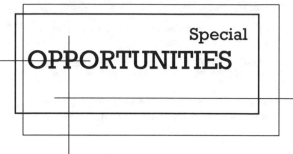

Special

OPPORTUNITIES

Here are the qualifications for additional opportunities for Scouts, Venturers, and Sea Scouts to improve their skills and to serve others. To earn special recognition in these fields you must meet these requirements:

50-Miler Award

The 50-Miler Award is presented to each qualifying individual for satisfactory participation in an approved trip. In order to qualify for the award, the group of which the individual is a member must fulfill all of the following requirements.

1. Make complete and satisfactory plans for the trip, including the possibilities of advancement, conservation, leadership, and service.

2. Cover the route of not less than 50 consecutive miles; take a minimum of five consecutive days to complete the trip without the aid of motors for the qualification of the 50-mile distance. For example, in the case of water treks and the use of motors, qualification distances exclude maneuvering in or out of slips or ports, safety/weather transverses, managing tidal currents, and accessing the open water. (In some areas, pack animals may be used.) **Note:** Qualification for the 50-mile distance does not have to be continuous, provided the primary purpose objective is met.

3. During the time on the trail or waterway, complete a minimum of 10 hours each of group work on projects to improve the trail, springs, campsite, portage, or area. If, after checking with recognized authorities, it is not possible to complete 10 hours each of group work on the trail, a similar project may be done in the

unit's home area. (There should be no unauthorized cutting of brush or timber.)

4. Unit or tour leader must then file the 50-Miler Award application with the local council service center.

Boardsailing BSA
REQUIREMENTS

1. Before fulfilling the following requirements, you must successfully complete the BSA swimmer classification test.

2. Review how each point of BSA Safety Afloat applies to boardsailing.

3. Explain precautions for the following environmental factors: dying wind, high wind, offshore winds, currents, waves, and lightning.

4. Discuss the prevention, recognition, and treatment of the following health concerns that could arise while boardsailing: hypothermia, sunburn, dehydration, and heat exhaustion.

5. Properly rig and prepare the sailboard you are using. Identify each of the following: uphaul, outhaul, downhaul, cleat, leach, tack, clew, foot, luff, skeg, centerboard, wishbone boom, and universal. Explain luffing. Explain how to steer the sailboard by adjusting the center of effort.

6. Demonstrate your ability to uphaul the sail, find the neutral position to the wind (sail luffing), and control the board's position with foot movement.

7. With supervision from your instructor, sail a course that involves beating, reaching, and running. Change direction by tacking into the wind.

BSA Stand Up Paddleboarding

REQUIREMENTS

1. Review the BSA Safety Afloat policy. Explain to your instructor how this applies to stand up paddleboarding.

2. Before fulfilling other requirements, successfully complete the BSA swimmer test: Jump feetfirst into water over the head in depth, level off, and begin swimming. Swim 75 yards in a strong manner using one or more of the following strokes: sidestroke, breaststroke, trudgen or crawl; then swim 25 yards using an easy, resting backstroke. The 100 yards must be completed in one swim without stops and must include one sharp turn.

3. Explain safety considerations for stand up paddleboarding in the following environments: lake, moving water, whitewater, open ocean, ocean surf.

4. Review the characteristics of life jackets most appropriate for stand up paddleboarding and understand why one must always be worn while paddling. Then demonstrate how to select and fit a life jacket for stand up paddleboarding.

5. Describe the appropriate type of leash to wear in different water venues.

6. Name and point out:

   (a) The major parts of a stand up paddleboard

   (b) The parts of a paddle for stand up paddleboarding

7. Discuss:

   (a) The different types of stand up paddleboards

   (b) How to correctly size and hold a paddle for stand up paddleboarding

8. Using a properly outfitted stand up paddleboard, demonstrate the following:

   (a) How to safely carry a stand up paddleboard

   (b) How to safely paddle away from a dock or shoreline (on knees)

   (c) How to stand and balance on a board in the neutral position

(d) How to appropriately fall off a board

(e) How to remount the board

(f) Forward stroke

(g) Back stroke

(h) Forward sweep

(i) Reverse sweep

(j) Draw stroke

(k) One self-rescue technique—lay on your stomach and paddle with your hands

9. With supervision from your instructor, paddle a course that involves:

(a) A straight line for 25 yards and stop within one board length

(b) A figure 8

(c) Moving abeam to the right 10 feet and to the left 10 feet

Complete Angler

The Complete Angler recognition was established by the BSA's National Fishing Task Force to honor well-rounded youth anglers.

REQUIREMENTS

1. Earn the three fishing related merit badges: Fishing, Fly-Fishing, and Fish and Wildlife Management.

2. Successfully complete one or more of the following projects:

(a) Teach a Fishing or Fly-Fishing merit badge skill to your troop or crew as part of a unit program activity.

(b) Help instruct Cub Scouts on fishing skills or fishery management as part of a Cub Scout meeting or outing.

(c) Participate in a local fishing derby or tournament, either a Scouting or community event.

(d) Complete a conservation project that will benefit a local fishery.

Cyber Chip

REQUIREMENTS FOR GRADES 6–8

1. Read and sign the Level II Internet Safety Pledge from NetSmartz. (BSA Cyber Chip green card)
2. Write and sign a personalized contract with your parent or guardian that outlines rules for using the computer and mobile devices, including what you can download, what you can post, and consequences for inappropriate use.
3. Watch the video "Friend or Fake," along with two additional videos of your choosing, to see how friends can help each other to stay safe online. (www.netsmartz.org/scouting)
4. As an individual or with your patrol, use the EDGE method and mini lessons to teach internet safety rules, behavior, and "netiquette" to your troop or another patrol. You are encouraged to use any additional material and information you have researched. Each member of the patrol must have a role and present part of the lesson. (www.netsmartz.org/scouting)
5. Discuss with your unit leader the acceptable standards and practices for using allowed electronic devices, such as phones and games, at your meetings and other Scouting events.

REQUIREMENTS FOR GRADES 9–12

1. Read and sign the Level II Internet Safety Pledge. (BSA Cyber Chip green card)
2. Write and sign a personalized contract with your parent or guardian that outlines rules for using the computer and mobile devices, including what you can download, what you can post, and consequences for inappropriate use.
3. Discuss with your parents the benefits and potential dangers teenagers might experience when using social media. Give examples of each.
4. Watch three "Real-Life Story" videos to learn the impact on teens. (www.netsmartz.org/scouting)
5. As an individual or patrol, use the EDGE method and the Student Project Kit to teach internet safety rules, behavior, and "netiquette" to your troop or another patrol. You are encouraged to use any additional material and information you have researched. Each member of the patrol must have a role and present part of the lesson. (www.netsmartz.org/scouting)
6. Discuss with your unit leader the acceptable standards and practices for using allowed electronic devices such as phones and games at your meetings and other Scouting events.

Note: All Cyber Chips will expire annually. Each Scout will need to "recharge" the chip by going back to the NetSmartz Recharge area. This space will hold new information, news, and a place for the Scout to recommit to net safety and netiquette. Then, with the unit leader, the Scout can add the new date to the Cyber Chip card or certificate.

Den Chief Service Award*

REQUIREMENTS

1. Serve the pack faithfully for one full year.
2. Complete online Den Chief Training (or in person, conducted by the council or district).
3. Know and understand the purposes of Cub Scouting.
4. Help Cub Scouts achieve the purposes of Cub Scouting.
5. Be the activities assistant in den meetings.
6. Set a good example by attitude and uniforming.
7. Be a friend to the Cub Scouts in the den.
8. Take part in weekly meetings, or as often as the den meets.
9. Assist the den at the monthly pack program.
10. Meet as needed with the adult members of the den, pack, troop, ship, or crew.
11. Complete FOUR of these projects:

    (a) Serve as a staff member of a special Cub Scouting event, such as a Scouting show, bicycle rodeo, etc.

    (b) Serve as a staff member of a Cub Scout day camp or resident camp.

    (c) Advance one rank.

    (d) Assist in recruiting three new Cub Scouts.

    (e) Assist three Cub Scouts to become Webelos Scouts.

    (f) Assist three Webelos/Arrow of Light Scouts to join a troop.

    (g) Help to plan and carry out a joint pack-troop activity.

    (h) Recommend to your Scoutmaster, Skipper, or Venturing Advisor another Scout, Sea Scout, or Venturer to be a den chief.

---

*See *Den Chief Handbook*, No. 33211, for detailed requirements

Firem'n Chit

This certification grants a Scout the right to carry fire-lighting devices (matches, lighters, etc.) to build campfires. The Scout must show their Scout leader, or someone designated by their leader, an understanding of the responsibility to do the following:

1. I have read and understand use and safety rules from the *Scouts BSA Handbook.*

2. I will build a campfire only when necessary and when I have the necessary permits (regulations vary by locality).

3. I will minimize campfire impacts or use existing fire lays consistent with the principles of Leave No Trace. I will check to see that all flammable material is cleared at least 5 feet in all directions from fire (total 10 feet).

4. I will safely use and store fire-starting materials.

5. I will see that fire is attended to at all times.

6. I will make sure that water and/or a shovel is readily available. I will promptly report any wildfire to the proper authorities.

7. I will use the cold-out test to make sure the fire is cold out and will make sure the fire lay is cleaned before I leave it.

8. I follow the Outdoor Code, the *Guide to Safe Scouting*, and the principles of Leave No Trace and Tread Lightly!

The Scout's "Firem'n Rights" can be taken away if they fail in their responsibility.

Historic Trails Award

To earn the award, members of your unit must plan and participate in a historic activity. A unit historic activity requires members to:

1. Locate a historic trail or site using http://bsatap.org/bsa-historic-trails-index/ or by contacting local councils. Have participating Scouts study materials regarding the historical aspect of the trail or site using council-provided pamphlets, web-based resources, local historic societies, or the library.

2. Hike or camp two days and one night along the trail or in the vicinity of the site.

3. Conduct a substantial service project or trail/site restoration under the supervision or permission of the owner or sponsoring agency of the trail or site. An alternative to a project can be a historic pageant, ceremony, or other public event related to this trail or site. Such an event should be large enough to merit coverage by the local press.

4. Your unit leader must then file the Historic Trails Award application with your council service center.

FRANÇAIS

Interpreter Strip
(UNIFORM INSIGNIA WORN CENTERED ABOVE "BOY SCOUTS OF AMERICA" OR "SCOUTS BSA" STRIP)

Youth and adults may wear this strip if they show their knowledge of a foreign language or the sign language for the hearing impaired by:

1. Carrying on a five-minute conversation in this language.

2. Translating a two-minute speech or address.

3. Writing a letter in the language.*

4. Translating 200 words from the written word.

---

*Does not apply for sign language.

Morse Code Interpreter Strip

Youth and adults may wear this strip if they show their knowledge of Morse code by:

1. Carrying on a five-minute conversation in Morse code at a speed of at least five words per minute.

2. Copying correctly a two-minute message sent in Morse code at a minimum of five words per minute. Copying means writing the message down as it is received.

3. Sending a 25-word written document in Morse code at a minimum of five words per minute.

Kayaking BSA
REQUIREMENTS

1. Before fulfilling the following requirements, successfully complete the BSA swimmer test.

2. Do the following:

   (a) Describe various types of kayaks and how they differ in design, materials, and purpose.

   (b) Name the parts of the kayak you are using for this exercise.

   (c) Demonstrate how to choose an appropriately sized kayak paddle and how to position your hands.

3. Do the following:

   (a) Tell what precautions must be taken for a safe trip afloat.

   (b) Demonstrate how to select and properly fit a life jacket.

   (c) Explain the importance of safety equipment such as life jackets, air bags, grab loops, and helmets.

4. Demonstrate your ability to aid yourself and others in the event of a capsize:

   (a) Capsize your kayak in water at least 7 feet deep, perform a wet exit if necessary, and swim the boat to shore.

   (b) With assistance, if needed, ready the capsized craft for use.

   (c) Show how to approach a capsized paddler in your kayak and tow them to shore.

   (d) While upright in your kayak, right a capsized kayak, empty it of water, and assist the paddler aboard without returning to shore.

5. As a solo paddler, demonstrate the following:

   (a) Entering and launching a kayak from shore or dock

   (b) Landing or docking and exiting a kayak

   (c) Forward stroke

   (d) Sweep stroke

   (e) Reverse sweep

   (f) Draw stroke

   (g) Rudder stroke

   (h) Back stroke

6. As a solo paddler, do the following:

   (a) Paddle forward in a reasonably straight line.

   (b) Move the kayak sideways to the right and to the left.

   (c) Pivot 360 degrees to the right and left.

   (d) Stop the kayak.

Mile Swim BSA
(SWIMSUIT EMBLEM ONLY)

REQUIREMENTS

1. Explain how regular exercise contributes to good health and why swimming is one of the best forms of exercise.

2. Tell what precautions and procedures a swimmer and escort must follow for distance swimming over open water.

3. Under the supervision of a currently qualified certified aquatics instructor or equivalent, participate in four hours of training and preparation for distance swimming (one hour a day maximum).

4. Swim one mile over a measured course that has been approved by the trained instructor who will supervise the swim.

National Court of Honor Lifesaving, Meritorious Action, and Heroism Awards

National awards for lifesaving, meritorious action, and heroism are made only for outstanding and unusual acts that demonstrate unusual heroism, skill, or bravery and reflect Scouting ideals, based on the following criteria:

1. **Honor Medal With Crossed Palms.** Has demonstrated unusual heroism and extraordinary skill or resourcefulness in saving or attempting to save life at extreme risk to self.

2. **Honor Medal.** Has demonstrated unusual heroism and skill or resourcefulness in saving or attempting to save life at considerable risk to self.

3. **Heroism Award.** Has demonstrated heroism and skill in saving or attempting to save life at minimal personal risk.

4. **Medal of Merit.** Has performed an act of service of a rare or exceptional character that reflects an uncommon degree of concern for the well-being of others.

5. **National Certificate of Merit.** Has performed a significant act of service that is deserving of special national recognition. *Note:* If the action is deserving of merit but does not qualify for a national award, the Scout may be eligible for the Local Council Certificate of Merit, No. 606760.

Heroism is defined as conduct exhibiting courage, daring, skill, and self-sacrifice.

Skill is defined as the ability to use one's knowledge effectively in execution or performance. Special attention is given to skills earned in Scouting.

National Medal for Outdoor Achievement

The National Medal for Outdoor Achievement is the highest recognition that a Scout, Sea Scout, or Venturer can earn for exemplary achievement, experience, and skill in multiple areas of outdoor endeavor. As is the case for the National Outdoor badges, outdoor activities completed as part of an approved Cub Scouting, Scouts BSA, Sea Scouting, Venturing, or Exploring program may be used if they meet the requirements. In order for a youth to earn the National Medal for Outdoor Achievement, the youth must complete the following requirements:

1. Earn the Scouts BSA First Class rank *or* Sea Scout Apprentice rank, *or* complete Venturing Ranger Award requirements 1 through 6.

2. Earn the National Outdoor badge for Camping with a silver device.

3. Earn any two additional National Outdoor badges, each with two gold devices.

4. Complete the requirements for all of the following: Backpacking merit badge *or* Ranger Backpacking elective; Emergency Preparedness merit badge *or* Ranger Emergency Preparedness core; Nature merit badge; and Wilderness Survival merit badge *or* Ranger Wilderness Survival core.

5. Complete a 16-hour course in Wilderness First Aid from the American Red Cross, Wilderness Medical Institute, or other recognized provider.

6. Become a Leave No Trace Trainer by completing the 16-hour training course from a recognized Leave No Trace Master Educator.

7. Plan and lead, with the approval of your unit leader, an outing for your troop, ship, crew, or patrol in two of the following activity areas: hiking and backpacking, aquatic activities, or riding. Include in each outing a service element addressing recreational impacts resulting from that type of activity. With the approval of your unit leader, you may plan and lead the outings for another Cub Scout pack, Scout troop, Sea Scout ship, or Venturing crew.

8. Complete at least one of the following:

    (a) Plan and lead, with the approval of your unit leader, an adventure activity identified in the National Outdoor badge for Adventure for your troop, ship, crew, or patrol.

    (b) Successfully complete a season on a council summer camp staff in an outdoor area, such as aquatics, Scoutcraft, nature/environment, climbing, or COPE.

National Outdoor Awards

The six badges of the award recognize a Scout, Sea Scout, or Venturer who demonstrates both *knowledge* and *experience* in camping, hiking, aquatics, riding, conservation, or adventure. Youth earning the National Outdoor badges have demonstrated that they are knowledgeable, safe, and comfortable in the outdoor activity covered by the badge. Outdoor activities completed as part of any BSA program (Cub Scouting, Scouts BSA, Sea Scouting, Venturing, or Exploring) may be used to satisfy the requirements of the National Outdoor Awards so long as conducted as part of an approved unit, district, or council program. This is referred to as "under the auspices and standards of the Boy Scouts of America" in the requirements.

National Outdoor badges may be earned in the following areas.

Camping. A Scout, Sea Scout, or Venturer may earn the National Outdoor Badge for Camping upon successfully completing the following requirements:

1. Earn the Scouts BSA First Class rank *or* Sea Scout Apprentice rank, *or* complete Venturing Ranger Award requirements 1 through 6.

2. Complete the Camping merit badge requirements.

3. Complete the requirements for two of the following three: Cooking merit badge *or* Ranger Cooking core; First Aid merit badge *or* Ranger First Aid core; or Pioneering merit badge.

4. Complete 25 days and nights of camping (Sea Scouts may be on a boat), including six consecutive days (five nights) of camping, approved and under the auspices and standards of the Boy Scouts of America—including nights camped as part of requirements 1 through 3 above. Youth must complete six consecutive days (five nights) of the 25 nights at a BSA accredited resident camp.

   A gold device may be earned for each additional 25 nights of camping. A silver device is earned for each additional 100 nights of camping. The youth may wear any combination of devices totaling his or her current number of nights camping.

Hiking. A Scout, Sea Scout, or Venturer may earn the National Outdoor Badge for Hiking upon successfully completing the following requirements:

1. Earn the Scouts BSA First Class rank *or* Sea Scout Apprentice rank, *or* complete Venturing Ranger Award requirements 1 through 6.

2. Complete the requirements for one of the following: Hiking merit badge *or* Backpacking merit badge *or* Ranger Backpacking elective.

3. Complete the requirements for one of the following: Orienteering merit badge *or* Geocaching merit badge *or* Ranger Land Navigation core.

4. Complete 100 miles of hiking, backpacking, snowshoeing, or cross-country skiing under the auspices of the Boy Scouts of America, including miles hiked as part of requirements 2 and 3.

A gold device may be earned for each additional 50 miles hiked, backpacked, snowshoed, or skied as outlined in requirements 2 and 3 above. A silver device is earned for each additional 200 miles of hiking. The youth may wear any combination of devices totaling his or her current number of miles hiked.

Aquatics. A Scout, Sea Scout, or Venturer may earn the National Outdoor Badge for Aquatics upon successfully completing the following requirements:

1. Earn the Scouts BSA First Class rank *or* Sea Scout Apprentice rank, *or* complete Venturing Ranger Award requirements 1 through 6.

2. Complete the requirements for the Swimming merit badge and either the Lifesaving merit badge or the Venturing Ranger Lifesaver elective. (For Sea Scouts, Swimming merit badge requirements are an Ordinary rank requirement, and Lifesaving merit badge requirements are an Able rank requirement.)

3. Complete the requirements for the Mile Swim BSA Award.

4. Complete the requirements for at least one of the following: Canoeing, Fishing, Fly-Fishing, Kayaking, Rowing, Scuba Diving, Small-Boat Sailing, Water Sports, or Whitewater merit badge or Venturing Ranger Fishing, Scuba, or Watercraft electives. Complete at least 25 hours of on-the-water time, applying the skills that you learned in the merit badge or Ranger elective.

5. Complete at least 50 hours of any combination of swimming, canoeing, fishing, fly-fishing, kayaking, rowing, scuba diving, small-boat sailing, stand up paddleboarding, water sports, or whitewater activity under the auspices of the Boy Scouts of America, including time spent in requirements 2 through 4.

A gold device may be earned for each additional 25 hours of aquatic activity listed in requirement 5. A silver device is earned for each additional 100 hours of aquatic activity. The youth may wear any combination of devices totaling his or her current number of hours of aquatic activity.

Conservation. A Scout, Sea Scout, or Venturer may earn the National Outdoor badge for Conservation upon successfully completing the following requirements:

1. Earn the Scouts BSA First Class rank *or* Sea Scout Apprentice rank, *or* complete Venturing Ranger Award requirements 1 through 6.

2. Demonstrate the safe use of five of the following conservation tools: pick or pickax; shovel or spade; ax; bow saw; crosscut saw; pry bar; sledgehammer; loppers or shears; fire rake or McLeod; and/or Pulaski. Discuss the ethical use of the tools you chose.

3. Complete the following requirements:

   (a) Environmental Science merit badge *or* Sustainability merit badge *or* both Ranger Conservation core and Ecology elective

   (b) Soil and Water Conservation merit badge

   (c) One of the following merit badges: Fish and Wildlife Management *or* Forestry *or* Mammal Study

4. Complete 25 hours of conservation work under the auspices and standards of the Boy Scouts of America, including hours worked as part of requirements 1 through 3 above.

   A gold device may be earned for each additional 25 hours of conservation work. A silver device is earned for each additional 100 hours of conservation work (for example, the first silver device is earned at 125 hours total conservation work). The youth may wear any combination of devices totaling his or her current number of hours of conservation work.

Riding. A Scout, Sea Scout, or Venturer may earn the National Outdoor Badge for Riding upon successfully completing the following requirements:

1. Earn the Scouts BSA First Class rank *or* Sea Scout Apprentice rank, *or* complete Venturing Ranger Award requirements 1 through 6.

2. Complete the requirements for at least one of the following:

   (a) Cycling merit badge *or* Ranger Cycling-Mountain Biking elective and 100 miles of cycling

   (b) Horsemanship merit badge *or* Ranger Equestrian elective and 20 miles of horseback riding

   (c) Motorboating merit badge *or* Ranger Watercraft elective and 100 miles of motorboating

   (d) Skating merit badge *or* Ranger Winter Sports elective and 20 miles of skating

3. Complete 200 miles of riding activities, including cycling, stock riding, skating, motorboating, mountain boarding, or snowmobiling (including ATV or PWC riding at an approved council program) under the auspices of the Boy Scouts of America, including the miles in requirement 2 above.

   A gold device may be earned for each additional 100 miles of riding set forth in requirement 3 above. A silver device is earned for each additional 400 miles of riding. The youth may wear any combination of devices totaling his or her current number of miles of riding.

Adventure. A Scout, Sea Scout, or Venturer may earn the National Outdoor Badge for Adventure upon successfully completing the following requirements:

1. Earn the Scouts BSA First Class rank *or* Sea Scout Apprentice rank, *or* complete Venturing Ranger Award requirements 1 through 6.

2. Complete the requirements for one of the following: Wilderness Survival *or* Search and Rescue *or* Emergency Preparedness merit badges; *or* Ranger Wilderness Survival core *or* Ranger Emergency Preparedness core *or* Ranger First Aid elective.

3. Complete 10 of any combination or repetition of the following adventure activities under the auspices of the Boy Scouts of America:

(a) A backpacking trip lasting three or more days and covering more than 20 miles without food resupply.

(b) A canoeing, rowing, or sailing trip lasting three or more days and covering more than 50 miles without food resupply.

(c) A whitewater trip lasting two or more days and covering more than 20 miles without food resupply.

(d) A climbing activity on open rock, following Climb On Safely principles, that includes camping overnight.

(e) Earn the National Historic Trails Award.

(f) Earn the 50-Miler Award.

(g) Attend any national high-adventure base or any nationally recognized local high-adventure or specialty adventure program.

Items 3a through 3g may be repeated as desired. A single activity that satisfies multiple items in 3a through 3g may be counted as separate activities at the discretion of the unit leader. Similarly, a single activity that doubles an item in 3a through 3d may be counted as two activities at the discretion of the unit leader. A gold device may be earned for each additional five activities. A silver device is earned for each additional 20 activities. The youth may wear any combination of devices totaling his or her current number of activities.

National Park Service Resource Stewardship Scout Ranger

The Resource Stewardship Scout Ranger program invites Scouts and Cub Scouts to participate in educational and/or volunteer service projects at national park sites. The goal is to spark the Scouts' awareness of the national parks while giving them the opportunity to explore the parks and learn more about protecting our natural and cultural resources. Scouts are awarded certificates and/or patches for participating in the program.

Scouts can earn a certificate or patch by participating in

- organized educational programs
- volunteer service projects

To earn a troop certificate, troops must participate for a minimum of five hours at one or more national park sites.

To earn a patch, Scouts must participate for a minimum of 10 hours at one or more national park sites.

Qualifying organized educational programs:

- Ranger-guided interpretive tours
- Junior Ranger programs
- Environmental education programs
- Any other official NPS education program (campfire program, ranger-led hike, etc.)

For more information, visit www.nps.gov/subjects/youthprograms/scout-ranger.htm.

Additional information may be found at www.nps.gov/fost/learn/kidsyouth/upload/Scout-Ranger-Brochureonepage7-20-09-2.pdf.

Nova and Supernova Awards

The Boy Scouts of America's STEM Nova Awards program incorporates learning with cool activities and exposure to science, technology, engineering, and mathematics (STEM) for Cub Scouts, Webelos Scouts, Scouts BSA, Sea Scouts, and Venturers. These activities and associated awards stimulate interest in STEM-related fields, and show how these subjects appear in everyday life and the world around us. Counselors and mentors help bring this engaging, contemporary,
and fun program to life for youth members.

THE NOVA AWARDS

There are multiple Nova awards for BSA program: Cub Scouts, Webelos Scouts, Scouts BSA, Sea Scouts, and Venturers. Each award covers one specific subfield of a STEM subject area. As of January 1, 2019, the Scouts BSA Nova awards are Shoot!, Splash!, Let It Grow!, Start Your Engines!, Whoosh!, and Designed to Crunch, with additional awards being added as they are approved.

Upon earning their first Nova award, Scouts receive the distinctive Nova Award patch. For each Nova earned after that, a Scout earns a separate pi (π) pin-on device that attaches to the patch.

THE SUPERNOVA AWARDS

Supernova awards were designed to motivate Scouts and recognize more advanced achievement in STEM-related activities, and thus have more rigorous and in-depth requirements than Nova awards. Scouts can earn the Dr. Bernard Harris Supernova Bronze Award and then the Thomas Edison Supernova Silver Award. These two Supernova awards are available to all Scouts who have earned First Class rank. The Dr. Bernard Harris Supernova Bronze Award requires the Scout to have earned three Scouts BSA Nova awards, in addition to other requirements. The Thomas Edison Supernova Silver Award requires completion of a fourth Scouts BSA Nova award, in addition to the Harris Award and other requirements.

For the Supernova awards, a registered and council-approved mentor, who serves much like a merit badge counselor, is required.

For complete requirements and more information about the Nova and Supernova awards, go to www.scouting.org/stem-nova-awards.

Outdoor Ethics Action Award

The Outdoor Ethics Action Award challenges Scouts and Scouters to take affirmative steps to improve their outdoor skills. The requirements are as follows:

1. Do the following:

    (a) Unless already completed, earn the Outdoor Ethics Awareness Award.

    (b) Complete the BSA outdoor ethics course.

    (c) Explain how each of the four points of the Outdoor Code (www.scouting.org/outdoor-programs/outdoor-ethics) guides your actions when outdoors.

2. Do the following:

    (a) Read chapter 7 of the Scouts BSA handbook on outdoor ethics.

    (b) Teach a skill related to the Outdoor Code or Leave No Trace to another Scout in your troop or another Scouting unit.

3. Complete one of the following:

    (a) Successfully complete a term as your troop outdoor ethics guide.

    (b) Participate in an outing that emphasizes the complete set of Leave No Trace (http://lnt.org/learn/7-principles) or relevant Tread Lightly! (www.treadlightly.org/learn) principles. All members of the troop participating in the outing should use outdoor ethics and the specific skills needed to minimize impacts from their use of the outdoors.

4. Follow the Outdoor Code, Leave No Trace, and Tread Lightly! principles on three outings. Write a paragraph on each outing explaining how you followed the Outdoor Code, Leave No Trace, and Tread Lightly! Share it with your unit leader or an individual who has completed the BSA outdoor ethics orientation course.

5. On a troop outing, help your troop on a service activity that addresses recreational impacts related to the type of outing. The project should be approved in advance by the landowner or land manager and lead to permanent or long-term improvements.

6. Participate in a report at a court of honor or similar family event on the service activity in requirement 5.

Outdoor Ethics Awareness Award

Scouts interested in learning more about outdoor ethics and Leave No Trace should begin by exploring the Outdoor Ethics Awareness Award. The requirements are as follows:

1. Recite from memory and explain the meaning of the Outdoor Code (www.scouting.org/outdoor-programs/outdoor-ethics).

2. Watch the National Park Service Leave No Trace video (www.nps.gov/havo/planyourvisit/leave-no-trace-video.htm).

3. Complete the Leave No Trace online course (http://lnt.org/learn/online-awareness-course). Print the certificate.

4. Complete the Tread Lightly! online course (https://tread-lightly. teachable.com/p/online-awareness-course). Print the certificate.

5. Participate in an outdoor ethics course, workshop, or training activity facilitated by a person who has completed the BSA outdoor ethics orientation course or is a BSA outdoor ethics trainer or master.

Paul Bunyan Woodsman

(TRAIL PACK OR BLANKET EMBLEM)

Study the Scouts BSA handbooks and the *Camping* merit badge pamphlet, and demonstrate to your Scoutmaster or other qualified person the following:

1. Explain the most likely hazards you may encounter while participating in camping activities and what you should do to anticipate, help prevent, mitigate, and respond to these hazards.

2. Show that you know first aid for injuries that could occur while using woods tools.

3. Earn the Totin' Chip.

4. Help a Scout or patrol earn the Totin' Chip, and demonstrate to them the value of proper woods-tools use.

5. Earn the Firem'n Chit.

6. Be familiar with the proper and safe use of woods tools including:

   (a) Ax   (e) Pulaski

   (b) Hatchet   (f) Saw

   (c) Loppers   (g) Shovel

   (d) McLeod

7. With official approval and supervision, using woods tools, spend at least two hours doing one of the following conservation-oriented projects:

   (a) Clear trails or fire lanes.

   (b) Trim a downed tree, cut into 4-foot lengths, and stack; make a brush pile with the branches.

   (c) Build a natural retaining wall or irrigation way to aid in a planned conservation effort.

Religious Emblems

A Scout is reverent. A Scout is reverent toward God. A Scout is faithful in fulfilling religious duties. A Scout respects the beliefs of others.

To encourage members to grow stronger in their faith, religious groups have developed the following religious emblems programs. The Boy Scouts of America has approved of these programs and allows the emblems to be worn on the official uniform. The various religious groups administer the programs. Check with your local council service center or contact the religious organization directly to obtain the curriculum booklets.

African Methodist Episcopal Church—God and Church; God and Life. Local council service center or P.R.A.Y., 11123 S. Towne Square, Suite B, St. Louis, MO 63123; telephone: 800-933-7729; email: info@praypub.org; website: https://ameced.com/scouting/ and www.praypub.org/bsa

African Methodist Episcopal Zion Church—God and Church; God and Life. Local council service center or P.R.A.Y., 11123 S. Towne Square, Suite B, St. Louis, MO 63123; telephone: 800-933-7729; email: info@praypub.org; website: www.praypub.org/bsa

Anglican Catholic Church—Servus Dei. Anglican Parishes Association, 800 Timothy Road, Athens, GA 30606; telephone: 706-546-6910

American Sikh Council. P.O. Box 932, Voorhees, NJ 08043; telephone: 607-269-7454; email: contact@americansikhcouncil.org and sikhscoutsusa@gmail.com

Anglican Church in North America—God and Church; God and Life. Local council service center or P.R.A.Y., 11123 S. Towne Square, Suite B, St. Louis, MO 63123; telephone: 800-933-7729; email: info@praypub.org; website: www.praypub.org/bsa

Armenian Apostolic Church of America (Western Prelacy)—Saint Mesrob. 6252 Honolulu Ave., Suite 100, Los Angeles, CA 91214; telephone: 818-248-7737

Armenian Church of America (Eastern Diocese)—Ararat. Department of Youth and Education, Diocese of the Armenian Church of America, 630 Second Ave., New York, NY 10016; telephone: 212-686-0710

Bahá'í—Unity of Mankind. Bahá'í Committee on Scouting, Bahá'í National Center, Education and Schools Office, 1233 Central St., Evanston, IL 60201-1611; telephone: 847-733-3492; email: schools@usbnc.org; website: www.bahai.us/unity-of-mankind-scouting-award-program

Baptist—God and Church; God and Life. Local council service center or P.R.A.Y., 11123 S. Towne Square, Suite B, St. Louis, MO 63123; telephone: 800-933-7729; email: info@praypub.org; websites: www.praypub.org/bsa and www.baptistscouters.org

Buddhist—Sangha. National Buddhist Committee on Scouting, 415 42nd Ave., San Mateo, CA 94403-5005, telephone: 650-574-4527; fax: 408-756-3288; email: odagawas@aol.com; website: bcascouting.org

Catholic, Eastern—Light Is Life; Pope Pius XII. Local council service center or National Catholic Committee on Scouting, 1325 West Walnut Hill Lane, P.O. Box 152079, Irving, TX 75015-2079; telephone: 972-580-2114; website: www.nccs-bsa.org

Catholic, Roman—Ad Altare Dei; Pope Pius XII. Local council service center, National Catholic Committee on Scouting, BSA Supply Group; telephone: 800-323-0732; websites: www.nccs-bsa.org and www.praypub.org/bsa

Christian Church (Disciples of Christ)—God and Church; God and Life. Local council service center or P.R.A.Y., 11123 S. Towne Square, Suite B, St. Louis, MO 63123; telephone: 800-933-7729; email: info@praypub.org; website: www.praypub.org/bsa

Christian Methodist Episcopal Church—God and Church; God and Life. Local council service center or P.R.A.Y., 11123 S. Towne Square, Suite B, St. Louis, MO 63123; telephone: 800-933-7729; email: info@praypub.org; website: www.praypub.org/bsa

Church of Christ, Scientist (Christian Scientist)—God and Country. P.R.A.Y., 11123 S. Towne Square, Suite B, St. Louis, MO 63123; telephone: 800-933-7729; email: info@praypub.org; websites: www.christianscience.com/youth and www.praypub.org/bsa

Church of Jesus Christ of Latter-day Saints (LDS)—On My Honor. LDS Relationships—BSA; 15 West South Temple, Suite 1070; Salt Lake City, UT 84101-1579; telephone 801-530-0004

Churches of Christ—Good Servant; Giving Servant. Members of Churches of Christ for Scouting, 401 Cypress, Suite 406, Abilene, TX 79601; telephone: 325-370-1679; email: info@goodservant.org; website: www.goodservant.org

Community of Christ—Path of the Disciple; Exploring Community Together. P.R.A.Y., 11123 S. Towne Square, Suite B, St. Louis, MO 63123; telephone: 800-933-7729; email: contact@cofchrist.org or info@praypub.org; websites: www.cofchrist.org/world-community and www.praypub.org/bsa

Eastern Orthodox—Alpha Omega. P.R.A.Y., 11123 S. Towne Square, Suite B, St. Louis, MO 63123; telephone: 800-933-7729; email: www.eocs.org/contact or info@praypub.org; websites: www.eocs.org/religious-awards and www.praypub.org/bsa

Episcopal—God and Church; God and Life. Local council service center or P.R.A.Y., 11123 S. Towne Square, Suite B, St. Louis, MO 63123; telephone: 800-933-7729; email: scouting@brothersandrew.net or info@praypub.org; websites: www.brothersandrew.org/Ministries/scouting.html and www.praypub.org/bsa

General Church of the New Jerusalem (The New Church)—Open Word Award. Chairman, Boy Scout Relations Committee, General Church of the New Jerusalem, P.O. Box 277, Bryn Athyn, PA 19009; telephone: 215-938-2542; fax: 215-938-2617

Hindu—Dharma, Karma. North American Hindu Association, 847 E. Angela St., Pleasanton, CA 94566-7568; telephone/fax: 925-846-3811; email: info@naha.us; website: www.naha.us

Islamic—In the Name of God. National Islamic Committee on Scouting, Mr. Syed Naqvi; telephone: 732-801-1283; email: islamicbsa@aol.com; websites: www.islamicscouting.org and www.islamiccouncilonscouting.org

JAINA—Federation of Jain Associations in North America. Jaina Headquarters, 722 S. Main St., Milpitas, CA 95035; telephone: 510-730-0204

Jewish—Ner Tamid; Etz Chaim. P.R.A.Y., 11123 S. Towne Square, Suite B, St. Louis, MO 63123; telephone: 800-933-7729; email: www.jewishscouting.org/contact-us/ or info@praypub.org; websites: www.jewishscouting.org/boy-scout-emblems/ and www.praypub.org/bsa

Lutheran—God and Church; God and Life. Local council service center or P.R.A.Y., 11123 S. Towne Square, Suite B, St. Louis, MO 63123; telephone: 800-933-7729; email: info@praypub.org; websites: www.praypub.org/bsa and www.nlas.org

Meher Baba—Compassionate Father. Committee for Meher Baba and Scouting, 912 Ninth Ave. S, North Myrtle Beach, SC 29582; telephone: 843-272-3498; Meher Spiritual Center, 10200 N. Kings Highway, Myrtle Beach, SC 29572; telephone: 843-272-5777

Moravian—God and Country. The Moravian Church, Drawer Y, Winston-Salem, NC 27108; telephone: 336-722-8126; Rev. Franklin Jones, the Moravian Church, 4609 Valley Drive NW, Rochester, MN 55901; email: fatherjones@juno.com

National Association of Anglican and Traditional Catholic Scouters— God and Church; God and Life. Local council service center or P.R.A.Y., 11123 S. Towne Square, Suite B, St. Louis, MO 63123; telephone: 800-933-7729; email: info@praypub.org; website: www.praypub.org/bsa

Nazarene—God and Church; God and Life. Local council service center or P.R.A.Y., 11123 S. Towne Square, Suite B, St. Louis, MO 63123; telephone 800-933-7729; email: info@praypub.org; website: www.praypub.org/bsa

Polish National Catholic Church—God and Country (Bog I Ojczyzna). Mr. Richard Daum, 11 Everette Place, Wayne, NJ 07470; telephone 973-694-9457; email: rodaum@verizon.net

Presbyterian Church in America—God and Church; God and Life. Local council service center or P.R.A.Y., 11123 S. Towne Square, Suite B, St. Louis, MO 63123; telephone: 800-933-7729; email: info@praypub.org; website: www.presbyterianscouters.org and www.praypub.org/bsa

Presbyterian Church (U.S.A.)—God and Church; God and Life. Local council service center or P.R.A.Y., 11123 S. Towne Square, Suite B, St. Louis, MO 63123; telephone: 800-933-7729; email: info@praypbub.org; websites: www.presbyterianscouters.org and www.praypub.org/bsa

Protestant and Independent Christian Churches—God and Church; God and Life. Local council service center or P.R.A.Y., 11123 S. Towne Square, Suite B, St. Louis, MO 63123; telephone: 800-933-7729; email: info@praypub.org; website: www.praypub.org/bsa

Religious Society of Friends (Quakers)—Spirit of Truth. Friends Committee on Scouting, 7140 E. Buddy Lane, Camby, IN 46113; email: clerk.quakerscouting@yahoo.com; website: www.quakerscouting.org; Bart McLeroy, email: bmcleroy@gmail.com; Friends Committee on Scouting (Quakers) email: clerk@quakerscouting.org; website: http://quakerscouting.org

The Salvation Army—God and Church; God and Life. P.O. Box 269, Alexandria, VA 22313; Eastern Territory, telephone: 914-620-7427; Central Territory, telephone: 847-294-2112; Southern Territory, telephone: 404-728-1363; Western Territory, telephone: 310-544-6434

Sikh—World Sikh Council, America Region. P.O. Box 3635, Columbus, OH 43210; toll-free telephone: 888-340-1702; fax: 888-398-1875; email: contact@worldsikhcouncil.org or sikhscoutsusa@gmail.com

Unitarian Universalist Scouters Organization—Living Your Religion. Unitarian Universalist Association, 24 Farnsworth St., Boston, MA 02210; email: religiouseducation@uua.org; website: www.uua.org/children/scouting; Dr. Harold Yocum, Unitarian Universalist Scouters Organization, 2716 Julies Trail, Edmond, OK 73012; email: drhal2@cox.net

United Church of Christ—God and Church; God and Life. Local council service center or P.R.A.Y., 11123 S. Towne Square, Suite B, St. Louis, MO 63123; telephone: 800-933-7729; email: info@praypub.org; website: www.praypub.org/bsa

United Methodist—God and Church; God and Life. Local council service center or P.R.A.Y., 11123 S. Towne Square, Suite B, St. Louis, MO 63123; telephone: 800-933-7729; email: info@praypub.org; websites: www.praypub.org/bsa and www.umcscouting.org

United Pentecostal Church International—God and Church; God and Life. Local council service center or P.R.A.Y., 11123 S. Towne Square, Suite B, St. Louis, MO 63123; telephone: 800-933-7729; email: info@praypub.org; website: www.praypub.org/bsa

Unity Worldwide Ministries—Light of God; Fillmore Youth. P.O. Box 610, Lee's Summit, MO 64063; telephone: 816-524-7414; email: kid@unity.org; website: www.unity.org/emblem

Zoroastrian—Good Life. The Zoroastrian Association of Greater New York, c/o Ms. Temilyn Mehta, National Coordinator, The Good Life Program, 12 Rockwell Circle, Marlboro, NJ 07746; telephone: 732-972-6527; email: tghad@hotmail.com

Scuba BSA

REQUIREMENTS

1. Before doing other requirements, successfully complete the BSA swimmer test. To begin the test, jump feetfirst into water over the head in depth, level off, and begin swimming. Swim 75 yards in a strong manner using one or more of the following strokes: sidestroke, breaststroke, trudgen, or crawl; then swim 25 yards using an easy, resting backstroke. The 100 yards must be completed in one swim without stops and must include at least one sharp turn. After completing the swim, rest by floating.

2. Discuss the importance of using the buddy system at all times while scuba diving. Explain that a dive buddy is there to assist with the donning and doffing of equipment, to lend assistance in case of emergency, and to share in the underwater experience. Remember, always dive with a buddy—***Never dive alone!***

3. Review hazards associated with scuba diving, including causes of decompression incidents, and safety procedures to avoid them. Explain the importance of never using scuba equipment unless you are enrolled in a training exercise, or have completed a diver certification program, taught by a certified instructor.

By the end of a Water Skills Development session, the participants will be able to meet the following requirements in clear, confined water:

4. State the purpose of the following pieces of basic diving equipment: mask, fins, BCD, BCD inflator, regulator, air gauge, and alternate air source.

5. Describe how to locate the air gauge, and explain how to recognize the "caution zone" on it.

6. Don and adjust mask, fins, snorkel, BCD, scuba, and weights with the assistance of a buddy, instructor, or certified assistant.

7. While underwater, demonstrate and recognize the following hand signals: OK? OK!; Stop; Up; Down; Out of air; Come here; Ears not clearing; Slow down/Take it easy; Something is wrong; Watch me; Check your air supply.

8. Inflate/deflate a BCD at the surface using the low-pressure inflator.

9. In shallow water, demonstrate proper compressed air breathing habits; remember to breathe naturally and not hold the breath.

10. Clear the regulator while underwater using both exhalation and purge-button methods, and resume normal breathing from it.

11. In shallow water, recover a regulator hose from behind the shoulder while underwater.

12. In shallow water, clear a partially flooded mask while underwater.

13. Swim underwater with scuba equipment while maintaining control of both direction and depth, properly equalizing the ears and mask to accommodate depth changes.

14. While underwater, locate and read submersible pressure gauge and signal whether the air supply is adequate or low based on the gauge's caution zone.

15. Describe how to avoid hazardous aquatic life (if applicable to your confined water location).

NOTE: The counselor for Scuba BSA must hold an instructor rating and be in current teaching status with PADI, NAUI, SSI, or another member of the RSTC in accordance with BSA scuba policies. Instruction must meet the minimum training standards for introductory scuba experiences set by the RSTC and guidelines provided in the Scuba BSA pamphlet, No. 430-515. BSA scuba policies are also provided in the *Guide to Safe Scouting*.

Snorkeling BSA
REQUIREMENTS

1. Before doing other requirements, successfully complete the BSA swimmer test: Jump feetfirst into water over the head in depth, level off, and begin swimming. Swim 75 yards in a strong manner using one or more of the following strokes: sidestroke, breaststroke, trudgen, or crawl; then swim 25 yards using an easy, resting backstroke. The 100 yards must be completed in one swim without stops and must include at least one sharp turn. After completing the swim, rest by floating.

2. Discuss the importance of using the buddy system at all times while snorkeling and list duties of a buddy, beginning with equipment checks.

3. Explain the function, fit, and selection of mask, fins, and snorkel. Discuss the use of inflatable flotation vests and life jackets when snorkeling in open water.

4. In confined, shallow water (about waist deep), demonstrate use of mask and snorkel:

(a) Show how to prevent the mask from fogging and how to equalize pressure in mask, ears, and sinus cavities. With your head underwater, flood the mask, observe the effect on your vision, surface, and drain the water from the mask.

(b) With your face in the water, breathe through the snorkel. Then submerge, surface, clear water from the snorkel, and resume free breathing without removing the snorkel from your mouth.

5. In confined, shallow water, demonstrate the use of swim fins: Do first using only fins, and then repeat with a mask and snorkel.

(a) Fit and adjust fins to feet.

(b) Walk with fins as if entering from a beach.

(c) Swim at the surface (10 yards) and underwater (three yards) using the flutter kick.

(d) Control direction without using hands while swimming with fins at the surface and underwater.

6. In confined, deep water (6 to 12 feet), demonstrate:

(a) Proper techniques for entering and exiting the water with snorkeling equipment from a dock or boat.

(b) Headfirst and feetfirst surface dives, including proper body position for safe ascent and descent.

7. Show knowledge of snorkeling signals:

(a) Demonstrate divers' signs and signals, both audible and visual, for use at the surface and underwater.

(b) Set out a diver down flag and explain its function.

8. In clear, confined water 8 to 12 feet deep that has a firm bottom, while swimming with a buddy, use mask, fins, and snorkel to locate and recover an object from the bottom.

9. Demonstrate basic survival skills:

(a) Float facedown for five minutes while breathing through a snorkel with a minimum of movement.

(b) Demonstrate survival floating for five minutes without use of a snorkel.

(c) Using fins, show how to tow an exhausted or unconscious buddy to safety.

10. Review and explain the eight points of Safe Swim Defense and BSA Snorkeling Safety. Explain training, preparations, and precautions required for snorkeling in open water. Explain environmental factors that affect snorkeling and discuss special precautions needed for oceans, streams, and lakes.

11. Explain pressure, buoyancy, and submerged optics and acoustics related to snorkel swimming and diving.

12. Discuss the effects of submersion on the body and how to handle potentially dangerous situations:

(a) What is hyperventilation and how is it avoided?

(b) What are the symptoms and consequences of hypothermia?

(c) Why is CPR training recommended for those participating in swimming and snorkeling activities?

Totin' Chip

This certification grants a Scout the right to carry and use woods tools. The Scout must show their Scout leader, or someone designated by their leader, that the Scout understands their responsibility to do the following:

1. Read and understand woods tools use and safety rules from the Scouts BSA handbooks.

2. Demonstrate proper handling, care, and use of the pocketknife, ax, and saw.

3. Use knife, ax, and saw as tools, not playthings.

4. Respect all safety rules to protect others.

5. Respect property. Cut living and dead trees only with permission and good reason.

6. Subscribe to the Outdoor Code.

The Scout's "Totin' Rights" can be taken away if they fail in their responsibility.

Whitewater Rafting BSA

Many Scouting units participate in rafting trips conducted by outfitters or councils. The Whitewater Rafting BSA award recognizes the challenge and adventure of such activities.

REQUIREMENTS

1. Before doing the following requirements, successfully complete the BSA swimmer test.

2. Do the following:

    (a) Name the parts of a whitewater raft.

    (b) Describe differences between a paddle raft and an oar powered raft.

    (c) Explain the importance of perimeter lines used on whitewater rafts.

    (d) Demonstrate how to choose an appropriate size paddle.

    (e) Demonstrate how to select and properly fit a life jacket.

    (f) Demonstrate how to select and properly fit a helmet.

    (g) Discuss the use of throw ropes in rescuing overboard paddlers.

    (h) Discuss common river hazards including rocks, strainers, broaching, standing waves, hydraulics, and foot entrapment.

3. Explain the importance of safety equipment used in whitewater rafting including throw ropes, helmets, and life jackets. Also discuss appropriate clothing and footwear for a whitewater rafting trip.

4. Under proper supervision and appropriate conditions, safely do the following:

    (a) Lift, carry, launch, and land an inflatable raft, with help, on calm or slow-moving water.

    (b) Sit in a raft as a paddler with proper foot position.

    (c) Swim a Class I rapid while wearing a life jacket, helmet, and attire appropriate for the water temperature. Demonstrate defensive and aggressive swimming positions as possible.

5. While on calm or slow-moving water, demonstrate the following

strokes in an inflatable raft with at least one other paddler and on command of a qualified paddle captain:

(a) Forward

(b) Back

(c) Sweep

6. While on moving water up to Class I, demonstrate the following maneuvers with at least 3 other paddlers in an inflatable raft and on the command of a qualified paddle raft captain:

   (a) Turn left.

   (b) Turn right.

   (c) Paddle forward in a straight line for 50 feet.

   (d) Back paddle reasonably straight for 15 feet.

7. While on moving water up to Class I, demonstrate the following maneuvers with at least 3 other paddlers in an inflatable raft and on the command of a qualified paddle raft captain:

   (a) A front or a back ferry

   (b) A shallow or a wide eddy turn

   (c) A shallow or a wide peel out

8. Participate in a whitewater rafting trip in up to Class III whitewater with a qualified paddle raft captain in each raft, using a minimum of two rafts and for at least one hour's duration.

William T. Hornaday Awards*

These awards are presented for distinguished service in natural resource conservation for units, Scouts, Venturers, Sea Scouts, and Scouters. Scouts may earn the Hornaday Badge or the Hornaday Bronze or Silver Medal.

WILLIAM T. HORNADAY BADGE

To be eligible for the Hornaday Badge, presented by the local council, a Scout must do the following:

1. Earn First Class rank.

2. Plan, lead, and carry out at least **one project** from one of the categories listed (see the next page).

3. Complete the requirements for any **three** of the merit badges listed in bold. In addition, complete any **two** of the others listed.

WILLIAM T. HORNADAY BRONZE OR SILVER MEDAL

To be eligible for these awards, granted by the National Council, a Scout must do the following:

1. Earn First Class rank.

2. **For the bronze medal:** Plan, lead, and carry out at least **three projects from three separate categories** listed. Earn the Environmental Science merit badge, plus at least three additional badges shown in boldface, and any two others listed.

3. **For the silver medal:** Plan, lead, and carry out at least **four projects from four separate categories** listed. Earn all six merit badges listed in boldface, plus any three others listed.

PROJECT CATEGORIES

- Energy conservation
- Soil and water conservation
- Fish and wildlife management
- Forestry and range management
- Air and water pollution control
- Resource recovery (recycling)
- Hazardous material disposal and management
- Invasive species control

---

*For complete requirements, see the applicable award application form at www.scouting.org/ awards/hornaday-awards/forms and the *Hornaday Award Conservation Project Workbook* at https://filestore.scouting.org/filestore/pdf/Hornaday_Award_Conservation_Project_Workbook.pdf.

MERIT BADGES

- **Energy**
- **Environmental Science**
- **Fish and Wildlife Management**
- **Forestry**
- **Public Health**
- **Soil and Water Conservation**
- Bird Study
- Fishing
- Fly-Fishing
- Gardening
- Geology
- Insect Study
- Landscape Architecture
- Mammal Study
- Nature
- Nuclear Science
- Oceanography
- Plant Science
- Pulp and Paper
- Reptile and Amphibian Study
- Weather

World Conservation Award

You can earn this award by earning the following merit badges:

1. Environmental Science OR Sustainability merit badge
2. Either Soil and Water Conservation OR Fish and Wildlife Management merit badge
3. Citizenship in the World merit badge

NOTES

NOTES

NOTES

NOTES

NOTES

NOTES

NOTES

NOTES